A
CHRISTIAN VIEW
OF
RUSSIA

In Thanksgiving for the Spilt Blood of Jesus

A
CHRISTIAN VIEW
OF
RUSSIA

DAVID ZIOMEK

Bridge Publishing, Inc.
Publishers of:
LOGOS • HAVEN • OPEN SCROLL

All Scriptures are taken from the King James Version (KJV) unless otherwise identified as: *The Jerusalem Bible* (TJB).

Contents

Flow, flow, O bitter tears,
Weep, O Christian soul,
Soon the enemy will come and darkness will fall,
Darkness black and impenetrable.
Woe, woe unto Russia,
Weep, weep, O Russian people,
Hungry people!

> The prophetic last lines of
> Modest Mussorgsky's opera
> *Boris Godunov*

Then spake Jesus again unto them, saying, I
am the light of the world: he that followeth me
shall not walk in darkness, but shall have the
light of life.

> John 8:12 KJV

Hail O Cross, my only Hope.

> The often-repeated words of Edith
> Stein, a Jewish believer who died in a
> Nazi concentration camp in Poland
> during World War II.

Introduction

I think I owe the reader an explanation of how this book came to be. I began working in the Soviet Union in 1975 as a guide/tour director for an American travel firm. During my frequent trips to Russia, I was able to keep a diary of my observations about Russia and the Russian people. For two consecutive summers, I had the unforgettable experience of living in Leningrad, first as a language student in the university, then as my company's resident representative. Altogether, I spent more than two years on Russia's well-protected soil.

The book which grew out of a variety of these experiences, was, in its genesis, little more than an ego-trip. To be honest, however, I did want to tell the story of the Russians' search for their Saviour. Nevertheless, the book was all me, and the Lord only here and there, wherever he conveniently fit in.

The book was first completed in the spring of 1979. The manuscript met with consistent rejection from a variety of publishers. I could not understand why, but the Lord finally showed me. In an emotional moment, I cried out to my parents in hurt and disappointment. "You don't understand. This book, Russia—it's my life." The truth of these words made me freeze in my tracks. It was terribly true. I had created an idol.

A CHRISTIAN VIEW OF RUSSIA

Leaving the book behind, I set out for Washington, D.C. This time I was letting the Lord lead. He directed me to a Christian ministry with an outreach to the U.S.S.R. It involved a letter-writing campaign to individual Russians. The Lord kept me working on the project for nearly two years, nurturing me in His Word and revealing himself to me in a most powerful way. Then one day, the Lord led me home to Massachusetts. His will was that the project not go forward; the vision was not for the present time. The disappointment was heartbreaking.

Little by little, the Lord showed me what He was preparing me for. My life was now Jesus, He was Saviour and Lord; He was everything. I had been tested. I was now ready to write for Him. He opened the doors to the publication of this book, and He gave me His Word as the spiritual lens through which to observe the Russia I knew. My growth in the Lord in Washington, my quest for His Spirit, has made this book possible. And I praise Him for this!

When I re-read my first attempt to portray Russia, I found it empty and lacking. The Lord who was now my life was nowhere in it. I felt humbled and ashamed, but it was glorious to know that I had really changed. I now had a new pair of eyes and I could see with the eyes of Jesus. Whether I was a receptive instrument as I reworked the book, is a judgment you the reader must make. There is still much of me in these pages, but beyond that, I praise Him for using my foibles and weaknesses in portraying this land of Russia.

My heartfelt prayer is that the Holy Spirit open you to the cry and hunger of the Russian people for their Saviour. We don't often think of Russia as an area of ministry, but it is, and one of truly great need. The vineyard is ready, waiting to be harvested of its fruit. If the Lord has anointed my writing, the hungry Russian soul will be imprinted in your heart.

Finally, a loving expression of thanks to my mother and

Introduction

father. Without them, this book, this dream, would have remained only in the depths of my soul. I dedicate this book to them and Father Gleb Yakunin, a Russian Orthodox priest and a member of the Christian Committee to Defend the Rights of Believers.

In August 1980, Fr. Yakunin was sentenced to five years in a labor camp and another five years of internal exile for his activities in trying to help other believers. Although I have never met Fr. Yakunin, I feel a deep bond with him in the love of Jesus. Through the power of the Holy Spirit, I pray that his longing for Russia to rise again to new life in Christ will become your daily prayer.

1

Russian Children, Soviet Pioneers

It was you who created my inmost self, and put me together in my mother's womb; for all these mysteries I thank you: for the wonder of myself, for the wonder of your works.

(Psalm 139:13-14 TJB)

Communism as a political theory holds that when pure communism is achieved all classes will disappear. Russia is now in transition from "developed socialism" to communism; at least this is one of the propositions that the latest Soviet Constitution of 1977 maintains. If communism ever is achieved in Russia, one thing is certain; the Russian brand of communism will still foster one privileged class: children.

Watching Russian children became my favorite preoccupation. And, like all children, their enthusiasm is invigorating, their happiness and innocence contagious. I remember watching a class of kindergarten children in the eastern city of Bratsk merrily going their way hand in hand through a park, a few breaking the line to stop to pick up twigs and stones as the unsuspecting teacher led her troops forth. A little boy walked just behind his teacher holding high an unfurling red revolutionary flag. A few little girls giggling at one another had their hair in ponytails and tied back by a pretty red ribbon which complemented their light-colored

1

blouses. On the other side of the park little tots were riding the seesaws while older girls were playing hopscotch á la Russe, the seven square boxes drawn on the pavement with chalk.

In Leningrad, the cradle of the Russian Revolution, I saw children frolicking on the snow-covered slides in the park across from St. Nicholas' Cathedral. (St. Nicholas' Cathedral is the largest functioning Russian Orthodox church in Leningrad.) Their tiny legs were tightly bundled in thick cotton-like socks to protect them from the frigid Leningrad temperatures. As Moscow welcomes the spring season, Muscovite children make the most of the warm weather by having fun in a playground only a stone's throw from impressive Red Square. I saw children scooting about on miniature bikes as a three-year-old, overdressed for the warm temperatures, began to cry when her unwanted playmate smashed her pail into the moist sand cake which decorated the edge of the sand box. The vigilant grandmothers jumped up from a nearby bench to intervene.

And outside the farmers' market in Kiev, I struck up a conversation with two shy pre-teenage girls whose faces with peaches and cream complexions are uniquely Slavic. Munching sunflower seeds, a popular Russian snack, they began to inquisitively study me when they learned that I was an *amerikanets.* "I'm Olga, I'm Ira, I'm a Pioneer, I'm a girl," they say, speaking the few random phrases they best remember from their English language class in an almost perfect American accent.

The Lord is truly sovereign, even in the U.S.S.R. Strange as it may sound at first, it's wonderfully true. The perceptive observer inside Revolutionary Russia need not strain to catch glimpses of the handiwork of the Lord; signs of His divine presence are everywhere. Indeed, everywhere, nearly everywhere, there are merry Russian children, the bright, bright dots that cover the plain Soviet landscape. For me, they often became a welcome breath of spiritual fresh air in a rather heavy and ponderous society. They were then, and are now, signs of His Kingdom that is within us.

Children, what the Psalmist called, "a heritage of the Lord,"[1] but what Soviet Power prefers to call, "the privileged class," seem to fare pretty well in Russian society. Foreign tourists often notice how well Russian children are dressed; shirts and blouses are freshly laundered and skirts and trousers neatly pressed, an easily recognizable sign of the generous attention that Russian parents lavish on their children. Watching children and parents together leaves the impression that overprotectiveness is a common parental trait. Perhaps the average small size of today's Russian urban family, where one child is almost the norm and more than two unusual, is partly responsible for the excessive pampering that "the privileged class" receives at the hands of their parents and grandparents.

Judging by the many afternoons that I frequented the parks located on the grounds of Aleksandr Nevsky Monastery across from the Hotel Moskva in Leningrad, Russian mothers and grandmothers are forever telling their little ones that what they're doing is good, bad, shameful or forbidden. I rarely saw a child get slapped, nothing more than a love tap, though it certainly must happen. Children can provoke their parents by continuing to do what they are told is *nelzya*, which seems to produce a parental plea for better behavior rather than perhaps some needed disciplining.

Being without the Word of the Lord, Russian parents are maybe just a little uneducated in how to drive out the foolishness that can sometimes get bound up in the heart of a naughty youngster. Sparing the rod, the Russians spoil their

---

[1] Psalm 127:3 KJV

children, but, as we shall see, Soviet officialdom has its socialist ways to train up her littlest citizens. Russians are taught patience from a system that demands it from everyone. So parents have had quite some time to develop the virtue of patience, long before they have children.

Russia's children can always count on a vacant seat on the usually jam-packed public transportation system. Signs on the windows of metro trains, trolleys, buses, and trams indicate that seats located by the exits are reserved for passengers with children. While invalids are likewise afforded such a privilege, it is not uncommon to see an elderly man or woman give up their seat to a kindergarten-age boy or girl, something you rarely or never see in America. Parents will almost always stand, giving an empty seat to their youngster, another oddity for the foreigner.

This deference shown to Russia's youngest citizens has, however, a real practical value. Since few Russians can afford the exorbitant cost of an automobile, nearly everyone relies on public transportation. This makes all such systems usually dangerously overcrowded. A little one, for instance, surrounded on all sides by pushing and shoving adults trying to maneuver in and out of a subway car could easily become injured in the scuffle.

Even amid the great media propaganda barrage in evidence everywhere in Russian life, parents can escape with their children to a cartoon film such as the popular series, "Nu pogodi!" ("Hey, wait till I get a hold of you!") about the traditional antics of the dumb wolf and clever rabbit. The circus, too, testifies to the discrimination in favor of Russian children. Clowns will always actively involve children from the audience in their tricks, like balancing a spinning ball on the finger of a giggling boy. And when it comes time to present a floral bouquet to the circus performers, chances are one of Russia's littlest spectators will do the honors.

Russian Children, Soviet Pioneers

Count Leo Tolstoy, a Christian and one of the pre-revolutionary giants in Russian literature, is said to have remarked that the upbringing and development of a child should begin from the first day in the womb. The Soviet government however generally must wait at least three years before its socialist rearing can actively begin. Although some nurseries will accept infants as young as three months old, Russian mothers seem to prefer to keep their children at home during the formative years. The vast limitations of mighty man and the unsearchable sovereignty of an Almighty God are certainly mysteries to be pondered.

How reassuring it is to know that long before Soviet education can inaugurate its mind-changing program, Our Heavenly Father has already placed His divine imprint on each of His beloved children. It was He that formed their inmost being, knitted them securely in their mother's womb, carefully watching as each bone took shape. The blond-haired boy holding high an unfurling red flag, and the ponytailed little girl frolicking on the snow-covered slide are known intimately and individually by the Lord. Before time had commenced to be, each and every one of their "little Revolutionary days" had already been listed, catalogued, and determined. Intricately and wonderfully made, these little Russian tots have been fashioned with a precious void that only God Himself can fill. Looked at in this way, our trip through Red Revolutionary Russia begins with some needed divine perspective.

Tourists are sometimes invited to visit kindergartens which can often be the highlight of the planned activities in a given city. Arriving at *Detsky Sad* (kindergarten) *#740,* about a half-hour ride from Red Square on a crisp autumn morning, the sand box in the playground became for myself and thirty Americans the focal point of attention. The pile of sand, about two and a half feet high, which looked perfect in form and symmetry, seemed created, not played in. Shovels and other playbox toys were neatly stuck in the sand mound. What looked like brand-spanking-new dolls decorated the borders of the sand box. Was this an ordinary kindergarten or a showcase? That was the inevitable question we all asked ourselves as we were introduced to the director of the pre-school institution.

Taking our seats on miniature chairs designed for the toddlers was a rather comical sight. The more plump among us could have used at least another chair for additional propping up, as did the broad-shouldered husky director who sat down to address us. The desks and chairs, as well as lockers and benches, were of various heights to accommodate the different sizes of Russian children.

Parents bring their children to the kindergarten at seven in the morning where they remain until seven in the evening. Some kindergartens operate almost as permanent baby-sitters around the clock supervising and caring for the children of parents who work nights. "Most parents," we were told, "send their children to kindergarten because it gives both spouses an opportunity to work, and they know that the upbringing will be good. Grandmothers can only feed their children, but the kindergarten helps the child to grow and develop."

But although it wasn't mentioned, these Russian grandmas aren't considered noble Revolutionary teachers. Untutored and uneducated in Soviet ways, these seventy- and eighty-year-oldsters are the heritage of the pre-revolutionary days when Holy Russia reigned and devotion to Christ was a great Russian tradition. I found it rather interesting that the New Testament makes only one lonely reference to grandmothers, in fact to Timothy's grandmother, Lois by name. St. Paul writes of Timothy's sincere faith coming to dwell first in his grandmother, and then his mother, Eunice.

Russian Children, Soviet Pioneers

The passing of the faith down through the generations is a precept that the Bible teaches; it is not surprising that even atheists have also learned the lesson, and learned it well. Although no one will admit it, wrinkle-faced grannies are considered threats to the Soviet goal of building communism; like grandmother Lois of Paul's day, Russian *babushki* can feed their children with real spiritual food.

The preparatory aim of the pre-school institution is to bring up children in the arts, music, physical education, and the Three R's so that youngsters will develop into well-rounded adults. The typical day at kindergarten #740 begins between 7:00 A.M. and 8:00 A.M. when the children arrive. At 8:15 A.M. physical education, 8:30 A.M. breakfast, 9:00 A.M. study lessons. The lessons in drawing, clay molding, dancing and music appreciation run for various periods of time depending upon the age of the children. Classes are broken down into three small groupings of 20-25 children each: 3- and 4-year-olds, 4- and 5-year-olds, and 5- to 7-year-olds. First category kindergarteners would probably have perhaps two lessons during the first study period, each lasting for fifteen minutes. The other children might have three different lessons lasting for twenty to thirty minutes each.

"As you know all children are creative," the director smiled proudly, "and so we have different exercises to stimulate their creativity. For instance, the children are shown a picture and then asked to make up a story about what they see." Looking about the classroom I saw only two pictures on the walls, one illustrating a Russian fairy-tale, the other of a revolutionary tale in the life-size portrait of Vladimir Ilich Lenin, the father of "the Great October Socialist Revolution." Perhaps they were both the context of study.

In the spiritual context, there was another lesson to be learned here. In his farewell address to the Israelites, Joshua, Moses' successor, raises the great question: "Choose you this day whom ye will serve . . . ."[1] For Soviet Power today, this three-thousand-year-old question is still a very valid one, one that has been officially answered, and answered for everyone.

Vladimir Ilich Lenin, architect of the revolutionary events of October 1917 is theatrically heralded as a god of a radical new way of life. He is the leader of the Soviet people, the guardian of the Soviet state. It is here in the quiet of the kindergarten that Soviet breast-weaning begins. It is here that the first standardized helpings of Marxist humanism and Soviet atheism are gently and carefully spoon-fed. The portrait of this man Lenin is a powerful, dramatic statement that man is supreme, the creator of his own and his society's destiny.

The presentation continued as we moved into the cafeteria just down the corridor. We were informed that at noon children have lunch, followed by a nap and then games. A second light lunch is served in mid-afternoon, but children have supper with their parents at home. And for all this parents pay no more than 12.50 rubles a month, depending on their salary.

Like everything else in the conformist Soviet society, the format and method of teaching has been standardized throughout the country. And naturally, there is only one kind of school, the state-run type. Private and parochial schools, whch thrived in czarist times, went out with the Revolution.

Children with outstanding abilities are sent to special schools to develop their natural talents. There are also special schools and sanatorium camps for the retarded and the handicapped where an effort is made to cure speech defects and various childhood diseases. "But the parents must make such a decision themselves," the director carefully added,

---

[1] Joshua 24:15 KJV

perhaps so as not to give the impression of a totalitarian state usurping in every area parental prerogative for the advancement of society.

"What about the recalcitrant child? How is he or she treated in terms of discipline?" was the question raised by a tourist who had a knack for making insightful inquiries. The answer revealed a little bit of what goes on inside Russia today. "There is no basic punishment. We try to convince the child that what he or she is doing is wrong. Often there is a moral type of punishment. The child is advised by his teachers not to take part in games, and this usually works. We point out children who have better conduct, who set a better example, and this helps too." Clearly, the social conditioning process teaches children at an early age the importance of conformity to what is demanded of them. The Soviet process has sought to capture the wisdom of the proverb: "Train up a child in the way he should go: and when he is old, he will not depart from it."[1]

We were taken on a brief tour throughout the school which confirmed our initial impression of the institution's showcase quality. Covers on many of the books seemed new and untouched. Cages of birds, parakeets, squirrels, and an aquarium of fish created a pleasant atmosphere for children, but it somehow seemed overdone. Dolls without a single fingerprint or other sign of use were beautifully arranged in the corner of the room. "There are two of each doll, and one set is black," the director said. "Why? So everyone will have the same. When it comes time to play, one child cannot boast that she is the only one with a certain doll."

As usual we were getting our fair share of propaganda. Now the tenets of communism were being manifested right down to the number of dolls and trucks. It was a serene little

---

[1] Proverbs 22:6 KJV

world of equality and conformity, or at least this was the idea behind the demonstration.

In a few of the rooms were wall-charts titled *Dezhurnye*, meaning "the monitors," with a space for the name of the child on duty. Every child has his or her turn to share in the social responsibilities of sharpening pencils, dusting black-boards, watering the plants and gardens, and helping out during meal times. Instilling a sense of social awareness in pre-schoolers shapes the mold for forming Soviet Man.

This brief orientation whetted our appetite to see the products that *Detsky sad #740* had created. Six- and seven-year-olds, pretty as a picture, decked out in attractive shirts and blouses, with each girl wearing a veil, greeted us in unison with a warm, resonant "Hello!" Following the ancient Russian tradition of welcoming guests to one's home, a little girl presented us with *khleb* and *sol*, bread and salt, the two root words that make up *khlebosolstvo*, the Russian word for hospitality.

As the children stood staring around the room's perimeter at the huge adults in miniature chairs, we were introduced to the two teachers responsible for this particular group of about fifteen children. The introduction and formalities over with, it was time to meet the children. The natural silence and tenseness which followed began to subside as a little boy was selected to play checkers with the American who asked good questions. Immediately the children encircled the checker board and watched their seven-year-old classmate polish off his senior of a good sixty years in what looked like a fair game.

The recital which soon followed was a combination of songs and dances; the overflowing pride in each child's eyes was well-merited. And in the background watching it all, the portrait of Vladimir Ilich Lenin, his image ever-present, inescapable. When the recital was finished the children extended their hands inviting us to dance to the piano accompaniment. Before bidding us *do svidania* (goodbye), the children chanted in choral unison, *"Mir, druzhba, mir, druzhba,"* echoing the offical Soviet entreaty for peace and friendship. No one could be unimpressed with the sentiments expressed.

There is no single word in the official Soviet vocabulary more popular, more widely used, than this word "peace." In the Christian context, however, peace has a peculiar richness, a spirit that transcends the meaning of the mere absence of conflict or war. Christian peace is the fulfillment of a longing that comes from within, a desire to embrace that which comes from above. For the Christian, peace is in the person of Jesus, the Good Shepherd, the Prince of Peace.

In the Lord's eyes, were these little ones lost baa-baa-baaing lambs running through the Soviet maze without a shepherd? At least for me, the innocent, heartfelt cry for peace is more, much more than the final scene of a children's recital. Nor is it merely the impressive accomplishment of Soviet political instruction. It is evidence that these Russian children are indeed fearfully and wonderfully made. It is also a reminder that the Good Shepherd's words to Simon Peter, "Feed my lambs,"[1] is an invitation extended to us all.

I gave the little girl I danced with a pack of "bourgeois" chewing gum, which immediately made her eyes twinkle and her face radiate with happiness. Taking the little treasure she glanced about the room, apparently to check who was watching. Then, with a genuine reluctance, she went straight up to her teacher and presented her with my gift. Her happiness had just turned sour. It was obvious that the gum would be distributed to all the children. Here was living proof of the success of the educational process.

Charity is a virtue, indeed the greatest of Christian virtues. But in a society where man is the sole and supreme teacher,

---

[1] John 21:15 KJV

11

and the building of a communist utopia is the goal, sharing takes on a distinct social-political significance. To the spiritually-minded, this effort to create a spirit of charity without the loving Spirit of God must seem a bit strange. Nevertheless, it does raise the question, can an atheistic and humanistic society engender in its citizenry a genuine desire to be altruistic and generous? Certainly, it is an interesting experiment.

As we were leaving the administrator pulled out the official comment book, asking my group if they'd care to leave their impressions. Politely, many of the tourists lavished praise on the capable and obliging director, as well as the strong points of the character and educational development which the Russian kindergarten system attempts to foster. Yes, there was unquestionably something here that we as Americans, even as Christians, could not but admire, and perhaps even be a bit jealous of. Here we found a wholesomeness, a feeling that respect and responsibility toward one's fellow man, toward one's socialist brothers and sisters, was being lived out in the little community called *Detsky sad #740*. But at the same time there was something that caused concern, maybe even fear. In everything we saw, there was a feeling of uptightness. The spirit did not seem free; it appeared yoked. There were everywhere too many signs of regimentation.

The experience was a good one, and the consensus of my group was that we both could learn from each other. The happy medium to be achieved was somewhere between the lack of discipline of the American system, and the constraint and lack of spontaneity in theirs.

Outside in the playground the children were busily running around having fun; they didn't seem to be the same little angels who had just entertained us. Inhibition had given way to a free-wheeling spontaneity. The little girl to whom I had given the gum came running up to me excitedly, wanting to know how much a package of *zhvachka* costs in America. "We can only get *zhvachka* abroad," she told me openly, shedding the almost adult-like manner which she had demonstrated only minutes before. "My grandfather can only get it when he goes abroad," she continued. The contrast was stunning.

Inside, I hadn't been able to get this little one to say literally one solitary word. She could only turn to her teachers in reaction to my casual questions, as if to ask, "Now what do I do?" For all practical purposes, this convinced little collectivist was dumb. But now—Praise the Lord!—she was just like any other seven-year-old, inquisitive, spirited and very real. She was the same little girl the Lord created in the solitude of her mother's womb.

Most foreigners would probably be surprised to learn that Russia too has cub scouts. They are not called scouts, but Pioneers, and both boys and girls are members of this state organization. Pioneers, who fall into the age category between ten and fourteen, are recognizable by a knotted kerchief worn around their neck. And naturally it is red, the color of the Soviet flag and the symbol of revolution. Monday through Saturday at about 2:30 P.M. when the school day comes to a close, Russia's Pioneers can be seen making their way home. The boys wear blue pants, a white shirt and a navy sportcoat, and the girls are usually attired in dark blue skirts and white blouses.

Russian boys and girls do not automatically become Pioneers; they must be accepted into the government organization. "There is only one qualification for membership," a Moscow guide explained to one of my tourist groups. "A child must be a model in society of good behavior. And once a member, a child may be expelled from the organization because of poor behavior. But the threat helps Pioneers to behave." Although nearly everyone becomes a member of the Young Pioneers, the threat of being rejected or expelled certainly must have an effect on Russian youngsters whose desire is for acceptance, not nonconformity. Laying the right foundation becomes critical as Pioneers grow to become productive citizens called on by the state to give of themselves, not only mentally and physically, but also spiritually, to their goal of building communism.

Likewise, in the tradition of the American scout, portrayed some years ago when I was a boy by helping an elderly lady cross a heavily-trafficked street, Pioneer members are brought up to respect their parents and their fellow man. I casually asked a young teenage boy in the Russian bath one day, what the responsibilities of those belonging to the Pioneers were. He broke out in a broad grin and immediately tried to conceal it. "We must help our comrades," he said. "Do you see that old man over there sitting on the bench? He's an invalid and had trouble hanging his clothes on the hook, so I helped him. And if we see someone on the street in need, we should also help out." A slight smirk on his face was still visible, but I couldn't tell if he was embarrassed, ashamed or just plain Russian proud.

But it is here that the comparison between Pioneering and scouting comes to an abrupt screeching halt. Scouting is for fun, for the development of the mind, body and character of young boys and girls. Pioneering is for the development of Soviet ideals and attitudes; its goal is to form Soviet men and women dedicated to communism. The motto of the Lenin All-Union Pioneer Organization makes this clear. "Be prepared for the struggle for the cause of the Communist Party of the Soviet Union!" Russian children are asked to pledge their commitment to this cause by answering in unison, "Always prepared!" The distinction between what Pioneers and scouts do becomes clear with a look at Pioneer Day, an annual celebration that takes place each May 19.

As the holiday drew near, I noticed on trams and buses little posters: "Birthday of the Pioneer Organization." I casually approached a few Pioneers, that is, as casually as a foreigner can start up a conversation with a young Russian boy or girl on the street. With a feigned sense of perplexity, I asked what activities would be taking place to celebrate Pioneeer Day, 1978.

The children, quite expectedly, looked a little puzzled hearing a strange accent and watching the antics of a foreigner prying uninvited into their little Russian world. But each Pioneer listened patiently and attentively as I pretended to be "new in town." The sense of respect shown to me was evidence that the Pioneer code wasn't just in the books; it had reached the level of practice. A few thought a demonstration would take place; others claimed that nothing was planned. And then there were those who just sort of looked at me with an expression that needed no translation: Are you crazy or something, mister?

"Who would demonstrate?" I asked.

"Only the very best Pioneers," a cute little ten-year-old girl told me, "will share this honor."

As I expected, the festivities were to be political.

"But how do they know who are the very best?"

The little girl smiled at my cultural peculiarity for posing such questions on the middle of busy Nevsky Prospekt, the main thoroughfare of Leningrad.

"They just know," she assured me. "They watch everyone and grade them. High scores on exams, that's important too."

"Oh, by the way," I continued, showing off I was familiar with the Pioneer motto, "what are you supposed to be prepared for? Everything?"

"No," was the rather serious, if not solemn reply. "We should be prepared for the work of Lenin."

Another Pioneer, a boy, maybe about twelve years old, pointed out that while academic achievements are significant, those who excel in their socialist responsibilities have a good chance of getting picked to participate in the festivities. Leaving the Pioneers on the eve of their anniversary, I congratulated them, *Ya pozdravlyayu tebya.* Each thanked me; the gleam in their eyes told me they were deeply proud.

On Palace Square, in front of the former Winter Palace, which on the night of October 25-26 (November 7-8),* 1917 was stormed by the Red Guards, I watched the proud privileged Pioneers, "the very best." Contingents of them marched across the historic square as the announcer blasted out the school or region they represented. But merely identifying student groups would be too commonplace, too uninspiring for a Soviet shindig. The recitation of the communist praises added drama and glory to the demonstration. Passions had to be rallied to serve the cause of communism, to raise up Revolutionary boys and girls, and they were. "LONG LIVE THE GREAT SOVIET PIONEERS!" "LONG LIVE THE GREAT OCTOBER SOCIALIST REVOLUTION!" "LONG LIVE COMMUNISM!" The young demonstrators answered the echo with loud cries in unison, *"Ura! Ura!* (Hurrah!)" *Communism is Our Goal!" "Ura! Ura!"*

Like the poster of V.I. Lenin that was the focal point in the kindergarten, here too, man was taking his rightful place on center stage. This time it was the Pioneers' turn. They were deserving of praise for they too wanted to create a noble society where boys and girls shared their toys and bubble gum, practiced serving at meals, and came to the aid of the disabled and infirm. These Pioneers, "the very best," knew well the Marxist game plan; the task was now to execute it.

---

* The Russian Revolution took place on the night of October 25-26 under the Julian Calendar (Old Style). When Russia adopted the Gregorian Calendar (New Style) in February 1918 the holiday was then celebrated on November 7.

Russian Children, Soviet Pioneers

Watching the exhibition on Palace Sqaure in 1978, I was watching Russia's future of the beginning of the twenty-first century. Here were those apparently dedicated to the Communist Party's vision of a rather unique futuristic society. Indeed a society that would become the most humanitarian in all of recorded human history. For the Christian, it all couldn't but come across as a great anomaly, a gigantic contradiction in terms. If the Lord is the beginning of every good and perfect thing, then how in the world could Soviet Power erect such an extraordinary society without Him, in fact denying Him?

What indeed is this Revolutionary way of thinking called communism anyway? Is it man at his best trying to do what up to now has been an impossible dream? Or is it some kind of perverted attempt to erect a Soviet Tower of Babel? And could it work, at least partially?

2

Communism: The Spotless Leopard

*Therefore if any man be in Christ, he is a new creature: old
things are passed away; behold, all things are become new.*
(2 Corinthians 5:17 KJV)

Russia's socialist economic system has turned the proud
Russian into a proud Soviet, a point not always brought out
by Western observers. The steady, monotonous political
assault of the Soviet media points an accusing finger at the
Western capitalist governments for failing to provide a job for
each able-bodied citizen, indirectly praising the fruits of
Lenin's coup d'etat which guarantees every Soviet citizen the
right to labor. Russians take every opportunity to boast that
they have no unemployment. Even a casual conversation
with a maid or waiter can often produce the leading question,
"Do you have unemployment?" Then will follow the methodically spoken words that are exuberant with old time Russian
nationalism: "Everyone in our motherland has a job."

In terms of surface politics, Soviet ideology has grasped one
of the teachings of the early Christian church. In his Epistle to
the Thessalonians, Paul gives the community rule that today
has become the collective rule for an atheistic order. Do not
give any food to those who will not work. The first Bolshevik
Constitution of 1918 proclaimed the same principle: "He who

does not work, neither shall he eat."

In the name of the Lord Jesus Christ, the Apostle Paul exhorts those living in idleness to mend their slothful ways and return to work. But if any man refuses this counsel, Paul advises his brethren to have nothing to do with such a person. Such action, however, was intended to correct, not to condemn. "Yet count him not as an enemy, but admonish him as a brother."[1]

In Soviet community, comrades refusing to join the ranks of the working proletariat are regarded as parasites on society and liable to prosecution under the criminal code. Christian brotherhood and Soviet justice reveal the distinction between the spirit and the law. Indeed, it is because of the law that the Soviets may boast, "Everybody in our motherland has a job."

Rising early in the morning was never one of my cherished practices in America, but at times it became a preoccupation in Russia. Like a reporter out for a scoop, I'd often just meander along the lonely boulevards early in the morning, just before the hordes of workers began the shove, pull, jostle, and jockey routine on the public transportation system. I was often overrun with tourist duties during the day, only if it meant just being visible to a group of sometimes unbelieving Americans who really hadn't accepted the fact that they were in Russia and needed my expert assurance. At six thirty in the morning, it was hard to find real juicy material, like a bank hold-up, and so I had to settle for the less exciting, like the entry below on "liberated" Russian women.

"In the wee hours of the morning of this frigid mid-November day, the landscape of the Soviet capital's broad boulevards is dotted by the colorful kerchiefs of Russia's charwomen raking sidewalks and gutters with hand-made

---

[1] 2 Thessalonians 3:15 KJV

Communism: The Spotless Leopard

mongrel brooms consisting of hard stringy branches tied to the end of a handle-like stick. They go about their work dressed in dark skirts and wear thick cotton long johns to protect their ample legs. The unmistakable sense of earnestness so strikingly contradicts the lackadaisical, if not plain lazy, general Russian approach to work. The few bits of paper ice cream wrappings and the *papirosy* butts, the remains of the popular peculiar three-inch-long cigarette, are the only signs of what the Russians did the night before.

"The sounds of a pair of approaching street sweeping trucks are carried through the invigorating crisp Moscow air, but the *babushki* seem oblivious to this technological intrusion into their domain. And so the cleaning goes on . . . ."

According to the great philosopher Hegel, all of life is an ongoing process that follows a certain inevitable path. His famous formula of thesis meeting antithesis and producing a new synthesis may seem strangely inappropriate to our discussion of the Soviet proletariat. And yet no one schema is better suited to describe all of Russian life than Hegel's. For *every* statement about Russians and Russian life, there is a somewhat contradictory statement which is equally true. Hard-working older women, the thesis, may be paired with its antithesis, the general population of work-shirking Russians. The synthesis of these polar opposites is the peculiar Russian expression of work in today's Soviet Union.

And Russian officialdom will surely be the first to tell you that Russians and work don't necessarily mix. At the University of Leningrad, while we were practicing developing our Russian adjective vocabulary, our teacher unexpectedly touched on this topic.

"*Trudolyubivy*," Zoya Sergeevna wrote on the blackboard. [In the Russian culture, it is always considered polite to address someone by using both his first name and his patronymic. The patronymic, which in Russian is called *otchestvo*, is derived from the given name of the father. For example, Zoya's father's name is Sergey, which makes her patronymic Sergeevna.] Then she asked, "Who can use it in a sentence?" My American classmate came out with a rather uncomplicated subject predicate sentence, perhaps hoping to chalk up a few brownie points. *"Russkie trudolyubivye."* Translation: "Russians are work-loving."

"Nyet," Zoya Sergeevna grinned, writing on the board another adjective, *Lenivy.* "Russians are lazy," she corrected.

Even Soviet tour guides will sometimes bare the Russian soul in this regard, mentioning in passing that, "Some of our people shop or have their hair done in the salon when they should be working." I was finding this true all over Russia. People who should have been behind desks or in their offices were nowhere to be found. Even in a hospital I remember finding the doors to the blood analysis lab locked tight in mid-afternoon.

"Where's the technician?" I asked a girl in the adjacent office.

"Oh, I don't know," she shrugged her shoulders. "She must have left." And this is totalitarianism! No, this is communism. I thought to myself; why, the Russians are freer than most workers in the "free" Western world. But it was all very understandable. As an Intourist guide told one of my groups, "Every single person in our society is guaranteed a job and no one is afraid of getting fired. The feeling is, I'll have my job one way or another."

Pavel, a young factory mechanic, explained the ritual you have to follow when your boss asks where you've been hiding for the last hour. "Well, you make up a story, like this went wrong, and then you had to fix this and do that . . . ." This sort of hemming and hawing are the unwritten rules of the game. But if the chief actually catches you goofing off, it might be serious. "You might get your pay cut, but as for getting fired," Pavel continued, shaking his head with a sense of confidence, "it's very difficult."

Nowhere is this attitude of Soviet workers more evident than on the multitude of unfinished construction sites with towering, lanky, idle cranes which identify the "work" areas from a distance. In Moscow, especially before the Olympics, in all directions as far as the eye could see, buildings were going up; but how these usually unmanned structures were erected is mind-boggling to any observer who has spent only a few days in *Moskva*. At least sixty percent of the time there isn't the slightest evidence of a single worker. And during the rest of the time it's difficult to find literally more than eight members of the working class represented and working.

"From each according to his ability . . . ." This, the first half of Karl Marx's historic precept originally meant that each worker in his visionary society would give his all in performing his particular profession. Although this too is the lesson Russia's littlest Pioneers are taught, for the adult population, Marx's philosophy of work hasn't left the crusty textbook. Men and women on the work force might be encouraged to delight themselves in the ways of proletarian labor, but so far, Soviet officialdom has failed to give them the desires of its revolutionary heart. If we could envision a Soviet citizen quoting Scripture to share what's on his heart, it would probably come from the book of Ecclesiastes. "What profit hath a man of all his labor which he taketh under the sun?"[1]

The second half of Marx's formula for communism—"to each according to his needs"—has an unusual mathematical application in Russian society today. Theoretically, a Soviet citizen is entitled to a minimum of nine square meters of

---

[1] Ecclesiastes 1:3 KJV

living space (the equivalent of a room ten feet square), although in practice many are forced to cope with much less. For the average-size urban family of three, the government should provide two rooms with a total of approximately twenty-seven square meters. The dimensions of the hallway, the kitchen, and the bathroom and toilet are not included in the government-set formula.

The shortage of government apartments and the steady annual increases in the number of new flats being constructed are two themes which Russian tour guides always develop in their presentations. "By 1945 when the war ended, 25 million people were left homeless. That means," the guide continues, "that here in Leningrad alone, almost every third building was completely destroyed or heavily damaged during the blockade. And in 1948 we had restored them all. We started all over again after the war." True enough, but the housing deficit must likewise be attributed to the lopsided emphasis during the Stalinist years on heavy industry at the expense of light industry. Whatever the reason, the average waiting time for a government flat reads like a prison sentence: seven to ten years.

Families waiting for their own self-contained apartment, roughly one-third of the urban population, live in communal flats with private living quarters, but share with others a communal kitchen, bath, toilet and telephone, if they have one. Sharing here becomes much more than a kindergarten lesson or an ideological goal; it's the beginning of communism with a capital C. The quality of life in the communal flat depends to a great extent on how poorly or how well its inhabitants co-exist.

The few communal apartments that I saw didn't exactly correspond to my image of a tiny kitchen with one little stove and a scarcity of cabinet space. In one communal flat, occupied by five people, either widowed, divorced or unmarried, each member of the "commune" had two to three designated burners on one of the four gas stoves, in addition to a sufficient amount of cabinet space for storing food, plates and other accessories. My best friend Grigory, who had just completed his third year in the foreign language institute, lived in a spacious room which looked much bigger than nine square meters. Sitting on the cot next to his two-foot-high refrigerator, Grigory related how sharing a kitchen and bath with only four others really wasn't that bad, considering that some families live in one small room and commune with ten and fifteen. *"Byvaet,* it happens," he smiled.

Even the sacrificial side of Soviet housing is not without a Christian precedent. "The faithful all lived together and owned everything in common; they sold their goods and possessions and shared out the proceeds among themselves *according to what each one needed."*[1] And yet the real bond for the believers was not the living space and food they shared; it was the lordship of Jesus Christ to which each was willingly and devoutly subject. Again, in juxtaposing Christianity and communism, external parallels fade into insignificance. For the early Christian community, communal life was the outgrowth of spiritual desire. For Soviet citizens, communal flats are the result of a housing deficit, and at the same time part of a political experiment. In this way, Christianity puts communism in perspective and vice versa.

Most of the communal apartments are located in the older, stately looking structures of pre-revolutionary vintage found in the urban centers. Many of the "old timers" I was told actually prefer the communal setups even though it means jointly sharing the facilities, and at times long lines. It certainly seemed understandable for those who had lived in the familiar environs of a particular building and apartment

---

[1] Acts 2:44-45 (Italics mine) TJB

not to want to move into the comparatively luxurious, newly-constructed private apartment dwellings constantly going up in the outskirts of the cities.

The pre-Bolshevik architectural masterpieces in Leningrad, for instance, are colorfully painted in pastel yellows and cool greens. Many of the facades are decorated with stucco friezes of characters from Greek mythology, in stark contrast to the row after row of depressing, basically off-white Soviet apartment buildings that are architecturally sterile. The rigid conformity of each new complex to those previously built, even down to the small protruding balconies, is ideologically sound in the Marxist framework of a classless society.

Russia has her private homes. Some are called *dachi*, which are equivalent to the log cabin in the country, or the cottage along the shore. And then there are the permanent residences which are found mainly outside of the city limits. Those who live in their own houses in the country or in the suburbs are mostly the collective farmers, who jointly work the farm acreage near their homes, though some are city workers who commute on buses and trains.

Naturally, the conveniences are not what they are in the modern apartments, but as one private owner put it, "It's mine." The fences which set off the small perimeter of land that each family for all practical purposes can call its own, though technically and constitutionally only the government can own land,* demonstrates vividly the natural human desire for personal ownership. In a broader sense, this too further delineates the differences between the communism of the first believers and that of present-day Russia.

Putting aside the tedious theories of Marx and Engels, there is one tenet of communism that may be regarded as

---

* "In the U.S.S.R. . . . the socialist state alone is the sole, exclusive owner of all land . . ." (See the *Great Soviet Encyclopedia*, Vol. 9, p. 313.)

Communism: The Spotless Leopard

spiritual. When pure communism is achieved, the state, with all its trappings of power, the militia, elected representatives, city hall, the courts, even tax collectors, will all "wither away" into the garbage heap of history. Man will have become "born again," incapable of doing any wrong or evil; he becomes, for all intents and purposes sinless. His human greed will be replaced by a collective outlook. Man will then, according to the script, consider the rights and needs of others as earnestly as he does his own. Philippians 2:3-5 becomes the perfect code of conduct: "Always consider the other person to be better than yourself, so that nobody thinks of his own interests first but everybody thinks of other people's interests instead."

Am I my brother's keeper? These words that Cain spoke to the Lord after he slew his brother Abel, are symbolic of man's relationship to man down through the ages. The biblical record shows man to be innately selfish; by nature he does not want to be his brother's keeper. But as far as the Marxists are concerned, the Word is wrong, dead wrong. In their futuristic society, natural man, Soviet Man, will live according to the great Communist Party principle: "Man is friend, comrade, and brother to man." The key to the great transformation process lies in a new economic order. In a classless society, self-centered men and women will be transformed into collective-minded comrades.

Soviet power also has a substitute for sin, and it is called exploitation. The inclination to do wrong, to mistreat another, springs from the depravity of a political system, a class system, like the capitalist one. Stealing, murder, cheating, quarreling—sins of man against man—all exist because economic wealth in society is distributed on the basis of greed not need.

Let me be more specific about Soviet thinking. In the Soviet view, the problem begins with the curse of private property, specifically, the private ownership of the means of production.

A CHRISTIAN VIEW OF RUSSIA

Those that control the farms and factories, the bourgeoisie, exert their privileged position to viciously exploit the labor of the proletariat, the working class. It is through this system of class antagonism that evil made its way into a relatively peaceful world. Violence, hatred and oppression became the instruments of the bourgeoisie for imposing its class will on the poor working people.

If private property is both the supreme reason for the class system, and the source of all sin and greed, then the solution is simply to get rid of it. And presto, you're well on your way to the ultimate perfectability of man, the goal of Soviet communism. At one stroke, man's seemingly eternal exploitation problem is dealt with and dealt with forever. The desire, indeed the very lust to sin, to oppress one's comrades for the sake of profit, becomes politically dissolved in and through a classless society. Purifying the modern world of the antagonistic class structure, man is wonderfully born anew into a collective righteousness. All things become new!

Even though the laws of history are supposed to be marching on toward the long-awaited communist millennium, today's Marxists would rather not wait for the inevitable. History must be given a good shove forward; man must do his share. The communist regeneration of the person is to come by means of violent political struggle. And so Soviet Power continues to hold out global class warfare against capitalism as the way to man's true freedom and development.

But when will the great communist millennium begin? When will political power finally cease to exist? For as Marx pointed out in *The Communist Manifesto*, political power "is merely the organized power of one class for oppressing another." In the classless society force will no longer be necessary to keep the peace. By socializing the farms and factories, men and women become imbued with a new social consciousness, a sinless one. The source of all hatred, strife and warring is gone. We are all delivered from evil; we are all good again.

Well, ironically enough, the Soviets have now had their eyes on communism for about sixty-five years, since the October Revolution of 1917. And yet the absolutely most tactless, most dangerous question you could raise in the workers' state is: "When will we reach communism?" Using a creative bit of ideological gymnastics, Soviet Power claims to have reached the stage of *razvitoy sotsializm*, developed socialism. But as far as the revolutionary utopia goes, the ideologists prefer to say only that the Soviet Union still has classes, but not class antagonisms or class warfare. And although class exploitation has been done away with, a residue of the private-ownership mentality still remains in the minds (and hearts) of some Soviet people.

Translated into simple English, I think this means that some of the comrades are still sinning, but that only little itsy-bitsy sins are involved. By whatever standards you measure Soviet society, one thing seems certain. Evil still exists and man has yet to become perfect.

How can a Christian respond to this lesson in Soviet Marxism? Can economics change human nature? And can man himself fashion a truly sinless heart?

The Soviets need to listen to the Apostle Paul. "But the natural man receiveth not the things of the Spirit of God: for they are foolishness unto him: neither can he know them, because they are spiritually discerned."[1] Denying the spiritual realm, Soviet wisdom fails to see that the real battle is not being waged between the upper and lower classes, but between the willing spirit and the weak, very weak, flesh.

Both the Christian and the Marxist don't like natural man

---

1 Corinthians 2:14 KJV

as he selfishly stands. They are in agreement that he can become better, altruistic and truly concerned for his brothers and sisters or comrades. But the way to perfection for each is divided by an enormous chasm. Christian communism and communism without Christ clash in much more than an ideological way.

The Scriptures teach that regeneration of the soul is a divine process; alone, man is helpless to rid himself of the fruits of Adam's rebellious sin. Only the Creator can change a stony I-Me-My heart into a heart of flesh. It is His Spirit dwelling within us that inspires the selfless desire to seek another's interest before our own. For the Christian, regeneration begins with repentance, turning away from sin.

Regeneration is not a magical process that takes place inside a new, radical economic order. Neither is it a goal. Rather it is a gift, and it is free. Baptized into Jesus' death on the cross of Calvary, our old selfish self becomes once and for all nailed to the shameful tree. And in accepting Him as Lord and Saviour, we become "a new creature: old things are passed away; behold, all things are become new."[1]

"Can the Ethiopian change his skin, or the leopard his spots?"[2] Speaking through Jeremiah the prophet, the Lord thus admonished a prideful and impenitent Jerusalem. As easy as it is for a Negro to turn into a Caucasian or a leopard to lose its spots, that's how easy it is for evil men to do good. In a symbolic way, is the Soviet "classless society" formula a revolutionary spot remover for sinful man?

Foreigners who know little of the Soviet Union tend to believe that everyone in Russia is a communist. Yet by her own admission, Russia is only a socialist country moving toward communism; she acknowledges that her leopards are

---

[1] 2 Corinthians 5:17 KJV
[2] Jeremiah 13:23 KJV

Communism: The Spotless Leopard

still somewhat spotted. Beginning with the false assumption that Russia is a communist country, it is a short step to the conclusion that all Russians, indeed all Soviets, must be members of the Communist Party. However, the official statistics show that only about 17.5 million of the Soviet Union's approximately 268 million citizens belong to the Communist Party, i.e. less than 7 percent of the total population.

Everyone, or nearly everyone, simply by virtue of age, takes membership in the three political organizations that introduce citizens to the communist way. There are the Little Octobrists, youngsters between the ages of seven through ten who are preparing for Pioneerhood, the Pioneers, whom we already discussed, and finally, the Komsomol, the Young Communist League, which accepts children at the age of fourteen. But membership in the final political organization on the ascending ladder, the Communist Party, is officially held out as an honor and a privilege for those who are willing to serve as models of Soviet men and women striving toward the grand goal of communism. Most aspirants who seek Party membership will often do so in their mid-twenties, thereby surrendering their Komsomol status which officially continues until the twenty-eighth year.

Do Party members have privileges in society? This was the straightforward question I put to my instructor, Zoya Sergeevna. True, it was a rather blunt and leading question, but I was in the university to learn, a little bit about Russian grammar, and a little bit about Soviet life. Anyway, Zoya, who in appearance and mannerism, came across as a prim and proper librarian, had been so truthful in her admission that Russians are lazy. I had to try. I had always found her rather candid in talking with her American students about Soviet life, though she would never say anything against the system. When one of us would unthinkingly say something undiplomatic about her Mother Russia, Zoya Sergeevna would remain silent, exhibiting but a trace of a smile as if to say we were forgiven for the unkind faux pas.

The answer to my provocative question was an unsteady *nyet.* "Party members have no privileges," she told us. There was a pause, and then came a slight qualification. "Only if you're very high up are you given privileges," she continued. Such a bold admission about Russia's bigwigs was certainly no state secret, but it spurred me on to try out more of my basic Russian grammar for bigger and better things.

"If two engineers were being considered for a promotion, one a party member, and one without party status, would the party member receive preferential treatment?"

"Yes," she agreed, quickly turning red in embarrassment.

"Why?" I probed, when I should have had the Christian charity to stop my political interview.

"It's complicated," she replied, perhaps regretting having been so truthful and impulsive. It was her job to teach us that there was no discrimination in this future-oriented society, but Zoya's gentle personality wasn't suited to the task. We returned to our lessons on prefixed verbs of motion, leaving behind the sensitive issue of privilege and the Party.

Grigory, my good university buddy, was much less reluctant than Zoya to field my many mainly political queries. We grew to trust and confide in each other over the years, leaving the suspicion and rivalry of Soviet-American relations to our capable leadership in Washington and Moscow. Following in his father's footsteps, Grigory had quickly joined the Party when he was twenty-two. Whether Zoya herself was a Party type, I never knew, and asking such a question, even for me, would have been a big no-no.

But, like Zoya, Grigory too could become a little embarrassed when he revealed the darker side of revolutionary life. I can recall his nervous laughter before a group of his closest

Communism: The Spotless Leopard

buddies as he told of a rather humorous incident. It seemed that there was this administrative position that was much sought after, and the first prerequisite was sitting for a difficult examination. Well, after everyone had completed the test, the proctor announced that those candidates who were Party members were to stay for a few minutes. "When nearly everyone had left the room," Grigory grinned, "they congratulated us for passing the exam."

I wasn't really surprised to hear such gossip. Although Soviet teachings proclaim the indissoluble unity of Marxist-Leninist theory and practice, I was learning otherwise. The dialectical balance was tilting heavily toward the theoretical side of things. Grigory was a good person, a trusted confidant who often listened to my personal and business problems. But I must admit that he was not a living example of the Pioneer code in action. We both had our faults, failings and weaknesses. I was still a sinner and he was still wearing his leopard spots.

Membership in the Soviet Communist Party, what Lenin labeled the "mind, honor and conscience of our epoch," may make life a little bit easier, but it also involves responsibilities and the commitment of time. For many, these are trade-offs which apparently are not considered worthwhile. Besides regularly attending meetings and lectures, and making dry speeches to one's fellow comrades, for those who have elected (and been accepted) to serve as beacons of revolutionary light in Soviet society, there is also the duty of performing social work. Apparently, anything that advances the goal of achieving communism falls under the heading of social work. Setting an example of how a Soviet worker should give his all, mind, body and spirit to fulfilling the industrial quota, and pointing out the erroneous, unscientific and religious views of others are two examples that a Leningrad guide singled out.

A CHRISTIAN VIEW OF RUSSIA

"Actually," another university instructor who had joined the Party informed me, "everyone has a duty to perform social work, but in practice only party members fulfill their obligation." I sensed in her attitude the classical snow job that so many official Russians have a flare for. When I inquired what her forté in social work was, the forced solemnity of it all proved too much as she turned to her husband (who was not a Party member), while giggling like an adolescent through her testimony. "Well," she said, "my work is to go to the dormitory and sit down and talk with students and try to straighten out the drunks and hooligans among them." It was not a commanding performance; I had seen much better.

On the road to the revolutionary utopia, there are signs, very real ones, that Soviet Russia is making some headway. According to official pronouncements, Russia's crime rate is three to four times less than what it was in the 1920s and 1930s. How valid in fact this assertion is seems to me less significant than the experiences I had of living, working and studying in Russia off and on for a total of more than two years. Admittedly, I lived in a shell, sharing a dormitory room with other Americans, and residing in Intourist hotels where doormen examined admission passes, and the militia patrolled the premises here, and seemingly everywhere, around the clock. Nevertheless, these experiences are my only basis for judging Soviet Russia.

Perhaps some of the most mind-boggling scenes that I can still recall quite vividly are of Russian mothers leaving their infants in baby carriages outside of a grocery store while they did their shopping. This was something I witnessed in both Moscow and Leningrad, altogether about six or seven times. The sight of a baby carriage parked outside on a snow-covered sidewalk in frigid Leningrad weather is something I know I'll never forget. Even in my own motherland—the United States, nominally a Christian nation—no one in their right mind would dare do such a dangerous thing.

What impressed me nearly as much, was what appeared to be an almost total lack of fear or apprehension, or even caution, among Russians about walking on the streets at night. Walking down a rather dimly lit, untrafficked street, with neither motorists nor pedestrians, I often came up behind a lonely girl or woman, my approaching footsteps breaking the silence of the evening. And as I'd pass the stranger, I'd always glance over at her, expecting that this time I'd be sure to get some kind of a response to show that she was at least conscious of my presence. But each time the reaction was the same. No one seemed concerned that I was there.

My limited experiences, however, also taught me that Russia has her madmen, rapists and thieves. Some examples come to mind. An American co-ed at the University of Leningrad had been seeing her Russian Romeo for about a week when one day he slipped her into a taxi, passed a few rubles to the driver, and headed for his flat. His plans were disrupted when her screaming in English drew the attention of some onlookers who realized that she was not his drunken wife as he claimed. In a popular Leningrad restaurant, one of my American tourists took the last dance with a handsome Russian, who quickly and professionally removed her necklace. And in a routine conversation with Brian, our company representative in Moscow, I was told how just minutes before, outside the Intourist hotel, a Russian madman swinging an ax had hacked and killed two Swedish tourists.

For Russia, seeking to re-do man such that he can not sin against his fellow man, reporting on the incidence of crime falls into the realm of politics. Consequently, there can be no reliable figures on the number of robberies, homicides, and other violent crimes that take place inside the U.S.S.R. If however, the baby carriages in front of grocery stores and my experiences on Russia's lonely streets are more than isolated examples, they represent an undeniable freedom in atheistic Russia.

The goal of eliminating or reducing crime in society takes us and the Soviets back to the inevitable question, sin. For the Christian believer, man is through and through a helpless, defiled sinner; nothing can change, modify or soften this reality. But there is Good News! To reconcile us to the Father, Jesus endured the rugged cross; in Him we have our righteousness.

Beginning with the Genesis story, the inescapability of sin forms a constant theme throughout the Scriptures. Adam, after he had sinned, sought to cover up his nakedness and sin. For generations, centuries, down through the ages, the human race has been sinning, falling short of God's glory. Some have tried to ignore sin, others have denied it, and still others, like the Soviet leadership, have tried to redefine it in an impersonal way. But try as they may, the ugly reality of sin remains; it will not disappear. With the Psalmist, we too must say, under the conviction of the Holy Spirit, "I acknowledge my transgressions: and my sin is ever before me."[1]

Revolutionary Russia, however, will not join in this penitential chorus. The claim that the crime rate has plummeted under more than sixty years of Soviet Power is taken as evidence that the Marxist experiment is succeeding; the spot remover is said to be working well. It all goes to prove that crime stems not from human nature—a purely bourgeois view—but from the social conditions of an exploitive society. Whatever crime Soviet Russia admits still exists is said to be related to the "birthmarks" of old czarist society that still taint socialist society. When the blemishes finally fade away, communism will emerge victorious.

---

[1] Psalm 51:3 KJV

Communism: The Spotless Leopard

In Soviet thinking, evil is reduced to the external, the measurable, the touchable, and more importantly, the controllable. Doubtless, the serenity on Soviet streets and the freedom of unattended baby carriages points to the effectiveness of Soviet law and order. But that is all. If leopard spots were merely the by-product of a political system, if all unrighteousness could be done away with by doing away with homicides and assault and batteries, then, maybe then, the classless system might have a better chance. But is sin and selfishness, really, basically, an external matter?

The Word of the Lord says that it is not. Christ reproached the Pharisees of his day for the fact that though they devoted great attention to the observance of ritual and tradition, their hearts were not right. And this is where Jesus said was the birthplace of sin: the heart. No ideology, no matter how noble, no government, no matter how totalitarian, can deal with the evil that proceeds from the heart. Adultery, wickedness, pride, blasphemy—are all the leopard spots that Soviet cleansers must remove if man is to be truly born anew.

The biblical instruction on the deceitfulness and depravity of the heart is lost on a hardened leadership. And so, as it has for centuries, the wisdom of man must and will be confounded by the foolishness of God.

3

Blue Jeans, Half-Liters and Druzhinniki

But there is a spirit in man . . . .
(Job 32:8 KJV)

What has to be described as much more than a passing
infatuation in Russian society is the great penchant, primarily
among the under-thirty set, to be decked out in contemporary-
looking Western styles. And what is more Western, in the
capitalist sense, than advertisements? Wearing shirts and
blouses with foreign commercial slogans is a craze, and a
permanent one at that. Reviewing my notes, I find that *Love
Story*, Marilyn Monroe, Kent Cigarettes, Grank Funk Rail-
road and Pan American Airlines represent the range of things
Western that Russians advertise absolutely free of charge.
The Pan Am slogan is particularly worthy of attention: "Tell
your wife to pack for two."

I remember seeing a young man, perhaps in his early
twenties, who had on a pair of jeans featuring a large leather
label on his hip, "Made by West." What greater credit could be
given to his taste in jeans than this label! It was a mark of
sophistication, a bold way of showing off that his jeans didn't
come from rebellious Poland or socialist Czechoslovakia, but
from the West, where all good things come from.

In Russia, the apex of style and good taste in clothing is a pair of well-fitting jeans. As a Muscovite waiter aptly put it, "When you wear jeans, you feel like a king." And when it comes to jeans, Russians are connoisseurs. They know the names of all the popular American and European manufacturers, Wrangler, Levi's, Western, Lee, household words among the younger generation. Various cuts and styles in jeans rise and fall in popularity; today it is flare-bottom jeans, tomorrow it's the straight look. But jeans are never ever out of style or out of season.

Unfortunately for Russians, however, Soviet Power doesn't hold the same ideological view about a pair of snug-fitting jeans. Any young person will tell you, and without tongue-in-cheek, that the jeans problem in the U.S.S.R. is of national proportions. Nowhere do the Russians manufacture the popular denim material, although something that looks like jeans from a distance is sold in the shops. But the sad fact is, it's not "the real thing." And so Russians are forced to resort to the illegal black market where speculators act as brokers, buying jeans from foreign tourists and reselling them at a profit to their Soviet brothers and sisters.

A fine pair of Levi's might run a month's salary for the average worker, but for jeans, there's no question about it, they're worth every kopeck. Russians sporting hip-hugging jeans are a permanent fixture of the Russian landscape. During the almost two-minute-long descent into the unbelievably deep Leningrad subway system, I'd often count to see how many passengers were travelling in style. Coming up the packed escalator on the other side, I'd usually find that at least one out of every six Leningradians under forty had on a pair of fashionable jeans. But then again, Leningradians have a national reputation for their sophistication, perhaps a residue from the revolutionary city's pre-Leninist, aristocratic past.

Everyone, even the top men in power, beneath their crusty,

Blue Jeans, Half-Liters and Druzhinniki

dry exterior, have a hankering for jeans. This is behind a now somewhat dated Russian anecdote: President Carter arrives in the Soviet capital to pay an official visit on his counterpart in the Kremlin. As the two leaders embrace, Brezhnev whispers to Carter, "Did you bring the jeans?" Carter smiles, kissing Brezhnev on one cheek, "Yes, for you," he answers, and then turning to the other cheek, "and for Podgorny too." For the Russians, the joke is very humorous, since Podgorny was the formal head of state of the U.S.S.R. until he was quietly ousted in 1977.

Below jeans, the next great desire of things Western among the post-war Russian generation is Western music. A frequent topic of conversation among Russian youth is foreign rock and jazz music. And having engaged in a number of such discussions, I learned that Russians by and large know a great deal more than I do about European groups. Much to my embarrassment, many of my interlocutors could recite the names of American rock groups that I had never heard of. Some music lovers can quote a seemingly unending litany of the titles of fifty to one-hundred different groups, and all in English, although they don't know basic words like "book" and "house." I was surprised to learn how many Russians had heard about the fast-selling *Saturday Night Fever* album at the same time it was making its debut in America. Irony of ironies, even *Jesus Christ Superstar* has had its heyday inside the U.S.S.R.

Russians can pick up some radio stations in Western Europe without too much static, depending on how far away they are from the source, the quality of their equipment and, of course, the degree of jamming. Literature from abroad announcing new releases finds its way into Russian hands. And like the styles in jeans, tastes in music also differ. But the more consistently popular groups are Pink Floyd, Deep Purple, the Bee Gees, Chicago, the Beatles, Bonney-M, the

A CHRISTIAN VIEW OF RUSSIA

Rolling Stones and the Swedish group Abba. Artists like Paul McCartney, John Lennon, Tom Jones, Engelbert Humperdinck, Dean Reed, Cliff Richards and Demis Roussos have all been favorites at one time or another.

When young Russians gather to party the odds will almost always be in favor of such Western sounds rather than their own popular Russian artists. Soviet radio stations, which lopsidedly broadcast more news and propaganda than music anyway, will almost never devote any time to the Western "beat music" that Russians so long to hear. The government's taste in music tends to favor the nationalistic and patriotic melodies that have a distinct political flavor. So party time means a chance to chug down ample shots of bitter vodka and sip tasty wines, while relaxing to music about things romantic.

But as with the popular shirts that advertise, and the jeans that make you feel like a king (or queen), Russian shops do not stock Western discs. The Russians have, however, reproduced a few Western albums featuring such performers as Louis Armstrong and Engelbert Humperdinck; naturally, *Jesus Christ Superstar* never made it.

Chewing gum, of all things, takes its place alongside Western dress and music as another of the cherished imported commodities that add pizzazz to the Russian world. Multitudes of foreign tourists return from their Russian adventure with stories about Lenin and long lines everywhere, and gum, *zhvachka*, as the Russians affectionately call it. Even public servants like policemen have been known to make their plea for sticks of gum, which in one case was exchanged for the police officer's coat sleeve buttons, a coveted souvenir from "communist" Russia. But gum collecting shouldn't be seen as begging. In traditional Russian hospitality, a foreigner might be given in exchange a little souvenir as a way to say "thanks."

Blue Jeans, Half-Liters and Druzhinniki

I just took for granted that children relished gum because of its taste and chewy quality. But gum had yet another attraction, a psychological one. "We like to chew it because it makes us feel like foreigners," a group of boys told me as we chatted in a little garden across from the capital's gigantic Ukraine Hotel.

"But isn't it sufficient to be Russian?" I inquired.

"Yes," I was told quite seriously, "but it's good to be in fashion, to be modern." Pointing to his upper teeth, one youngster added, "and it's also healthy for your *zuby*." I was learning something new every day.

The invasion of Western tourists, armed with sticks of chewing gum and dressed in chic denims, has already had a profound effect on Russian society, and the increase in the number of cavities per capita is just one of them. Tourists have been discovering Russia, and Russians have been discovering a whole new world, if not another planet. Unfortunately, the Soviet invasion of Afghanistan has slowed down the tourist influx, especially the American kind; nonetheless, the Russians have already seen that there is another way to live.

There must be hundreds of examples which suggest that a good part of the Russian population has its gaze set westward toward the mecca of "the good life."

A race car being repaired in a makeshift garage on the grounds of the University of Leningrad exhibits an unlikely piece of graffiti written in Latin alphabet letters, "Frank Zappa." In a booth in a Moscow bar two Russian couples, sitting beneath a heavy fog of cigarette smoke, joke about their package of Russian cigarettes which is covered by a homemade wrapping with the intriguing symbol of the fictional British Secret Agent, James Bond—"007." The pale-colored walls of the new apartment of my Jewish friends, Nadezhda and Dmitry, are enhanced by a large pictorial poster of the Swedish group Abba and a hand-made lithograph of John Lennon.

More than a dozen empty packages of foreign brand cigarettes and a lonely bottle of Johnnie Walker (Red Label), also empty, decorate the bureau of Grigory's communal abode. An advertisement featuring a fashion model dressed in a stylish jacket is cut out of a German magazine and pasted on the wall of a restaurant in Kiev. A hotel administrator complains that the color changing mood ring I gave her eleven-year-old son is keeping him from his homework. A group of Russians stand gawking at a Western-made automobile of an embassy official parked on Karl Marx Prospekt in the capital.

"Why the obsession with things from the West?" I asked Tanya, an eighteen-year-old native of Leningrad.

"Well, we just like it," she replied, not giving a second thought to my philosophical inquiry.

Perhaps Tanya was right, basically. Russians are simply attracted to the shimmering, gimmicky life style of the bourgeoisie that take up residence on the other side of the revolutionary society. But there does seem to be another obvious reason behind the obsession. In a society anchored down by unimaginative, standard-cut clothing, the institutionalized sameness of Soviet housing and uninspiring ballads that praise the Red Army, anything that exhibits color, design, or real emotion is gloriously reveled in.

If it was the Divine Designer's desire that we all be near-look-alikes in dress, live in the same kind of humble abode, and even earn the same equal wage, I'm sure such an exhortation could be found in His Word. Somewhere! Like its formula for doing away with social sin, Soviet thinking here departs lock, stock and barrel from the Christian way.

Soviet designers cherish conformity, right down to the most delicate of details; the standardization of society produces a checkerboard landscape with each block in its appointed space. For instance, there are the crimson-colored kerchiefs that make known a Pioneer from afar and the protruding balconies that give all residents their proper view. There are the exclusively state-run schools that offer the same state-approved curriculum. And last, but certainly not least, there is the monotonous array of statuary and pictorial paraphernalia of V.I. Lenin that proclaims the one ideology.

In the Christian experience, it is Jesus who is the bond, uniting all believers as brothers and sisters in the Lord. But Christ is also the font of a wide variety of gifts, graces, and good things which together give us each our divine uniqueness. Drawing on the analogy of the human body, St. Paul tells us that just as our earthly bodies are composed of many diverse parts, so too is the Body of Christ. Together, we are able to become the hands and feet of the Master in the contemporary world.

Now what is the Christian application here to the sameness, the obsession with standardization that is the blueprint for erecting the revolutionary society. Well, first of all, it thoroughly contradicts the Scriptures, the great instruction manual on how to live a truly human and abundant life. The Apostle Paul's surrealistic Picasso-like creation of an entire human body made up of just one ear or one eye, is a good portrait of Russia today. There is just one monolithic mass of stuff made out of millions of smaller chunks, each a carbon copy of the other.

The omnipotent Creator however made us with different parts to our body obviously for a reason. Eyes, ears, legs, and so forth were designed to be intrinsically indispensable and interdependent, each member fulfilling its unique function toward the harmonious working of the entire body. As long as the Russian people are held back from becoming the unique creations that God intended them to be, Soviet society will not be able to grow to its full potential.

The very individuality that enables the greedy capitalist system to work so well, and let's admit it, at times so ruthlessly, has been stifled by the rigors of Soviet ideology. The different shapes, sizes, and colors that balconies come in, the diversity, indeed the disparity between what is and isn't taught in parochial and state-operated schools, and the crazy competition that goes on between Calvin Klein and Mr. Wrangler—they all demonstrate how the well-oiled demo-cratic-capitalist system propels itself forward.

The Russian blueprint is on the drawing board, but its radical architectural design has a long way to go before it becomes fully operational. Take a walk down busy Nevsky Prospekt in Leningrad, or spend an evening enjoying some traditional Russian hospitality, and you'll find that the Lord's blueprint is still holding up very, very well. There are signs here, there, and everywhere of a generation of young people who have risen up in quiet rebellion. Their desire is to liberate themselves from the mold of Soviet designers; "proletarian conformity" is not a popular style.

The pastel blouses that come in light greens and blues and the romantic music that speaks of the wonders of love are a few of God's clues that the Russian creative spirit is alive and well inside the U.S.S.R. Dare to go beyond the surrealistic Soviet design of life, and I guarantee you that you'll come across something spectacular and full of pizzazz. You'll touch the spirit in man.

Soviet architects have their hands full; they must contend with this new generation that knows too much about our capitalist class system. These young people have already taken a giant step away from the values of communism and defected to the ideals of another way of life. Exactly what percentage of Russian youth is moving in this direction no one knows for sure. But on the basis of these external trappings, to conclude that this Russian movement symbolizes a rejection of all that it means to be Russian is a temptation that should be avoided.

The spectacle of Russians dressed in the spectrum of bourgeois colors doesn't mean that the opening of Soviet frontiers would suddenly create a mass stampede Westward. The handiwork of Calvin Klein and his competitor, Mr. Wrangler must be put into Russian perspective. The historic Russian soul, nationalistic and deeply rooted in the Mother Earth, will not easily be prostituted. There is an axiom here that must be learned, and learned well: Not all Russians are in love with socialist Russia, but *every* Russian is in love, deeply in love, with their *rodina*, their motherland.

Tanya was right. Russians just like to be decked out in Western attire. In the paraphernalia of our commercial world these Slavs simply find a refreshing reprieve from a barren wasteland, a wasteland that obviously still hasn't suffocated and dried up God's creative power. The Russian people are searching, searching desperately for a reason, some kind of meaning to it all, a meaning which transcends, goes way beyond, the Marxist goals represented in the hurrah and hoopla of Pioneer Day, the communing that goes on in communal flats, and the security of a full employment system.

There is yet another popular way through which the Russians find comfort for their wearied soul. But it is not dazzling and spectacular; it's transparent and easily breakable. It is called the half-liter bottle. Alcoholism is one of the works of the flesh that the coming classless society is expected to deal with.

If you ask a Russian what he did last evening and he snaps his forefinger beneath his chin, the meaning in Soviet Russia is unmistakable. He tied one on, and most probably, it was with vodka. The Russians' ability to drink is phenomenal.

A CHRISTIAN VIEW OF RUSSIA

Foreigners who break from the pack of their sightseeing comrades to dine in a typically Russian restaurant can easily get the impression that drinking for Russians is a sport in which everyone excels. Spread out on a white linen table cloth will usually be such a mixture of hard liquor, Armenian cognac, Georgian wine, Soviet champagne, and of course, Russian vodka, that it's hard to believe that the partying is still going on above the table.

Every nationality has its drinking tales, but the difference in Russia is that they are all terribly true. It is virtually unthinkable for two men to sit down to dinner in a restaurant and not order a half-liter of bitter vodka. At the Uzbekistan Restaurant in Moscow, I sat absolutely mind-boggled across from two big-boned Russians who had neatly done away with two bottles each of Russia's most popular spirit and walked away with yet another bottle. Apparently, that would be properly attended to at home.

But where there is drinking, there is drunkenness. The alcoholic addiction problem among the Russian young people is terribly acute. Intoxicated adults can be found literally everywhere, the great majority being middle-aged men. Even boys, no older than sixteen or seventeen, staggering uncontrollably along the street, acting as pillars of support for each other, aren't a rare sight.

The high incidence of divorce in Russian society has been openly attributed to the alcoholic epidemic. "What happens when he comes home drunk?" Olga, a young Leningrad guide without a boyfriend or husband anguished. She seemed to be already anticipating the fate of an alcoholic spouse. "And worse yet," she continued, "what do you do when he comes home with his *sobutylniki,* his drinking buddies?"

The drinking habits of a large proportion of the Russian work force is reportedly a significant reason for absenteeism and low production output in factories. But Russia's vodka

Blue Jeans, Half-Liters and Druzhinniki

doesn't always get in the way of fulfilling the industrial plan. My Jewish friend, Dmitry, a factory engineer in his mid-thirties, explained. "Usually at the end of the month or the quarter when we've fallen behind on our production quotas, the director will come around and ask if you want to work overtime. He's always got to overfulfill the plan by 110 to 120 percent or so. And if the workers say no, he says, 'Okay, you can have your vodka,' so they stay on and work."

Young Russians when they gather to party will always have on hand as much liquor as their salary or modest university or institute stipend will afford. Soviet champagne and Armenian brandy seem popular with just about everyone. But because of their high prices, partying students will usually settle for Georgian or Bulgarian wine for the girls, and traditional vodka for the more experienced young men.

Soviet authorities couldn't hide this problem if they tried. They acknowledge that it exists, but shy away from talking about the cause. Why do Russians drink? There are lots of reasons, "Vsyakoe byvaet," any Russian will tell you, which there is no denying. But in Soviet Russia there is one factor that seems to predominate above all else. It is boredom. Russians are more likely to complain about the utter boredom of their Soviet existence after a few vodkas. "What else can we do?" Dmitry angrily complained. "You people in America, sure, you can drive your car out to the suburbs or go someplace to be entertained at night. But for us, it's just the bottle."

To say that Russia has little night life would be propaganda, for Russia has no night life, at least for her citizens. Bars in Intourist hotels, where only foreign currency is accepted, thereby excluding Soviet citizens, operate until early morning hours. But the closing time for the relatively few bars and restaurants where Russians can spend their not-so-hard-earned rubles is eleven in the evening. Department stores, cafeterias, and grocery markets usually close their doors by eight, and the last film showing isn't later than nine-thirty. Revolutionary Russia gives her Cinderellas and Prince Charmings plenty of opportunity for beauty sleep. But at the haunting hour of midnight, when the only lights illuminating Russian cities are from telephone poles and neon store signs, scores of Russians are at their homes, or in someone else's, escaping boredom with a bottle.

Consistent with the collective mentality, there is a Soviet way to deal with the fruits of the half-liter bottle. For the foreigner, untutored in the contortions of the Russian language, *druzhinniki* does not naturally slide off the tongue. But this is what they are called, the Voluntary People's *druzhinniki,* the public order squads identified by red armbands.

When Grigory's friend, Ivan, a nineteen-year-old vocational school trainee, told me that tomorrow he was going to help the police, I became mildly alarmed, wondering what his plans were.

"Ivan, what do you mean?" I asked, obviously showing a bit of apprehension.

He began to laugh. "I'm going to help the militia round up the drunks."

Patrolling public areas each evening, beginning about seven, the *druzhinniki* lie in wait for the staggering victims of the half-liter bottle. These nonprofessional volunteers, whose beats are the downtown streets, are more visible on Friday and Saturday evenings, which, like everywhere else in the world, are the two traditional nights for carousing.

Exactly what the *druzhinniki* decide to do with the apprehended seems to depend on their collective charity or lack of it at the given moment. Walking up to a member of the Leningrad community force, I casually got beyond small talk and proceeded to inquire about her group's modus operandi. "When I stop a drunk," the middle-aged woman began, "I'll first ask him where he lives and ask to see his passport or other documents. And if he's cooperative, I'll let him go and tell him to get on home. But if he gives me any trouble," she continued with a stern look, "I'll call the militia."

I was sitting opposite a group of *druzhinniki* in a small park in Leningrad across from the famous Maly Theater of Opera and Ballet. Duty called when two staggering drunkards unsuspectingly entered this protected turf. The three *druzhinniki*, two women and one man, left their comfortable park bench and approached the two middle-aged offenders.

"What's your problem?" the man snapped, surprising his two comrades.

Immediately both men tried their best to straighten up and act respectfully.

"I've had this terrible problem with my back," the taller, lanky man tried to explain as he placed his hand on his back, still unable to stand erect.

"It seems like your problem was with a half-liter," one of the women retorted. "Okay, you can go home," she continued sternly, "but stay away from Nevsky." The two drunks plodded along their merry way, using all their energy to appear as nonchalant as possible.

I approached the three guardians of social order and congratulated them on their Solomon-like decision which produced proud grins and a sincere *spasibo* (thank you). I asked what would have happened if they would have summoned the militia. The woman, who had remained silent during the incident, now spoke up.

"These two were just a little drunk, so most probably they'd only be held at detention headquarters for about three hours and then allowed to go home. But if they were completely drunk, they would be held overnight, washed, scrubbed down, and be fined twenty-five or thirty rubles. And sometimes a picture is taken to show the drunk what he looked like the night before. Offenders are also reported to their place of work and their behavior recorded."

"But being just a little drunk, that's permitted isn't it?" I teased.

"No," the other woman interrupted, "drunkenness on the street is forbidden." Her tone was emphatic.

"Then why did you let them go?" I quipped.

"Well, those were good men," I was told. Both women were grinning at each other, showing they were embarrassed. The Russian spirit was still surviving; charity was still a virtue of the people.

There are countless testimonies from men and women the world over who have sought the meaning to their earthly existence in the things of the good life. And for those whose lives were already without any semblance of meaning, the bottle, the half-liter or quart, became their consolation.

But temporary worldly fulfillment would only, inevitably, deepen the spiritual void gnawing away in the depth of the soul. Liquor could numb, but only for a while, slowly destroying its victims' sense of security and self-respect.

And the Russians too are no different. Their search for life's meaning is often a painful one, a scarred pathway of empty dreams, selfish desires, and broken hearts. Ideologies and cultures can and do influence, shape, mould and even confuse and distort. But man is man. And as simple as it may seem, the Lord purposely designed it that way.

Two-thousand years ago, a Nazarene called Jesus, claimed to be the Christ, the Messiah, God's only Son. He made a remarkable promise, one that men and women everywhere have found to be gloriously true: "Come unto me, all ye that labor and are heavy laden, and I will give you rest."[1]

Yes, it is true. Jesus Christ does satisfy! But this bold invitation is one that most Russians have still not heard.

---

[1] Matthew 11:28 KJV

4

"Are You a Believer?"

The fool hath said in his heart, There is no God.
(Psalm 53:1 KJV)

No single question occupied more of my time and energy inside officially atheistic Russia than the question of God. From the very beginning I was somehow mysteriously drawn to wonder what Russians really think about the Lord. At Georgetown University, where I studied Russian, all elementary language students were assigned ten- and twelve-line dialogues to memorize each week. One of the many questions which the exercises imprinted in my mind was *"Vy veruyushchy? Are you a believer?"*

I remember during my first trip to Russia in the summer of 1975, trying, as nonchalantly as I could, to put this question to the Russians I casually met. Cab drivers were usually the fated targets for practicing my unsophisticated language skills. But never did I dream that this question would become my calling card during my two years inside the U.S.S.R.

Asking someone how they feel about God anywhere in the world can be a highly personal question. But in Russia, where the state religion is communism and Lenin is god, the question is more than just tinged with politics; it's drenched. I developed a certain theatrical ability for making a smooth transition into my favorite question, thereby lessening the obvious shock value of the penetrating inquiry. Russians knew immediately that I was a foreigner, and small talk about where I was from and what I was doing in their motherland would always precede my loaded question.

In general, those I spoke with found the question engaging and controversial; belief in God in officially atheistic Russia, a great Christian nation for almost a millennium before the Revolution, is far from uncommon. Even more surprising was that almost all Russians would usually answer the question either *da* or *nyet*. Few refused to commit themselves or confronted me for prying into their conscience and ideology. Almost always I brought up the problem of God when I was alone with Russians, which naturally created a freer atmosphere and avoided the problem of too much publicity. I learned my lesson by putting the question to an elderly woman in a Moscow barber shop who was hacking away at my overgrown mop of hair. "Oh, yes, we have many believers," she smiled, which immediately prompted one of her younger colleagues working on another victim to hush her up. I was learning the methodology for polling the average Russian.

Yet Russia is too full of contradictions to make any one assertion stick. The foreigner who tries to put into words what Russia is all about quickly sees this as an exercise in futility. It was during my second visit to Russia, as I was walking up Gorky Street in Moscow, that I by chance stopped a Russian Orthodox priest and asked if he might know where I could buy some oranges. He told me that he was going to the fruit store himself and so I tagged along.

It seemed that on this late Saturday evening in February everyone in the big city had decided to stock up on citrus fruit. Judging by the length of the line, which neatly turned and twisted throughout the spacious market, you would think

"Are You a Believer?"

that they were giving away something. But it wasn't true; communism was still only on the horizon. There was no way I was going to stand in line for what I figured would be a good hour for a kilogram of Moroccan oranges, and neither would the young priest, who seemed to be about my age. He revealed what the Russians call *blat*, what we might call connections or clout. Cutting in front of the line, he opened his briefcase and handed a large wrapped package to the young salesgirl who was obviously expecting the gift. With great excitement she ripped off the paper covering revealing a beautiful icon. "Our Lady of Kazan," the priest told her.

"Is she a believer?" I whispered to the bearded priest.

"Ask her yourself," he grinned. Before the line of tired, patient shoppers I threw out my unlikely question. This time it was more than my accent that gave me away as a foreigner from a faraway land.

"Of course," she answered, gazing with admiration at her treasured artifact. I got my oranges, and the priest his apples and lemons (Sunkist), without waiting in line.

Russia continued to become more of a paradox with each new experience. The more I thought I understood her, the more I realized that I guess I didn't.

What confused me as I began to explore the dynamics of Russian spirituality was the question how *anyone* could believe. Living in this bleakly atheistic society, I myself, a practicing Roman Catholic, found my faith being questioned. The denial of God everywhere and in everything could, if you let it, easily become infectious. At times it was a constant struggle to keep my eyes fixed firmly on the Lord.

I remember vividly a middle-aged porter at Moscow's grand Rossia Hotel who took my bags to my room and watched while I emptied my pockets to find a sufficient number of kopecks to offer as a tip. Seeing my rosary beads in the heap of Soviet and foreign coins, the curiosity of the porter led him to ask, "*Chto eto* (What is this)?" I explained how what looked like a necklace was used for praying to Jesus through Mary, His Mother. He broke out in a roaring laughter, as if I had just told him I was the grandson of the last Czar, Nicholas II. "The Mother of God, the Mother of God!" he repeated emphatically, trying to comprehend the apparent contradiction in terms. He could only shake his head in disbelief and perhaps wonder what other fantasies my life in capitalist America had produced.

God was a difficult enough notion to grasp, but the Mother of God? This was asking too much. The idea was totally absurd. Taking his tip, he snapped his forefinger underneath his chin, the Russian sign for the half-liter bottle. "That's all you need for dealing with life's problems," he smiled. "Drink and then sleep it off."

The atheistic state was all around me. The Soviet void that the image of Lenin and communism tried to fill was everywhere inescapable. Lighted candles hanging before Russian icons in my favorite Russian Orthodox churches in Leningrad and the capital, and my pocket New Testament, were a few of the only physical manifestations that brought my busy and distracted thoughts to God. And what did the average Russian have, I thought, except maybe a believing grandmother who hadn't given up on her grandchildren, breast-fed on Russia's state atheism.

In conformist Russia, there is no private religious schooling or instruction. There is no religious programming on radio and television. In the public domain, religious literature is not available anywhere and passing out religious tracts is illegal. Officially, religion is viewed as a chosen instrument of the ruling class for deceiving and exploiting the masses. And God is defined, according to the *Great Soviet Encyclopedia*, as "an imaginary figure of a powerful supernatural being."

According to the highest law of the land, this is just the way things ought to be. Article 52 of the Soviet Constitution guarantees citizens the right "to perform religious worship or to conduct atheistic propaganda." Atheists may proselytize their inner convictions, but believers are forbidden to publicly account for the hope that is in them.

Was I in a nation rubbing elbows with a bunch of revolutionary fools who claimed there is no God? The question was inescapable.

I put a milder version of this question to a thirty-four-year-old engineer whom I casually met between acts of Puccini's opera, *Madame Butterfly.* Our conversation of small talk progressed to greater themes as we continued our discussion before a tempting buffet of caviar and ice cream inside the Kremlin's Palace of Congresses. We were learning more about each other, letting the performance six floors below proceed without us. He appeared to have immediately gained my trust for his answers seemed sincere. "We simply come to think about God on our own," he said. "I'm a Baptist. I have a Bible I can read, but they are very, very difficult to come by."

Another casual interlocutor said the same thing in a captivating way. "Each man wants only three things, food, a woman, and to bless himself." Such a simple obvious answer had escaped me. Believing in God doesn't require any instruction, the availability of a Bible, or for that matter the existence of a church; it only requires that a man be able to think.

A gregarious taxi driver, who told me he was a baptized Russian Orthodox Christian, not only knew the third commandment, he offered a marvelous way to prove the existence of God. "Well, you know that there are seven days to a week, six days for work, and then Sunday. It's always been a day of rest, going way back in the Bible. It's a day for God and religion. And no one," he raised his arms in emphasis, "no one has been able to change it. Not any of your presidents or any world or national leaders with all their power have been able to change this day. So," he concluded, just as we pulled up outside Leningrad's Baku Restaurant, "maybe there is a God."

I was learning more theology here in the world's first nation of mass atheism than I had as an undergraduate at Boston College.

Anna, a Soviet tour guide who befriended me, had the courage to confide in me how she came to accept the existence of God. For her, the magnificence of nature spoke of a living, almighty power. "You only have to take a look at a blade of grass to know that yes, there is a God." The puzzling inquiry at last had an answer. The Russians' search for meaning was not doomed to failure; it wasn't in vain. God had made an available way.

I guess in hindsight I hadn't given the Russian people enough credit; or maybe my faith in the unsearchable ways of the Lord needed a bit of strengthening. But on the other hand, my days in Russia had also brought me closer to the Lord. I grew to know Him in a more personal way. Inside the revolutionary society, I was finding that my prayer life wasn't drying up at all; it was really just beginning to burst wide open.

It was now clear. The wonder, glory, and sublime mystery of the Redeemer is everywhere and in everything; if only we're open to His Holy Spirit, we can see it. Even in a purely pagan land, the resting that goes on on Sundays and the blades of grass that poke through the crusty mother earth were more convincing than heaps and heaps of organized atheism.

But isn't this the very teaching of the Scriptures? Hasn't the Lord already placed in our hearts the divine truth about Himself. It all happened in the immense solitude of the womb where all of us, including the Russian Pioneers, were

"Are You a Believer?"

wonderfully and intricately made.

The Word tells us that since the creation of the world we have all witnessed, in the majesty of earth and sky, signs of a great eternal power. It is as plain as day, dark as night. And yet for those with hardened hearts, the enduring truth of God is imprisoned in their depraved, deceitful hearts. But for the many, many Russians who had the occasion to watch me flash out my calling card, this was not at all the case. The Lord, as always, proved sovereign over the so-called godless state.

Although officially subscribing to the atheistic platform of the Communist Party, my buddy Grigory, with the leopard spots, was no atheist. At times he couldn't understand or relate to my own walk with the Lord, but he would listen. I was talking about things that he still was just not prepared to see or maybe even hear. It could be frustrating, and sometimes appear hopeless, but even when I was a poor witness, I felt the hand of the Lord in it all. To Grigory, I was just a *veruyushchy*, and a rather strange one at that.

Although well acquainted with the writings of Marx, Engels, and Lenin on the peculiar problem of God, Grigory once whispered to me in the hot Russian baths, that there were times he turned to the Lord. Making the sign of the cross in Russian Orthodox fashion, he began to explain. "Yes, there are those times that I bless myself, like when I'm having a big problem, or just before an important examination. Maybe it helps," he smiled, "I don't know. And sometimes, but very rarely, I go to church when I'm really having a bad time of it, or when I'm having good luck, and I light a candle. Most young Russians aren't practicing Christians, but when they have or expect trouble, they turn to God. I know," he continued in a low voice, nervously giggling, "there's this girl, an acquaintance of mine. Always before an examination she goes to church, prays and lights some candles, but," he snickered, "sometimes she passes her exams and sometimes she doesn't, so what's the difference?"

Without the power of His Infinite Word, Grigory's search, Nadezhda's and Dmitry's search, indeed every Russian's search for God, could easily spin off into some kind of superstition. Denied the opportunity of spiritual formation, God, for the Russians, was often reduced to an external force so similar to Unholy Russia which wields absolute control over everyone. The distorted, unidimensional image of a totalitarian God pulling and pushing levers from inside the Kremlin towers up in the sky doesn't exactly inspire the Russian child of God to look heavenward crying, "Abba, Father."

The little Russian flock knows God not as Our Father, the source of all that is good and perfect from above; rather, He becomes an amorphous kind of fate which will order their existence either tragically or benevolently. The possibility of a personal, prayer relationship with the Lord for many seems ridiculous and quite amusing; it tickles their Marxist-conditioned funny bone. In this way some sixty-five years of Russian propaganda has taken its toll.

Especially for the younger generation, nurtured from birth on Russia's godless thinking, the idea of God can be a perplexing thought. One summer night I took my group of Americans on a slow riverboat ride down the Moskva River. I went into the captain's quarters to find out what time we'd be returning to the dock. As it turned out, I spent the river trip down and back with the captain and a young boy of about seventeen, who was responsible for tying up the boat at each stop so passengers could disembark.

Our conversation about God began as usual at my subtle prompting and lasted for nearly ninety minutes. The young mate wasn't a believer, although he admitted that he was most impressed with the ritualism and drama of the Russian

"Are You a Believer?"

Orthodox service. "Explain to me how a God can exist?" he confronted me curiously, taking advantage of a unique opportunity to talk to some kind of religious fanatic. Between dockings along the Moskva, I tried to explain St. Thomas Aquinas's famous proof of the existence of God. Unfortunately my grammar and poor vocabulary failed to convey much of the philosopher-saint's reasoning.

But for this Russian adolescent, the origin of life could be better explained as the interaction of molecules and dust particles, a simplified notion of the theory of chemical evolution. The very befuddled expression on his face told me that he wasn't buying my ideas, but I nevertheless proceeded. Looking back, I can see that Aquinas was a poor, very poor, place to start.

My argument led the young mate to pose what he thought was a challenging question, and one that many Russians of all ages and with different levels of education would invariably bring up. "If God exists, how can he stay up there?" he asked, pointing to the sky through the captain's window into the deep pitch darkness. "And why didn't our cosmonauts see God when they were in space? If there was a God he'd probably be angry that they were trespassing and he'd make them fall from the sky. But nothing happened."

Each time I was asked these questions I was struck by the Russians' spiritual poverty. In one sense it was comical, in another tragic. As I expected, pointing out that God was Spirit was too much theology for them to absorb in one sitting. I went even deeper into absurdity by explaining that there were three persons in one God. It all must have sounded like a fairy tale.

At times I felt that Russia's war babies were just teetering on the brink of becoming believers, but that one small step to faith was an enormously difficult one to take. They could not do it alone; they needed help. Ella, a Jewess in her early twenties, was a teacher who instructed Russia's Soviet Pioneers. Her mother had emigrated to the West, yet she chose to remain on Russian soil.

"Yes, I believe in God," she told me, then quickly rethought the force of her un-Soviet-like words. "Well, I often go to church and light candles. I like to watch everything in the church, the believers praying, the icons, the smell of candles burning." She seemed as if she was trying to prove to herself that she had some kind of faith. With a sigh of great frustration, she continued, "I just find it so hard to believe, but I really want to. It's such a positive characteristic if a person can believe in God."

"Do you ever pray?" I asked.

Ella answered my questions with questions of her own.

"How do you know the Lord listens, or if he talks to you? How do you really know?" She was asking me questions that I had at times asked myself. Somehow the differences between us were much narrower than I had previously thought.

In our spirits, yes, Ella and I were much alike; it was our respective societies that distinguished each of us, and did so in a most profound way. I had the freedom to be nourished and encouraged in the Word. I had access to books and tapes that shared how the Holy Spirit was working with other brothers and sisters. Ella lived in the revolutionary society; she had none of this.

Then there was Maria and Boris, a couple in their late thirties whom I met through a mutual friend. Well-off by Soviet standards, Maria and Boris had two children, a boy and a girl, the youngest no more than three or four years old. The setting was a reunion, a get-together to celebrate my unexpected return to their motherland after a long two-year absence. Surrounding the *zakuski*, Russian appetizers, which consisted of hefty chunks of beef and leaves of red cabbage, was, as I could well have expected, too, too much alcohol. The curse of the half-liter also seemed to plague my friends.

Seeking the Holy Spirit's guidance this time, I decided not to begin with Aquinas. Unexpectedly I caught sight of a small Russian Bible taking up space on a nearby table. Evidently smuggled into the country, it must have cost Boris, a wheeler-dealer himself, a small fortune on the black market.

"Hey, is that a Bible over there?" I began, as I made my way to the Word. The Spirit this time did the rest.

I quickly thumbed to John, the fourteenth chapter. Familiar with the text in Russian, I began to read slowly, meaningfully, and accentfully:

> Philip said, "Lord, let us see the Father and then we shall be satisfied." "Have I been with you all this time, Philip," said Jesus to him, "and you still do not know me? To have seen me is to have seen the Father, . . ."[1]

The intoxicated expression on the faces of my Leningrad friends became transformed; there was a quiet, spiritual intensity about the room. The loudness of their voices was muted, though my faulty Russian pronunciation was far from captivating. The Spirit of the Lord was moving.

"In the face of Jesus, we see the Father," I said, as I proceeded to tell of Jesus' supreme act of love. "Love, that's what it's all about. And it's all right here in this little blue book."

The momentary, spontaneous silence continued. Adorned in a rich looking, velvety bathrobe, the blond-haired, muscular Boris held his fingers to his lips in a contemplative spirit. Silently, peacefully, Maria smiled.

"I want to show you something. Come with me." Following Boris into his narrow bedroom, I was taken on a brief tour of Russia's religious art. Decorating the walls of the government

---

[1] John 14:8-9 TJB

flat hung perhaps a half-dozen or more icons. And just above the twin-size bed hung a crucifix, traditionally Roman Catholic in design, perhaps from nearby Poland.

Returning to the living room where closed curtains blocked my view of their little balcony, Maria, a roly-poly, spirited woman with distinct Russian features was ready with a question. "But David, now tell us," she said with a certain seriousness, smiling all the while at her husband. "What does the Bible say about a man having two women?" She then told me, much to Boris's embarrassment, of her spouse's affair with a certain woman.

I found the leading of the Holy Spirit in my words of exhortation as I continued to witness. Here I found confusion and distractions; maybe even spiritual ignorance is the better word. Revolutionary Russia in trying to destroy and rob the spirit in man, had succeeded in making the story of salvation, at least this foreigner's brief rendition of it, seem alien and very strange.

My friends needed to hear more.

In my travels, I had many discussions about the Lord, some casual, while passing the time with a mad taxi driver, others more intense, as with Boris and Maria. There were some who impulsively called themselves atheists. But if you were able to scratch the surface of their Marxist education and get them to bare their gut feelings, there was the instinctive belief, or at least a searching, to try to come to terms with this most fundamental question of all of life. Is there a God?

For others, like the twenty-five-year-old Galina from Kiev, the long search finally ended when she met Jesus. "I was studying French in an institute in Moscow. One day I was given a copy of the New Testament. I read Acts 2, the story of the first Pentecost, and I became a believer. And how I praise the Lord! Up to then, I had no real reason to live, but now I've found new hope in Jesus."

"Are You a Believer?"

I couldn't help but be amazed at Galina's powerful testimony. Here she was a former agnostic, now a practicing Pentecostal in an underground church. My finite mind could not make sense out of this apparent paradox. In everything in this Slavic land of mass atheism there was a denial, a militant negation, of all that is spiritual and supernatural. And yet, in spite of it all, Galina could say, "I believe."

But where were the great Billy Graham Crusades? I thought to myself. Where were the tape ministries and the Christian book publishers? Where were the street preachers and the television evangelists? Where were they?

There was only one way to understand Galina's rebirth, and it was not through the limited power of human reasoning. I had for a moment made the same mistake Nicodemus did when he questioned the Master about spiritual things. "How can a man be born when he is old? can he enter the second time into his mother's womb, and be born?" Jesus' poetic reply to the baffled Nicodemus was also my answer to Galina's new life. "The wind bloweth where it listeth, and thou hearest the sound thereof, but canst not tell whence it cometh, and whither it goeth: so is every one that is born of the Spirit."[1]

It was a rainy, dismal Leningrad evening, something that I was growing accustomed to, as I entered the Catholic church to attend the seven o'clock mass. A car had just pulled up outside of the church from which emerged what appeared to be a family, the parents in their mid-forties and their two daughters, both no more than nine or ten. I hadn't paid much attention to them, even though it did strike me as unusual to see believers chauffeured to church. The old believers always walked or used public transportation.

As I sat among the all-*babushki* congregation before the

---

[1] John 3:4, 8 KJV

illuminated golden tabernacle, I heard a little child's voice break the articulate silence. It was a few solid minutes before I was conscious of what I was hearing. The sounds of a child's voice in a quiet church are almost expected by many worshippers throughout the world. But in Russia, the sounds are out of place, unnatural, for little believers are a rare, though refreshing, sight.

As the sounds of the child's voice continued to register in my mind, I turned around and saw this young family standing before the tabernacle in the rear of the church. One of the daughters was standing just beside her father, who was prompting her along with what seemed to be a prayer. The difficulty with which she had been repeating the words suggested that she was a victim of cerebral palsy. Her words were incomprehensible, but her spirit-filled expression and innocent reverence was scriptural. "Above the heavens is your majesty chanted by the mouths of children, babes in arms."[1]

When the little girl had finished, she was helped by her father to kneel down and stand up again, the only way she was capable of genuflecting. The family then turned around and walked out of the church. Maybe they had prayed for a miracle, but I was the one who was truly blessed.

The image of the father praying with his paralyzed daughter captured my thoughts for the next few days. In this family I saw that the soul, the natural, spiritual response of a human being to God, could not be destroyed. The spirit in man could not be crushed. The natural inclination to look to the heavens, to make the sign of the cross, could not be eradicated by some atheistic propaganda. I felt good. I had a greater faith in all of mankind, but most of all in my Redeemer.

---

[1] Psalm 8:2 TJB

"Are You a Believer?"

The pieces of the puzzle were at last beginning to fit together. The sixty-five-year-old Moscow chauffeur who confided that he believed in Christ, and would often accompany his foreign tourists when they attended a Russian Orthodox service. The scores of Russians, young and old, who would give a few kopecks to a begging *babushka* outside of a functioning church—a tradition of giving to the poor and knowing in turn that you will be prayed for. The middle-aged woman on the tram who blessed me by saying, "God be with you," as I departed.

The young couple, familiar with the biblical teaching from their saintly mother, who grinned, "We haven't been able to prove or disprove the existence of God, so meanwhile, we're believers." The Polish Embassy official who claimed that during her last five years in Moscow, there seemed to be a steady increase in the number of Russians going to church. The lonely woman in tears praying in the twilight of Leningrad's radiant White Nights.

The bold grandmother that I met returning from an all-night Easter vigil celebration, who told me how at midnight she had met the Resurrected Christ. But her joy was tempered with anger. "But there were only a few young people at the service," she complained. "In your country, I know children are taught about God, but here, they aren't, and you know, I don't like it." The sight of two Red Army soldiers whispering to each other in the back of Moscow's sole Catholic church watching the rites of a funeral service. And finally, and most recently, the memory of my Jewish friends, Nadezhda and Dmitry, praying to their Messiah for the first time in their lives. Our petition—that the Red Sea would be opened, making a way for them to emigrate.

Even Intourist guides, who were supposed to be fine atheists, would sometimes bare the spirituality that lay hidden or dormant inside their official shell.

A CHRISTIAN VIEW OF RUSSIA

At a tourist gala dinner at the Sadko Restaurant in Leningrad, I was sitting alone with my two guides, Marina and Olga. After a bit of spirited Russian drink and a goodly number of spirited Russian folk songs, our conversation turned to God. This time I was not the culprit. "You know," Olga said, "sometimes I feel as if I want to enter a convent somewhere and dedicate myself to God and do what is pure and right." Needless to say, I was absolutely shocked to hear such words so sincerely spoken. Her girlfriend, who was looking on in silence, later turned to the Bible, admitting that for her it was a source of great wisdom.

Irina, a guide with great charismatic appeal, confided in me her sorrow that her girlfriend, also an Intourist guide, was near death. At the time I had with me a novena booklet to Our Lady of the Miraculous Medal. I explained to her the concept of the nine days of prayer and offered her the booklet which she took and immediately placed into her handbag. She was obviously touched by the gesture. The next day Irina told me that her girlfriend would make the novena and wanted to thank me for my concern. Months later, when I saw Irina again, she broke the sad news that her girlfriend had died only days before. She didn't mention anything about the novena, nor did I. Naturally, she must have felt let down and confused, but neither of us would soon forget the experience.

Even foolish guides with hearts hardened to the Lord could at times have their spirits freed. Whether pretty, petite Kira actually came any closer to the Lord, I can't say for sure. But after several weeks of patient, prayerful testimony by this American on how the Saviour has changed his life, I could feel the Good Shepherd seeking after another lost sheep.

Kira and I had spent more than a month together shepherding some thirty Americans over hill and dale. We had survived long sleepless nights when, contrary to confident official pronouncements, Aeroflot planes never

"Are You a Believer?"

lifted off the ground. We had suffered the heat of one-hundred plus degrees in sunny Soviet Central Asia and got thoroughly soaked when Leningrad's skies opened up wide. We had organized our battle tactics in the face of contingents of tourists who at times seemed to be plotting insurrection. But more importantly, we had done it all together.

There is something that just seems to happen when two tour guides, one Russian and one American, pool their resources, skills and patience to endure such trying conditions as these. The chemistry that takes place in becoming comrades is powerful; it creates a bond that goes deeper than the deep suspicion that marks the Soviet-American relationship. When you're out in the boondocks, far away from the attentive ear of Big Brother, and things start getting rough, it's just the two of you together. Confidant, friend, companion, patient listener—this is what each of Russia's guides, who were mostly young women, became to me. I hope I was, in some small way, the same to each of them.

It was our final evening together. You really can't put into words all the subtlety of emotion that such occasions evoke. Kira and I were returning home from a Georgian theatre performance with our now contented and tired flock. I flicked on the overhead bus light to push back enough of Leningrad's darkness to read a short poem I had brought along for this special time. The title of the piece was, "The Cross In My Pocket." I can still vividly remember the last verse:

> So, I carry a cross in my pocket
> Reminding no one but me
> That Jesus Christ is Lord of my life
> If only I'll let Him be.

"I'll pray for you every day, Kira, that the Lord will lead you to Himself," I said a bit hesitantly, not knowing what to expect. The twinkle in Kira's eyes was much more than a quiet tearful mist. She was no longer the same woman I had met several weeks before, always polite and helpful, but at the same time restrained and formal in her relationship towards me. A Party member who sincerely confessed to believe in the transforming power of communism, Kira had just let her hair down and her spirit out. It was beautiful to behold! Even the city of "the Great October Socialist Revolution" seemed a bit brighter.

"I sincerely respect what you've said," Kira began, "and I want you to know that I'll always cherish and keep this poem." Staring down at my gift, she read the verses herself, quietly, slowly. The memory of the soft light on a Russian bus in what they call an atheistic state still lives in my heart.

It just so happened, coincidentally (that is, if you don't know the ways of the Lord) that one of my thirty little sheep had already found the Good Shepherd. Ellen was a beautiful born-again believer. She radiated her love for the Saviour in a quiet, natural way. During our Russian adventure, I was able to share with Ellen what the Lord seemed to be doing with Kira. "I have a Bible I brought along," Ellen excitedly told me, "but it's pretty well marked up with personal notes and underlining. But do you think that—" "Pray about it," I quickly interrupted, excited myself to see how the Lord was moving. "If the Lord leads you to give Kira the Bible, He will make it known."

About ten days later, our Finnair DC9 lifted off from Leningrad's Pulkovo International Airport for the forty-minute flight north to Helsinki. Ellen was beaming, and it wasn't only because we were homeward bound. "She took my Bible and I even gave her a Scripture that the Lord gave me. Isn't it wonderful!"

Kira now had the opportunity to read the gospel for herself, to learn firsthand about this Person called Jesus who had so dramatically changed Ellen's life and my own. A seed had been sown, and with continued prayer, and by the grace of the Father, Kira would someday become a believer.

Discussions about God didn't always lead to inquisitive soul-searching. Like men and women everywhere, some Russians declared that they believed in themselves, and not in any supernatural being. Religion was "the opium of the people"; though believing in God made man's difficult and troubled life more endurable, such belief could easily become an instrument of oppression, used by the ruling class to keep those they ruled content with their earthly lot.

For others the whole notion of God was completely repulsive. It was for Lidia, a big city girl in her early twenties, whose entire life was studying English in the institute and listening to Voice of America and Western rock music. Her life was empty and depressing.

"Have you tried God?" I once asked, hoping to console her.

"I guess that's all that's left," she sighed.

But as I turned from the abstract to the New Testament and the person of Christ, she became disgusted.

"Stop!" she nearly screamed. "It's all deceit, don't talk to me about such trickery." Lidia's father was a university professor who taught atheism and even lectured on the subject on the radio. What he had sowed, I was now reaping.

A few guides derisively ridiculed me for announcing to my tourists the times of religious services. A customs airport agent, seeing a long line of tourists waiting to be processed, sarcastically commented, "Tell them to be patient like Christ."

And finally for a few others, God was merely a fairy tale creation, as much the product of a wild imagination as the story of Little Red Riding Hood. Flying from Sochi to Volgograd, I was seated beside a middle-aged woman who was wonderfully amazed as I shared about the Living God. "You're kidding," she said in jest, "do you really believe in

A CHRISTIAN VIEW OF RUSSIA

God? After all, you come from a civilized country."

Reviewing the Russian landscape with spiritual eyes, with the mind of Christ, there are signs of readied souls thirsting after the Lord. How often in my own prayer and reflection, I have been drawn to the words Jesus spoke at Jacob's Well: "Lift up your eyes, and look on the fields; for they are white already to harvest."[1]

Blades of green grass, lazy Russian Sundays, and beautiful old icons all serve to point unfoolish Russians towards their Saviour. But alone, these signs, spiritual as they are, will not reveal the Risen Lord. The Good News of Calvary and the empty tomb will not be transmitted by some kind of spiritual osmosis.

Nowhere does the New Testament record anyone coming to believe in Jesus as Messiah simply because their heart was gladdened or their spirit uplifted by the glories of nature. Yes, the harvest is ready; but it's the harvesters that are needed. In the Book of Acts, we read how the Lord quickened the spirits of both the Ethiopian eunuch and Lydia, the merchant of purple cloth. But it was those laboring in the vineyard, Philip and Paul, who evangelized, who preached the gospel of the Risen Lord.

Faith comes from preaching and preaching from the Word of Christ. The Christian perspective on Russia's confused, desperate search for her Saviour can be found in the words of the prophet Isaiah.

"Here am I; send me."[2]

---

[1] John 4:35 KJV
[2] Isaiah 6:8 KJV

5

The Marketplace

This is the day which the Lord hath made; we will rejoice and be glad in it.

(Psalm 118:24 KJV)

Russia's man on the street might not personally know the Lord, but that doesn't mean the Lord has forsaken his little Slavic flock. Yahweh is still the Father, the Potter, working with the clay, molding, reshaping. Unholy Russia foolishly competes with the Sovereign Designer, seeking to spin forth a vessel of Soviet proportions. And yet from what this author has seen from inside the Potter's House, Our Saviour has transformed the revolutionary wheel for His own good purposes. In the Soviet marketplace, He is using the trials and tribulations of an upside-down economy to refine and purify the Great Russians into a patient and long-suffering people.

There are few things in Russia which can be done quickly and with a minimum of effort, and buying something in the Soviet marketplace is a case in point. In order to make a purchase you must first get the price of the item, memorize it, and then queue up in the cash register line, which can sometimes take as long as five minutes. Your change and a small white sales receipt, often headed with the word, *spasibo*, in appreciation for the patronage, is never, ever handed to the client. The usually middle-aged, pleasingly plump matron will drop it into a plastic dish, usually brown (surprisingly not revolutionary red!), which is fastened to the counter of the cashier's box before which standing customers wait to pay. With receipt in hand, the customer makes his way to the appropriate counter and waits for his turn to hand the proof-of-payment slip to the saleswoman, whose thoughts often seem kilometers away.

Long lines mean waiting and aggravation, but they may also signal a good omen. A line of 200 shoppers running from a second floor cashier's desk down the stairs into the lobby and out onto the street might mean that these consumers know something that you don't. Many times too, I pushed and shoved to get closer to the display counter or makeshift table set up in New York fashion on a downtown Soviet street. The rationale was that the longer the line, the greater the chances that something good is for sale. Can a line of several hundred people patiently waiting to buy mean anything else?

The government doesn't need to advertise what there is for sale; the people take care of that. Casual conversations among Russians often seemed to be about where someone found a hard-to-get commodity like Polish cosmetics and crystal, comfortable Czechoslovakian bras, or even a kilogram of luscious imported bananas. It's all part of the survival kit that everyone needs to survive as best as one can.

And then there are the lines that form outside stores in the late morning before the shops open and in the early afternoon when shoppers wait for clerks to return from lunch. Unimaginative store signs spell out in one or two words the merchandise that might be in stock, for example, crystal, knitted goods, milk, building materials, and so forth. Shortages in a wide range of consumer goods taught me to be skeptical about shopping in Russia. You learn not to be sure

The Marketplace

that what you need is even *in* the store until you've purchased it.

I once asked a man "What's in stock?" while we were standing in a mid-afternoon line outside of a curtain and linen shop. He was a joker. "Egyptian vodka," he teased, which sent ripples of laughter through the otherwise stoic line. Perhaps they didn't have any imported Egyptian vodka; after all, they were supposed to be selling linens and things. But I wouldn't have taken five to one odds, or maybe even ten to one, that you could have found small hand towels or a pastel-colored tablecloth. It would have been too much of a gamble.

The memories of the daily lines of up to 150 patient Russians waiting in line to buy fatty Russian sausage, and sometimes 400 to 500 saintly women queuing up in twos outside of a Polish cosmetic store, will always remain vividly in my mind. Being a foreigner living in a hotel, I could generally escape the frustration of the line syndrome. But the memories of manning the lines for a mere kilo of vitamin-C rich oranges, bring back the aggravation that I patiently, but usually not so patiently, endured.

Besides reflecting on the insufferable Russian economic system, these burdensome lines foster the virtue of long-suffering, one of the divine attributes of a forgiving and gracious God. But for Russians, in order to maintain proper health of body and spirit, patience is also an absolute necessity. The difference between patience and impatience could very well mean the difference between normal blood pressure and the kind of readings that generally mean a stroke is just around the corner. Foreigners, especially Americans, who come to spend time inside Russia come to know this bit of wisdom only after a good amount of head-slamming against the cement walls of the system. Only after total immersion in the maddening Russian way of life did I humbly embrace the solace of the magnificent Russian saying, *"Chto delat* (What can you do)?"

As one of the fruits and gifts of the Spirit, however, patience is far richer and more rewarding than the Russian socialist experience. The Psalms poetically convey an image of a trusting servant waiting for his faithful and righteous God to pull him out of the fire, so to speak, to save him from his wicked enemies. And in the Good News, patience is portrayed as a perfecting process, deepening our perseverance and hope as we wait confidently for the soon return of our Lord Jesus Christ. Until the gospel can be better preached behind Soviet frontiers, however, the Russians will have little chance to learn of the Christian joy of waiting.

The random sampling (on the following page) of state-set consumer prices is not meant to be at all comprehensive, but rather to give the reader some idea of the buying power of the ruble in today's Soviet marketplace. Take for instance the typical Russian family of three. The husband works as a factory engineer and earns 180 rubles a month, his wife is a shop clerk and earns ninety rubles a month; after taxes, their combined take-home pay will be roughly 245 rubles a month. Living in a government flat, their subsidized monthly rent, plus all utility services, will be about fifteen rubles a month. They must set aside a whopping 150 to 200 rubles each month for food. The couple will have no major expenses for medical attention and education since both are basically free.

This typical Russian family then, after paying the rent, and buying the meat and groceries will have left over at the end of the month somewhere between thirty and eighty rubles. Now that's the amount they must spend for clothing, basic necessities, and entertainment. The chart illustrates the financial dilemma that confronts the typical Soviet family.

Self-fulfillment in the golden years is not the only, nor perhaps the main, reason why many Russian pensioners choose to work. Soviet pensions, like salaries, are meager

The Marketplace

1982 PRICES QUOTED IN RUBLES

Winter Coats: 78-265

Men's Suits: 75-175

Pants: 18-50

Shirts: 7-40

Blouses: 11-43

Dresses: 14-61

Sweaters: 23-60

Raincoats: 48-110

Nylons: 2-8

Slips: 8-17

Shoes: 10-35

Socks: 1-4

Kerchiefs: 3-14

Pocketbooks: 11-30

Refrigerators: 100-345

Air Conditioners: 325-375

Radios: 20-136

Black and White TV
(Floor Model): 200-336

Color TV (Floor Model):
720-800

Tape Recorders: 140-526

Photo Cameras: 15-166

Movie Cameras: 130-540

Stereo Systems: 178-1510

Albums: 1-3

Pianos: 675-690

Guitars: 15-33

Electric Guitars: 167-264

Electric Organs: 900-3,000

Stuffed Animals: 5-25

Dolls: 5-10

Briefcases: 10-25

Wrist Watches: 29-64

Umbrellas: 17-35

Sunglasses: 1-6

Electric Shavers: 14-30

Motorcycles: 540-1,050

Outboard Motors: 540-830

Automobiles: 5,300-15,000

Half-liter of Vodka: 5-7

Half-liter of Cognac: 10-16

Package of Cigarettes: .40-.60

Theatre Tickets: 1-3.50

Museum Entrance
Fees: .20-.40

when compared to the inflated cost of food and clothing. For a pensioner living alone, I was told, seventy to eighty rubles a month is the absolute minimum needed to live a modest life, but I found that many retirees received pensions as low as forty and forty-five rubles a month. The complaint was always the same, it's just not enough. "Everything is so expensive," a shoeshine kiosk operator shook his head. "Meats, groceries, they're all so very expensive."

A CHRISTIAN VIEW OF RUSSIA

Some retirees resort to collecting mushrooms or picking flowers and selling them on the street. Others knit hats and scarves and line up outside the farmers' markets to find buyers for their hand-made knitted goods. It's officially illegal, but no one seems to care. And begging kopecks from charitable passersby outside of a Russian Orthodox church seems the last resort for the more desperate. True, Revolutionary Russia may not have poverty, but many Soviet senior citizens live under severe financial constraints.

"A bottle of white wine," my friend Grigory told the salesgirl in the liquor store.

"Only red," she snapped, with a sense of indifference that couldn't have been plainer.

Walking out empty-handed Grigory was disappointed, though hardly surprised. "Only one firm, just one firm, the government. No one cares." He had put his finger on the problem of socialism. No one cares, because no one is given any incentive to care. The total lack of competition is why service is poor and so many consumer items in short supply. Shortages are likely to crop up at any time, and they do. Today white wine, tomorrow red. Yesterday the shops had insulated boots, but today they are nowhere to be found; perhaps it will remain this way indefinitely. Consumers learn to survive by stocking up on items when they are available, not when they are needed.

But there is yet another lesson which transcends the practical value of the Russian marketplace philosophy. Each day should be lived to the fullest, for Soviet Russia, in her awesome power, may choose at any time to rearrange the lives of her citizens. The popular restaurant across the way may be closed indefinitely because its patrons became just a little too rambunctious for their own good. Or maybe there isn't any apparent reason for the closing; there doesn't have to be. In a society of total, unadulterated control, the present

The Marketplace

moment becomes more precious than a hundred tomorrows.

The Russian outlook on life has a familiar Christian ring to it. Remember Jesus' teaching on the birds of the air and the flowers of the field. It is the Father's providence that wonderfully sustains all of nature; as sons and daughters of the King, we need only to have faith and to set our hearts on the Kingdom.

Unknowingly, the Russians have taken to their bosom the truth of the Messiah's words: "So do not worry about tomorrow: tomorrow will take care of itself. Each day has enough trouble of its own."[1] How ironical it is that we in the so-called Christian world with our plentiful and overflowing stores and supermarkets are the world's greatest worriers. And these so-called pagans behind the Iron Curtain are living, to some small degree, within the Christian experience. I firmly believe that we all need to take a closer look at what we really believe. And again, I just can't help but see the Lord confounding the purposes and design of the revolutionary potter's wheel.

As quick-paced and impatient as I often was, enduring long lines in frequently frigid or dismally rainy weather was a test my flesh dreaded. As far as the Russians were concerned, I was often an impulsive, frenetic foreigner that needed his metabolism slowed down drastically, or maybe even turned off. There were countless times that I gave up and walked away from those punishing lines. I just didn't possess the angelic patience to wait and wait and wait some more. I too was still on the Potter's Wheel.

Ice cream parlors, which also serve champagne to wash down the rich ice cream, are very popular with Russians. But like the restaurants and cafes, there are too few of them. The *pivnaya* (beer bar) is another Russian cultural institution,

---

[1] Matthew 6:34 TJB

where for a minimum entrance fee of less than a ruble you'll be brought a large beer and often a tray with pretzels, a sliver of raw fish, a piece of stale salted bread, and a Russian cucumber (without the seeds). These saloons, which draw mostly men, are notorious for being rowdy places where fights can break out at any time.

Almost like a fairy tale, all of Russia closes down at 11:00 P.M. to give her trolls and munchkins enough time to rush back to their institutionalized apartment complexes and crowded communal flats before midnight. But for the Russian people, it's not a fairy tale, or the script of an existential play; it's their life, their fate. It is all part of what it means to be a Russian in the revolutionary society.

In a society which proclaims there is no God, the state becomes, so to speak, a mother and more, a god. Mother Russia, Revolutionary Russia—together she seeks to provide material sustenance for her children, preparing the way for the ideological nourishment that only she can give. Playing the dual role is a delicate balancing act, a subtle trick. Most Russians would probably admit that in providing free education, socialized medicine, and a guaranteed job, Mother Russia does well in making a comfortable nest for her chicks to huddle in. Here, she shames the West nicely. The market-place, however, is another question; it is not a part of the comforting nest.

Here in the marketplace even the proudest Soviet citizen must acknowledge that Mother Russia is not the all-sufficient provider she proclaims to be. With a wave of her magic wand, presto, a sick economy doesn't suddenly become sound. And so the Russian consumer must wait patiently for many good and basic things.

Like everything else that happens to them, no one seems to know why, or at least no one says. What takes place behind the crimson walls of the ancient Kremlin is comically portrayed in lively anecdotes, but real analysis is strangely lacking. The proletariat find little common bond with their very distant government; they are pawns that are moved without their will on the Soviet chessboard. And what can they say but the old standby, "*Chto delat* (What can you do)?"

But there are certain pragmatic reasons that explain the critical state of affairs that exists in the Soviet marketplace. The top priority given to defense at the expense of light industry, and the near absence of incentive in the socialist set-up, are, to be sure, major factors.

There is still another reason. It is not empirical, but spiritual. Everything, literally everything, that exists in Soviet life has as its intrinsic purpose to fashion a true collectivist, one who will seek the ideological nourishment that flows from the fruits of communism.

"No servant can serve two masters: for either he will hate the one, and love the other; or else he will hold to the one, and despise the other."[1] How well Jesus knew our weak human nature, the conflicts that prey upon our minds and spirits. Living in the world as a pilgrim on a journey Home isn't always easy; it is difficult. We must continually place the world, material gain and ambition into perspective. The Christian believer must never lose sight of the fact that the Lord desires that we be His entirely. In the letter of James we read how dear we are to the heart of God: "Do ye think that the scripture saith in vain, The spirit that dwelleth in us lusteth to envy?"[2]

Raising herself up as the revolutionary Golden Calf, Soviet Russia too has her priorities. Anything that is a hindrance, a distraction from its official goals, must be done away with. And topping the "hit list" are religion and

---

[1] Luke 16:13 KJV
[2] James 4:5 KJV

consumerism. The thirst for the spiritual, the lust for the material—together they become an unexpected pair, but enemies of the state nevertheless. The more material comforts that a man has, the more he will seek. This syndrome of rising expectations can easily become a threat to the great Soviet experiment. The cult of communism then, seeks to form a generation of citizens that will look to the revolutionary Golden Calf as the center and awe of its human existence. More than a political ideology, communism is a very real form of satanic bondage, perhaps one of the better definitions of Soviet totalitarianism.

Anyone who tries to figure out how Russians budget their monthly earnings may have some trouble understanding Russian mathematics, as the following anecdote suggests. A foreign correspondent during an interview with Brezhnev asks the Communist Party leader what the typical monthly salary is in the U.S.S.R. "About 170 rubles," Brezhnev replies. "And how does the average person spend his money?" the journalist inquires. "Well," Brezhnev continues, "let's say fifteen rubles for rent, 100 or so for food, eighty for entertainment, then sixty for furniture, maybe 120 for clothes—" "But I don't understand, Mr. Brezhnev," the confused reporter interrupts, "how can your people spend so much when they have only 170 rubles to begin with?" Dumbfounded himself, Brezhnev shrugs his shoulders, "The heck I know!"

I recall when this great discrepancy between Russian expenses and wages first dawned on me. I was having dinner with Boris at the Uzbekistan Restaurant in Moscow, while Maria was home caring for the children. All about me I saw Russians feasting before tables loaded with Russian *zakuski*, such as caviar and sturgeon, and a generous supply of champagne and cognac; the setting was impressive, not what you'd call cheap. I quickly ran through some calculations in

The Marketplace

my head arriving at a figure of fifty to sixty rubles per table of four.

"Boris, on salaries of 160 to 170 rubles a month, how can they afford this?"

"Simple," he said. "What they'll spend tonight, it's not 'clean money.' It's their 'left money' from their business."

A whole new Soviet world was staring me in the face.

Fartsovshchiki is a popular word in the Soviet Union. It is the name given to black market speculators. These active professionals, who come mostly from the younger generation, make their money by buying sought-after Western clothing, albums, hard currency, etc., and then reselling them at a profit, usually a very sizeable one. Foreigners often unsuspectingly become the dealers in a *fartsovshchik* business operation by selling their fashionable Western clothing at attractive prices.

A pair of jeans can bring between 100 and 200 rubles, and even more. The Russian entrepreneur will approach a foreigner on the street asking to buy the jeans off his legs and probably the shirt and coat off his back. The enticing prospect of being able to earn the equivalent of two to three weeks salary in a matter of minutes is apparently a gamble that many Russians are willing to take. However, there are stiff jail sentences which may be meted out to the Russian trader caught exploiting his comrades.

Many foreigners are approached to exchange money in taxis, both the official and the gypsy kind. The drivers usually have a basic vocabulary in the popular languages that is sufficient for them to competently negotiate a successful bargain. Counting to ten and being able to say "change money" in German, Finnish and English seems to be a proficiency that quite a few taxi drivers possess.

Meat may often be scarce in the rural areas of the country but, according to urban Russian housewives, finding a good cut of meat is always difficult. The Russian butcher who dispenses this prized commodity has a number of potential ways to increase his earnings, *pod stolom*, under the table, of course. Although state guidelines determine the amount of fat that each cut of meat should have, a butcher need only add a little excess fat to each cut and pocket the difference. Or he can sell the best cuts to his steady customers, who naturally slip him a few rubles for his kindness. "When I buy my meats," a middle-aged economist confided, "I pay my butcher directly, not the cashier. That way I'll know I'll get the very best this time and the next time too." Officially, meat cutters earn an average wage, but in my travels I came across more than a few Russians who would have liked to have their business.

The restaurant business is a trade where there are a variety of ways for making money under the table.

"No Vacant Places" is the deceiving sign that often decorates the inside of the glass doors of Russia's limited bars and restaurants. Under the circumstances, the choices are rather clear cut; either pay, wait in line, or go home.

Waiters in Russian society are considered to make excellent money, but such jobs in the better restaurants are gotten only through pay-offs. One-thousand rubles would not be considered an outrageous sum to land a job at the aristocratic Astoria Restaurant in Leningrad. Officially a Russian waiter might earn between 130-180 rubles a month, depending on how much he brings in. But with the under-the-table monkey business, an unscrupulous waiter can net an additional twenty to fifty rubles a day. Besides taking friends and acquaintances out of the punishing lines, waiters are notorious for working along with the chefs and conspiring to serve smaller than standard size portions. Overcharging customers is yet another way. A Russian anecdote demonstrates how waiters are poor mathematicians. Forty kopecks plus forty kopecks is a ruble forty. (There are 100 kopecks in a ruble.)

Rubles can cut the waiting time for an apartment, a cooperative, and and automobile, and maybe even prevent a young man from tasting the discipline of the Red Army.

Russians planning to spend their vacations on one of the popular Black Sea resorts in Sochi or Odessa, I was informed, must be prepared to slip the director of the hotel 200 to 300 rubles before he can find you a place in "his" hotel. And then of course, you have to pay the other landlord, the government, for renting the room, which is considerably cheaper.

In the Soviet Union where everyone reaps the benefits of full employment, it is a crime to be unemployed. But living in Nadezhda's and Dmitry's apartment was a *fartsovshchik* who was busy full-time, wheeling and dealing on the street. He bribed his boss to take care of the paperwork which showed him as gainfully employed.

Despite the corruption that seemingly everywhere defiles the socialist marketplace, there is some intrinsic good that comes out of this systemic madness. People need people. In the high technology, computer-designed Western world, it is sad but true that progress has made people independent, self-sufficient, and perhaps even a little alienated from one another. Indeed, Soviet survival is not a completely dehumanizing experience.

"I never buy my clothes in our stores in the usual way," Elena, a young Russian housewife confessed. "I have friends who hold the good quality stuff under the counter for me. And naturally, I help them out too when I can." A family who was fortunate enough to own a car explained how they did little errands for their neighbors, who in turn helped them with the shopping. A mother of two, Olga complained that one person wasn't enough to do all the shopping that had to be done. "There just isn't enough time," she told me. "You need help."

Russians pride themselves on how they love to read, but good books, especially those by certain foreign authors and the Russian classics, are hard to find in the local bookstores or the *bukinisty*, the second-hand book shops. A friend however can be on the lookout for, for example, Dostoevsky's *The Brothers Karamazov*, which on the black market might run five times the government-set price.

"Ty mne, ya tebe," is the name of a very well received Soviet film which portrayed the side of Russian life which Russians call *po znakomstvu*, literally translated, through acquaintances. Colloquially the title of the film means I'll scratch your back, if you scratch mine.

The comedy opens in the waiting hall of the *banya*, the popular Russian bath where a long line of Russian men wait to relish the cathartic pleasures of baking and beating themselves shades of bright red. A funny scene, all too familiar for Russians, shows a masseur taking one of his acquaintances to the head of the line, for which he is rewarded with a few bottles of Western shampoo. The plot takes shape when the masseur's brother becomes ill and turns to his look-alike twin to secretly take over for him as the water quality control inspector of the region. The masseur sees in the opportunity a way to advance his own interests. And he does just that.

The imposter turns his back on his socialist duty when he judges a local river as meeting specified government criteria, even though the audience sees how polluted the water has become from the waste pouring out of a nearby factory. The director of the plant rewards the inspector for his cooperation with a brand new boat, but in the end the imposter stands accountable before the community for the ecological damage his self-seeking has wrought.

The Marketplace

One scene, heavy with social and political overtones, shows the masseur, together with members of the town, shamefully standing on the banks of the polluted river and watching dead fish float by. Naturally the film ends with the twin brother trying to go straight. Taking into custody a black marketeer he has just apprehended, the protagonist can now be seen by the audience as a socially responsible citizen.

"Please, don't take me in, you know how long they'll give me," the young wheeler-dealer pleads.

"Yes," the inspector grins, "no less than two years. The judge is a good friend of mine."

For the Russians the film was perfectly hilarious because it was perfectly realistic.

It is here in the marketplace that the Soviet people are stripped naked of their "socialist dress." How closely do we find them resembling their capitalist counterparts! And really, should we be surprised? Greed is the same ancient, false god that reigns in both the socialist and non-socialist world. "He that loveth silver shall not be satisfied with silver; nor he that loveth abundance with increase: this is also vanity."[1] So concluded the sage in the Book of Ecclesiastes. Yes, such is the way of vanity, but also of universal human nature.

If arbitrary Russia permitted dissenting voices to be heard, an unlikely film review to *"Ty mne, ya tebe,"* might find its way into the pages of the Soviet press.

"Viktor Osipov's brilliant portrayal of a masseur on the take reveals that socialism is still somehow helpless in getting rid of the selfish streak in man. Again, Soviet Man, this time going under cover in the baths, proved no match for the temptation to reach for power and ill-gotten gain. In a brilliant bit of socialist symbolism, film director Pavel Kamkin

---

[1] Ecclesiastes 5:10 KJV

shows us a panoramic view of the Russian River polluted with the stench of dead fish. Are we being reminded in a general way of the true nature of the revolutionary heart and the fruits of socialist sin? In the final scene, we find our masseur friend has not really turned over a new leaf, as again he tries to win friends and influence people, this time through the corrupt court system.

"This film is highly recommended to both Pioneers and adults alike who still may naively believe that a shrewdly devised political system can convict a man of the right way he should go. *"Ty mne, ya tebe,"* is a subtle comedy not just about fish and fudging, but about what happens when man decides to act as God."

6

Tower of Babel, Tower of Truth

*The name of Yahweh is a strong tower;the virtuous man runs
to it and is secure.*

(Proverbs 18:10 TJB)

Unofficially there exists in Russia an agency which the
Russians totally rely on for all their information needs. OBS
are the initials of the powerful, far-reaching organization
which is believed to have more reliable contacts than the
KGB, the Soviet secret police. The title of the underground
organization:"One Grandmother Said." In totalitarian Russia
where information flows like ice, word of mouth is the only
way that a lot of what is news can freely travel.

At the end of June each year, Leningrad traditionally
celebrates a holiday called *Alye Parusa*, Scarlet Sails.
Leningradians gather along the banks of the Neva around
midnight and wait in excitement for the traditional ship with
hoisted crimson sails. One year my date and I waited with the
throngs of romantic Leningradians for the ship that Russian
grandmothers predicted would come, but that never came. It
was like waiting for Godot.

There was no publication of the event, no mention of the
holiday on television or radio. People were just anxiously
asking one another when the ship would sail through as they

peered out onto the symbolic dark Neva that reflected the sparkling light of the surrounding row of light poles. "I don't know," a girl standing next to us answered, "I'm asking myself."

"Well, Tanya," I teased, "maybe the Scarlet Sails won't come this year."

"No," she insisted with confidence, a little irritated at my apparent lack of faith in her Mother Russia, "everyone says that the *Alye Parusa* will be here, and I know it will come too."

In trying so hard to control minds and convert hearts, Revolutionary Russia has turned herself into a society of truly imaginative madness. Only the script of your typical Woody Allen film could contain such fantastic comedy and create such unparalleled insanity. This humorous side of Soviet life temporarily softens the image of a monolithic regime out to sell its peculiar way of thinking.

The daily, true-to-life Soviet scripts include some of the following scenes.

Transportation lines are re-routed to avoid ongoing construction. But the passengers discover the change only when the bus unexpectedly turns left instead of right. Sorry! The railing on the bridge has just been freshly painted; the blue stain on your pants now matches your navy socks. Who would think to leave a sign "Wet Paint"? Nobody would, that's who. The morning service at the local Russian Orthodox Church has just been changed from eight to nine o'clock. "Why didn't they put up a notice?" a few irritated *babushki* complain among themselves, as they stand, numbed by the chilling Moscow wind, outside the locked doors of the church.

There aren't any more tickets for the foreign film festival, you say. Well, maybe this is what the crotchety sales attendant to the left of the ticket counter says, but why not try her colleague five steps to the right? *She*, it turns out, still has plenty left. According to the billboard, a new feature film will make its debut this afternoon at three; according to the theatre personnel, however, "We still haven't received that film."

The posted information at the dock house, which was confirmed by the ticket lady, not once but thrice, announced that the boat excursion up the Moskva also returns to the point of departure. But obviously the captain hasn't spoken with that ticket lady in a while. Halfway up the river it's time for a casual announcement: "Everybody gets off at the next stop." If you lose something in a hotel or restaurant, don't even try to check on it the next day, because an entirely new crew is working; you have to wait an additional day until the same employees return to work. Why should anyone write down what's been found or leave it in a designated spot?

A patient is terminally ill with cancer, but only the family knows. The doctor comforts the dying young mother and tells her not to worry. "You'll be feeling much better after the operation." And if you're fated to lose your tourist status and become a patient in Russia, I suggest you not become too excited when the orderly brings in your lunch and the nurse takes it away. You need blood work, remember! Welcome to Woody Allen's Russia!

The Russians are virtual masters at dealing with the institutionalized information freeze as they cope with frustrating realities. They have learned to provide careful diplomatic answers to straightforward questions that, one would think, call for a simple *da* or *nyet* reply. Experience has taught them that nothing, aboslutely, positively nothing, can be certain inside their very uncertain and disordered society. Ask a Russian in the middle of the day if a particular restaurant is open, and the odds are high, very high, that the response will be noncommittal, "It should be." "Oh, by the way, did you hear that they are closing that restaurant for life?" "*Vsyo vozmozhno*, (anything is possible)" will neatly cover the likelihood.

Without question, one of the royal frustrations in the study program at the University of Leningrad was the indescribable lack of information about what was going on in our unorganized program. In addition to the formal language training, there were also extracurricular activities, which usually were always more impromptu than organized. The problem of communication was hopelessly muddled. Schedules of optional excursions, meetings, and lectures were cancelled, or changed to another time and then cancelled, and later re-scheduled for another day. Then the confusion would start all over again. Free time ended up in an activity, and a planned activity often ended up not being anything, except a notice on the dorm bulletin board.

We learned to treat the official word as a farce, and rarely found it otherwise. One could never be sure whether the consistent inconsistency of the schedule was deliberate, or just the pervasive inefficiency in the Soviet socialist setup. But at times my Russian-conditioned intuition told me we weren't supposed to know what we should have known until it was time to know it.

A classic example of it all was the following. Program reads free time. At lunch time, as we queued up for cafeteria chow of beef in gravy and starchy macaroni, the word spreads that at 2:30 P.M. there is going to be a lecture on Dostoevsky. Now, don't get me wrong. It wasn't that I wasn't interested in Dostoevsky, it was just that I had learned to try to limit my dosages of Russian aggravation. The students who showed up to be enlightened about the great Russian novelist weren't totally confounded when they were told that the lecturer was in Moscow. For all we knew Dostoevsky himself had just returned to the city of his birth. We were all just getting used to being a little confused.

Tower of Babel, Tower of Truth

And then there was the time that a film at a Leningrad *kino* was substituted for classes. Well naturally, no one could complain about that. Following the film, we were bused back to the university. It was 10:30 A.M. and classes ordinarily ran until after noon. One hundred and sixty students and five American college profs stood around the university buildings like a bunch of lost sheep waiting to be led, somewhere, anywhere. It was time to play the waiting game again. Godot didn't make it this time either; Russia's grandmothers could have predicted that. In grand Soviet style, we were not let down. No one came, and so everyone slowly wandered off in different directions to play hooky or stare up at the cloudy sky. It was just another day.

Incidentally, making a phone call between cities in Russia also is part of the fun. You don't just pick up the phone and dial a friend one-thousand kilometers away. First of all, not everyone is fortunate enough to have his own private telephone. The shortage of phones is remedied by the abundance of post offices, since they also serve as the community's telephone exchange. It is there that most Russians will go to put through an inter-city call. As for the Russian that has his own phone, one option is to reserve the call in advance with the operator. Maybe it'll take an hour or two, and sometimes much longer. So you have to wait and wait, and probably then wait some more. If you're full of energy, as well as gifted with patience, perseverance and persistence, you can dial a designated code number, and then the telephone number, repeating the process until you strike it lucky. But not everyone has a disposition suited for such an endeavor. As everyone now knows, I didn't. The grayish tint of my hair is sufficient evidence of that.

I'm sure that the Lord in His divine humor can't but chuckle at the wisdom of man's plan for an earthly paradise. Blue streaks of paint on my trousers and a telephone testing that often sent me clear off the utopian deep end is, I guess, also what goes into making up the revolutionary way.

But one thing does seem certain amid this vast stretch of uncertainty. No one in the Heavenly Jerusalem will need to worry about brushing up against wet paint or getting on the right bus going in the wrong direction. There won't be any disorder in that Kingdom for, as we know, our God is not the author of confusion, but of harmony and peace.

In creation itself we witness a marvelous, enduring order. Poor Job, even covered with boils from the soles of his feet to the top of his head, could wonder at the great ordinances of heaven with each and every star remaining in its mysterious place. For him, as for us, the source and skill of this celestial order could only be evidence of the Wisdom of the Lord, guiding all things for the good.

Beside the comical side here, there is also, I believe, a spiritual dimension. The fear of the Lord, Proverbs tells us, is the beginning of wisdom. Unholy Russia, denying, indeed contradicting, the very source of all wisdom, can only be confounded in erecting its revolutionary Tower of Babel. The ancient city of confusion was broken down by the confusion and diversity of many different tongues. Will the stony Soviet tower totter and eventually topple as the information blitz covers a wider and wider area?

Maybe, maybe not. But there is a kind of certainty here, it seems. No one should expect to wake up to a classless utopia until telephone lines are unscrambled and bus lines become a little less arbitrary. Communism, like its capitalist counterpart, needs continuous communication.

There is a way to escape from this maze of confusion into the outer world. The way to cope, at least to some small degree, is called in the Russian tongue, *Golos Ameriki*, the Voice of America. For the afflicted Russian, the Voice, BBC (the British Broadcasting Corporation), and other free world stations are ways to learn of another world of ideas, ideas with a freshness, color, and often appeal that can stimulate the solitude and monotony of a cobwebbed mind. It is a way to take some time off from all the seriousness that building communism entails.

According to many Russians, prior to President Nixon's historic visit to the U.S.S.R. in May 1972, the Voice of America (VOA) was very efficiently jammed. In the Russian mind then, *Golos Ameriki,* is the fruit of President Nixon's summitry. "Do you listen to *Golos Ameriki?*" was one question that I repeatedly asked Russians from taxi drivers to an occasional Russian Orthodox priest. And, like with my other calling card, "Are you a believer?" I got a fair share of affirmative replies. If my polling of Russians is at all an accurate representation of what the Voice means to Russians, VOA can almost be considered a contemporary Russian institution.

For under 100 rubles, about two-weeks salary, a Leningradian or Muscovite can purchase a radio that can pick up VOA and other Western stations. The Voice provides a wide spectrum of information about life in the States, from literature and theatre to religion and government. Many listeners have their favorite programs and announcers. Especially for the younger generation, the Voice of America is popular because of its broadcasts of American jazz and rock music. Lessons in the English language and the peculiar American pronunciation are favorites of those that are learning for free in the institutes or quietly at home. And last, but certainly not least, Russians also turn to *Golos Ameriki* as another source of news to find out what's happening in the world outside the Soviet Union.

At a dinner party, when the conversation turned to American life, Larisa enthusiastically jumped in, adding her little tidbit of hearsay.

A CHRISTIAN VIEW OF RUSSIA

"I just heard over the VOA that American millionaires don't know from one day to the next if they are going to lose their fortune."

"Talking about fortunes," Lena, her girlfriend interrupted, "have you heard what they're saying about Onassis' daughter? She just married a Russian. And they are going to live in Moscow," she beamed.

A few friends admitted that they hadn't heard the news.

"It was only over *Golos Ameriki*, it wasn't in our papers," Lena explained, as if it was only natural that the Soviet press would omit such a newsworthy event. "And Voice of America says that her husband has a glass eye."

What must go through the Russian minds, I thought to myself, as they realize that they have to depend on foreign news programs rather than their own press for real information. I didn't ask, not wanting to confront a group of people that I had just met. But I had asked my friends such blunt, provocative questions before, so I could have predicted the reply. The tone of voice might have been jocular or serious. There may have been a hint of irritation or a sense of befuddlement. But the message would have been short and to the point, the Russian point, *"Ne znayu*, I don't know."

But how much of what is heard on VOA is believed is yet another question. Remember, both Soviet and American news sources are competing for the same audience, leaving the average Russian in a quandary as to where the truth actually lies. Those who would talk with me freely about the Voice would claim they don't buy everything, hook, line, and sinker. However, your casual conversation with "Ivan on the street" is certainly unlikely to lead to a completely honest appraisal of the popular American broadcast. Information in Russia falls into the realm of "high politics"; it is therefore instinctively skirted by Russians until they've won your trust.

Tower of Babel, Tower of Truth

Poor Zoya Sergeevna, my long-suffering language teacher! Never did she have a school day off from my political antics. When it was time to practice putting newly-learned verbs and verb forms into real live sentences, mine were not about the trees that grow tall in the forests. I usually liked to speak about more provocative themes, like the slogans that sit atop Soviet roofs preaching the same old socialist message.

My American classmates and I found that Zoya had a real interest in what life was really like in our faraway motherland. Our drill sessions often amounted to Zoya asking us questions about American hobbies and the peculiarities of the American character. I can still recall the time she entered the classroom with a fresh copy of *Pravda* in hand. The Soviet press did a quick article on the famous New York City blackout some years ago. Naturally, a good bit of attention was given to the endless string of looting that followed the unusual incident. Our conversation class that day made us reflect on the precariousness of our own American system.

Well, I thought, if Zoya so loves to talk about the good old U.S.A., why not bring up the good old VOA? And I did just that.

"There are many, many who listen," Zoya Sergeevna admitted before her all-American class.

"And how many believe?" I prodded unmercifully, not really expecting a revealing answer.

She smiled graciously at my consistently political questions, paused briefly, and then answered slowly, thoughtfully, and diplomatically.

"It's news, it's interesting, but I don't think we should discuss it any further."

The problem for Russians in evaluating who and what to believe, and who and what not to believe, was explained to me by my best friend, Grigory. "There is a lot of news on *Golos Ameriki* that we don't get in our press at all, so we don't have anything to compare it to. And it becomes even more confusing when our government says one thing and yours says just the opposite. Who do you believe?"

There were those who concluded that the Voice was as much propaganda as what they suffer from their own media. A regular listener of VOA put it this way, "Your government is simply out to show that life in the U.S.A. is better than over here. But I still like the programs." A few expressed anger that VOA would sometimes talk about their beloved motherland negatively. "We don't like it when they tell us how bad we live, that we have no freedom and all that," a group of young acquaintances complained.

At a birthday party, after food, drink, and conversation had been exhausted, VOA was turned on. The broadcast was about religion in America. "Do they want you to believe?" I asked. "Well," the young birthday celebrant said, "they are talking in general, but underneath it all, that's the idea." Everyone grinned, abashed that they were admitting that even my motherland was as much capable of propaganda as their motherland.

Russians are careful when it comes to digesting information. They seem to assume that Revolutionary Russia will never ever have anything good to say about the decadent West, especially its archrival, America. According to the script, according to ideology, it just has to be that way. Maybe some of the allegations about the "crises" in contemporary American life are empirically true, but then again, maybe not.

It took me awhile to realize that Russians are far from naive, especially the city-slickers who are much, much more politically sophisticated than the village people. They seem to take for granted that they are victims of a fierce propaganda attack, as much as we in the West accept the fact that we are vulnerable to the advertising blitz that invades our lives. Russians know only too well that politics is a nasty, nasty

Tower of Babel, Tower of Truth

business which is out to take control of their lives, to make them think in a certain way. Many Russians, in their own unassuming way, seem ready to meet the challenge.

The information marketplace is as prone to scarcity as the consumer marketplace. Here it is truth that is hard to find.

The biblical record on deceit and deception begins in Genesis when the subtle serpent first lied to Eve. In fact, the serpent insinuated that it was God who was the deceiver. "No, you won't die if you partake of the fruit from that forbidden tree. No, you will become like gods." Since that day in the Garden, deceit and falsehood, characteristics of the Antichrist, have marred all of human history, infecting *all* peoples, nations, systems and ideologies.

In the information marketplace, Russian shoppers hunt for bits and pieces of political truth. They seek to know the real story of the life that goes on behind their Iron Curtain. How well they already know the Russian Hollywood version!

What is the buying power of the dollar and the pound compared to the ruble? Do some Americans have gun holsters strapped around their waist in the tradition of the wild, wild west? What about American gangsters? Is New York, especially Central Park, the vicious jungle it's made out to be? Are the West's many unemployed starving to death on the streets? Was the American grain embargo purposely designed to starve us out? Is the neutron bomb a Western conspiracy to kill off as many Russians as possible? Does President Reagan want war?

But as liberating as the true answers to these and other political questions may be, such truths are still light years away from the promise of truth that Jesus made. Being politically astute and skillfully reading between the lines of propaganda is not the way to divine truth.

The Master's promise is the same today as it was centuries ago, transcending time, geographical limitations and political thought. Those who believe in Him and continue in His words would know the truth that would set them free. Jesus is the Tower of Truth that stands as an impregnable fortress in this revolutionary land of Babylon. But before anyone can find shelter in Him, they must know how to enter; they must be shown the way.

As I was relaxing in a small park on Arts Square in Leningrad, across from the Russian Museum, I caught the attention of a little mischievous ten-year-old who was running around the huge statue of Russia's most beloved writer, Aleksandr Pushkin. The blond-haired boy took a minute out of his playful antics to sit down beside me on the bench.

We started up a conversation which turned political when I mentioned that I was an American. "Bang! Bang! Bang!" he exploded, laughing nervously as he called out President Kennedy's name. I was annoyed by the distorted character-ization of the aspect of America he seemed to know best. He sat quietly for a few minutes, perhaps a little ashamed of himself. Then began the onslaught of questions I was now well accustomed to.

"Do you really have that much unemployment in America? Your fruits and vegetables, and especially your meat, they're much more expensive than ours, aren't they? Prices in America keep going up because of inflation and crises, right? Life here is better than in America, I know that, isn't it? Your food isn't delicious because of all the chemicals and things they put into it. That's what I heard. Right?"

I answered the array of queries as best I could, putting them in a way that a Young Pioneer could absorb. When he had covered all the bases, he peered up at me, raising his hand to block the sun from his eyes. "Who are you anyway? A diplomat? A commissar?" I explained what I was doing in his country, besides of course, contradicting the word of his government. He had gotten his answers from one of the horses' mouths and went away with yet another political view.

The truth was out there somewhere, but would this little blond-haired urchin find it? Or could he?

7

Mushrooms, Marriages and Metros

Whose skill details every cloud
and tilts the flasks of heaven
until the soil cakes into a solid mass
and clods of earth cohere together?
(Job 38:37-38 TJB)

On an unusually sunny Leningrad June morning, after my usual Russian breakfast of *sosiski*, the equivalent of American hot dogs without the additives, and a heaping portion of fried potatoes, I decided to make the most of the day off and get some rest and relaxation Russian style. Frank, an American engineer, who was in Russia to install one of his firm's computerized machines in a textile factory, was living on the same floor of the Hotel Moskva with me, decided to tag along.

I had received a number of suggestions from my Russian colleagues in the hotel service bureau about the good spots out on the Gulf of Finland where I might go to escape the tensions of the tourist scene. But, being a foreigner, I could not travel more than forty kilometers outside of the city, roughly twenty-five miles. No one seemed to know exactly how many kilometers his or her favorite countryside retreat was from the center, so when Frank and I set out for our *dikoe mesto* in the sun, literally the wild spot, the Lord was our guide.

A CHRISTIAN VIEW OF RUSSIA

Arriving at Finland Railway Station by subway, we jostled our way into a crowd of about three-hundred Leningradians who were stoically struggling to get onto the ascending escalators which would quickly transport them to the street level. A sea of people was constantly forming by the escalators as new train cars were pulling up at twenty-second intervals, disgorging a continuous stream of sprinting Russians, also anxious to find sanctuary in the Russian countryside. This mass of humanity which came together inside the railway station would have made the Thanksgiving Day rush at Penn Central look mild and controlled by comparison.

After purchasing their tickets at the *kassa* window, or through one of the coin machines, Russia's pioneers for the day would make a mad galloping dash for one of the five or six platforms where the trains waited or would soon arrive. No one was restrained or taking the matter in stride; it was Sunday, time for a great escape into the wilderness, a time to be free, and maybe just a little anarchic (that is, for Russians). For the time being, Revolutionary Russia would be left behind. The gentleness of Mother Earth was waiting to unloosen spirits and soothe souls. The Russian people were out to bathe themselves in nature's rejuvenating balm.

The train cars were overflowing with passengers; both the young and the old were off to commune with nature. Russia's fishermen were carrying their poles; each pole was carefully wrapped in a protective cloth covering, observing the quasi-Russian custom of covering in some way all hand-carried items, almost as if there was a felt need to hide the contents from one's comrades. Young people, together in bands of three and four, were strapped down with bulging knapsacks. What looked like stakes for pitching tents were protruding from cumbersome-looking canvas bundles. The stage was set for a day in the country.

These Soviet Slavs weren't the only ones that needed

Mushrooms, Marriages and Metros

spiritual resuscitation. The pressing problems and irritating nuisances inherent in being resident representative for a travel firm at times anchored down my own spirit. The suffocating void that the building of communism rendered inside me needed to be liberated by the sounds and smells of God's country. And so when Train #61 pulled out of the Finland Railway Station some joint Russian-American therapy was about to take place. Frank and I just sat back silently gazing out the window at the many brightly-colored, quaint-looking *dachi* that seemed to be resting so peacefully in the countryside. We caught glimpses of solitary Russian sun bathers lying in deserted fields of tall, dry, golden-colored grass. Nature was beckoning. Judging by the serene look on the Slavic faces of our fellow travellers, Mother Russia was being warmly welcomed.

As the numbers on the markers along the train platform rapidly approached the mid-twenties, indicating our distance from Leningrad, I decided to be extra cautious. I approached the train attendant who announced the stops, and asked her to please tell us when we were forty kilometers outside of Leningrad. At first the stout middle-aged conductor seemed a bit surprised by the unusual request, but when I explained the reason for it, I was assured that we would be told when to get off. When it comes to order, as we shall see, Russians will spare no effort to guarantee that everything is properly done.

A few stops later we pulled into a not-so-remote looking village city which the platform identified as Dyuny. The marker read exactly forty. A casual monotone voice announced the stop, adding, "This station stop is exactly forty kilometers outside Leningrad." Those around us seemed perplexed by this additional bit of information, but Frank and I were just reassured that our adventure would be according to the books, right down to the last kilometer.

Judging by the crowds that were getting off, Russian fate,

in the form of our visa limitation, had brought us to a popular resort. It was only when we began following the Leningradians straight ahead to the shore of the Gulf of Finland did we realize that with each advancing step, we were trespassing further and further into forbidden territory; we relished every minute of it. Along our path, we now got a closer view of the summer homes and the Russians relaxing outside as "the privileged class" were merrily frolicking about entertaining themselves.

We came across a park with a merry-go-round, which, as I recall, twirled at a slow, methodical pace. Surprisingly, there were almost no children in sight, which meant there was no line to ride the ferris wheel. It was an opportunity I couldn't pass up. You never look a Russian gift horse in the mouth! I stepped up to the tiny sales booth and plopped down ten kopecks which was the price of a child's ticket.

"I'm a little boy," I told the clerk, as I crouched down to appear smaller.

The relaxed, elderly attendant who was reading, looked up from her book, "You're a big boy," she grinned, "it'll be twenty kopecks." I paid the extra fee and got my first Russian merry-go-round ride. Frank passed up the chance "to spin around" in Russia, joking, though not completely, that after working in the textile plant, he had come to have little faith in Russian-manufactured items. After a few minutes of his teasing about how shoddily put together the seats of the ferris wheel looked, I begged the adolescent girl who controlled the gears, and who was now sun-bathing, to please take me down. But there were two little Russians who were enjoying the amusement, and so I had to wait and endure the full treatment. I was beginning to learn that I was just an individual; the collective always, always came first.

The *dachi* that we had seen, I assumed, must have been owned by the elite and the very wealthy. I was surprised to learn, however, that quite a few Russians whose salaries are more or less average had their own *dachi*, which cost between five and fifteen thousand rubles. But out in the middle of nowhere you can get what amounts to a wooden two-by-four for a much cheaper price.

The price for second-hand summer homes depend not only on the location of the property, but also whether the homestead has any gardens or groves, like a strawberry patch or apple or pear trees, assets which can significantly increase the asking price of the home. Although it's easier said than done, it's possible to rent a plot of land from the state, get a group of friends together, and build your own summer retreat.

Bathing in the wild river streams, pitching tents, cross-country skiing, fishing, picking wild flowers and berries, and hiking are popular ways to relax among the nature-loving Russians. But popular as they are, they take a back seat for many Russians during the mushrooming season. Collecting mushrooms seems to be the favorite wilderness sport. A mushroom enthusiast put it rather well. "We Russians like to hunt three things, animals, birds, and mushrooms." Industrial enterprises and other large employers frequently organize mushrooming outings for their proletariat. Russians were actually shocked when I told them that gathering mushrooms wasn't a national pastime in the United States. "But everyone in Russia collects mushrooms," I was repeatedly told by "hunters" who would then go on to describe their special recipe for preparing the delicacy, either by frying, baking, sautéing, marinating, or simply pickling.

Only days before I thought I would leave Leningrad for the last time, I decided that I would have to try my hand at mushroom hunting. I wanted to experience for myself what appeared to be much more than a hobby. On a Sunday afternoon, I took the train out to a nearby village community.

A CHRISTIAN VIEW OF RUSSIA

I was ready for my first lesson in the fine art of tracking down, picking, and last but certainly not least, relishing the wild and treasured mushroom.

My friends were real country people, born and bred on the pure Russian earth. It was purely coincidental how I met them. My parents had come to Russia while I was living in Leningrad. I took them on a rather off-the-beaten-track tour around the revolutionary city which just so happened to include a train ride into the Russian countryside. Just as I was preparing to snap a picture of my mother and father standing before a quaint-looking, bright yellow wooden home, this woman popped out of nowhere and into the picture. As you can imagine it was pretty funny. Well, we started up a conversation and before we knew it, my parents and I were inside a nearby Russian home sipping tea, enjoying some real home-grown hospitality, and naturally taking more pictures. Anna Aleksandrovna and her four children thus became casual friends of mine and introduced me to the sport of tracking down the wild, wild mushroom.

Anna Aleksandrovna stayed home to mind the kitchen and prepare for our dramatic return. Her husband Vladimir Igorevich and two of the children were my guides for the expedition. Each had a favorite jacket or sweater which in the past had brought good luck in the form of some outstanding mushroom find. I was given an old jacket to put on and a pair of oversized long rubber boots which came up well past my kneecaps. Armed with a "mushroom knife" and a bag for depositing the tasty treasure, I was ready to stalk the cunning fungus plant.

A sharp, well-trained set of eyes also came in handy to uncover the capped stems hiding under a broken limb or beneath the tall, wet grass of the swampy Leningrad forests. (I had the handicap of being the only one wearing glasses.) My friends quickly taught me to distinguish between a good mushroom and a *poganka,* a toadstool. And if in doubt I was told to slice the hat of the mushroom through the center. A reddish color meant that I should move on. The mushroom stem was never to be yanked up by the roots, but carefully sliced at the base to insure that another would sprout in its place. Respect for nature is not the only consideration here; there is also the collective to bear in mind, i.e. all the other mushroom hunters who will comb the same area in pursuit of this wonderful tiny plant.

Every few minutes the solitude of the forest would be shattered by a spirited cry of, "Hey, come here, come over here! Hurry up!" each time one among us wanted to show off an especially admirable find. Vladimir Igorevich had taken his camera along and never missed an opportunity to take a few shots at these priceless moments. Naturally, the pictures were always taken with the mushrooms exhibited in the forefront encircled by the happy hunters.

Gentle droplets of water falling from the treasury of the rains began to unexpectedly visit the Russian earth, showering both us and the hordes of mushrooms our skill had failed to uncover. But before a word of caution could be uttered, the drops that cometh from the vapors above came pouring upon us rather too abundantly. It was time to hurry home with our spoils.

Back at home, Anna Aleksandrovna, together with a gathering of family and friends seated around the community kitchen table, naturally was eager to see what the afternoon outing had brought us. We were all comparing who had fared best during the hunt. But no one boasted of having a lucky day. Stalking the sought-after wild mushroom was all a matter of skill and expertise.

Each treasure was gently taken and lightly bathed in an enormous mushroom pan. Coming across a mushroom perfect in size, shape, and texture, the hunters would pamper it, smell it, caress it, all but kiss it. (I'm sure, though, that if I had mushroomed long enough, I would have eventually witnessed such a display of tender loving care.) The intense pride that these little edible fungi seemed to evoke, reminded me of a fisherman proudly holding up his catch for a picture, the only difference being that fishermen usually don't fondle and smell their catch. But then again, I never went fishing in Russia. Once the ritual had run its course, we got down to what I was primarily interested in, devouring the find. The fresh, spongy mushrooms were fried with potatoes and onions and were delicious.

On the way out to the country I had seen Russians combing the forests engaged in this favorite sport. Now as I was returning to Leningrad in the late afternoon, I saw the results of their pursuit in the hand baskets brimming with mushrooms; of course a cloth was draped over them in typical Russian style. Many of these mushrooms would be bottled and served during the winter months when they would be relished even more (if that is possible).

On the crowded train back to civilization, I saw Russians carrying with them lavender flowers that grow wild in the fields, and freshly-cut budding branches, signs that they had partaken of the fruits of nature. Perhaps these flowers and branches would be placed in vases to decorate their flats, reminding them of their day in the country. But maybe they would also remind them of something else.

There is a very revealing passage in Acts that I believe sheds some scriptural light on the ritualized observance of mushroom-hunting. I commented on it earlier when I referred to a Russian friend's remark that even a blade of grass reveals the wonders of Almighty God. Addressing a crowd of pagans in Lycaonia, Paul speaks these great words. The Lord "did not leave you without evidence of himself in the good things he does for you: he sends you rain from heaven, he makes your crops grow when they should, he gives you food and makes you happy."[1] Praise the Lord! On this Leningrad Sunday, the Lord sure did it all! He sent the rain that watered the helpless little fungus plants, and which also put an end to our safari, giving us the blessed occasion to happily enjoy the delicate morsels of wild, spongy food.

All of Russian nature, in one form or another, had exulted and praised the Lord, the lavender blossoms with their exquisite beauty and the poor little mushroom with its tempting symmetry. If Joyce Kilmer had been born in Soviet Russia, I'm sure he would have loved the tiny mushroom. And chances are he would have enshrined his dearest affection for these tiny creatures with the words, "Only God can make a mushroom."

And what about the treasury of the rain? True, its tumultous torrents nearly drowned us, but didn't that sudden soaking also speak of a living divine presence? That same rain that flooded the earth in Noah's day, plagued the Egyptians at the time of Moses, and ceased to fall during Elijah's time, is today in Russia still testifying to the goodness of God.

The lavender blossoms that spruce up Soviet flats are, of course, fragrant, aromatic reminders of a great time in the countryside. They are that and much more. They are signs that the flowers that grow wild in the fields do not have to weave or spin. No, their majestic beauty is already miraculously theirs.

For centuries the Russian people have been acutely sensitive to the beauty found in nature. In pagan Russia, for instance, there were many myths connected with Mother Earth. Yet even when Russia became a Christian nation, the fertile, black Russian soil continued to evoke deep religious

---

[1] Acts 14:17-18 TJB

feelings in the Russian soul. Today, in officially atheistic Russia, the wild mushrooms that are borne of the Russian earth are infallible signs of the presence of an almighty, awesome power. And to those with open hearts, the Great Creator is very near.

The leap from mushrooms to marriages is of quantum proportions, for while Russian mushrooms are made in heaven, Russian marriages are made in palaces, Soviet ones. At least this is what the Soviets call them. The notion of being married in a palace has an attractive quality to it. It creates the feeling that the Revolution has made available the fruits of the czarist past to everyone, that is, everyone who gets married.

Early one Friday morning, the most popular day for Soviet marriages, I made my way to Leningrad's main Wedding Palace, not far from the American consulate. Lined up outside were a half-dozen black Volgas with large symbolic wedding rings fastened to their roofs. Fresh flowers, streamers, a baby girl doll and a teddy bear decorated the hoods and front grills. Small wedding parties composed of no more than fifteen or twenty guests were busily coming and going. Pictures were being taken of the newlyweds and those soon to be married. The spirit was a happy one.

Inside the palace lobby, immediately to the right, sat a couple of hefty-looking women. Sitting behind desks with official-looking record books were the bureaucrats whose job it is to take care of the paper work that becoming husband and wife entails. Just beyond these very business-like women were two spacious reception rooms where a bride and groom and their well-wishers were waiting to be summoned to begin the Soviet ceremony. Everyone seemed occupied in expending nervous energy. Some were snapping photographs for the wedding album. Others were standing in front of full-length mirrors, putting the final touches on stylish hair-dos. And as always, there were those who were just plain fidgeting.

Mushrooms, Marriages and Metros

The tension of the moment was suddenly broken by the melodramatic theme from Tchaikovsky's *First Piano Concerto*. Apparently, it was the signal to the bride and groom to begin the ritualistic promenade up the revolutionary red-carpeted stairs into yet another waiting hall in the palace. Bearing bouquets of beautiful flowers, everyone joined in the procession.

While two jittery Leningradians were waiting upstairs to become husband and wife, I was still waiting downstairs for permission to watch the state ceremony. The permission from the director of the wedding palace was conveyed to me by a young clerk who ushered me upstairs and through a set of huge, regal-looking doors into a chandeliered hall where my presence, or perhaps intrusion, was acknowledged by a dignified nod of the head from a stately-looking woman.

She was standing behind a long, sleek desk and was elegantly attired in a flowing golden-colored dress. Over her shoulders was draped a red banner displaying the emblem of the Russian Republic, which calls on the proletariat of the world to unite. But it was the striking hammer and sickle encircled by sheaves of wheat that drew my attention. Her garb and manner distinguished her as the officiator who would perform the ceremony.

A photographer, dressed in street clothes, broke the aura of regality and pomp as he fiddled to get his camera set up for the occasion. And standing just a few steps from me in the rear of the palace hall was another member of the staff. The officiator gave the O.K. sign to this young girl who revealed her function by swinging open the rear doors which connect to an adjoining room where the wedding party had been patiently waiting.

As the doors opened wide, the officiator quickly reached under her table and turned Tchaikovsky back on again. Everything was ready. Light bulbs began to flash one after another as the bride and groom, followed by their friends and relatives, made their entry into the ceremony room, separating to the left and right. Standing in the center of the room, directly in front of the officiator, the couple prepared to hear the set words that will make them *muzh* and *zhena*. But first the music must be turned off.

The actual ceremony was short, lasting no more than five minutes. Taking the silver platter on which lay two gold wedding bands, the officiator, in perfect posture, left her place behind the table. Slowly, gracefully, she stepped past the mad photographer, who seemed more nervous than the bride, and took her new position before the bride and groom. Once the couple had placed the rings on each other's fingers, the officiator invoked Soviet law and pronounced the couple man and wife. A brief but meaningful kiss sealed the nuptial pact and completed the state's work. The officiator returned behind the table and switched on the music, a gesture which seemed to be losing some of its artificiality.

The official paper work was the next order of business. Following the officiator, the newlyweds, as husband and wife, and two witnesses, were called upon to sign their names in a large open document book. While the signing ritual was taking place, the photographer awkwardly moved about taking pictures of the event, oblivious to the sense of solemnity that characterized the occasion.

The time came to say a few words of congratulation and encouragement to the newlyweds. While they were being reminded of their new moral responsibilities, the romantic music was turned off. The ceremony drew to a close as each member of the wedding party, again to the sounds of music, presented their floral arrangements to the beaming bride. Tears of happiness streamed down joyous faces, as lots of hugging and kissing made for an emotional ending to the, in my opinion, rather pretentious ceremony.

Mushrooms, Marriages and Metros

But the officiator seemed to barely notice. She had turned her attention to preparing for the next couple. She looked down at the big book, still holding a perfect posture. She had but a few minutes to memorize the full names of the next couple, the first name, the *otchestvo,* the second name which is derived from the given name of the father, and the last name. Such memorization before each performance obviously required concentration; she could not allow herself to be distracted by the emotion of the occasion.

Meanwhile another wedding party was preparing themselves in the antechamber. The same young girl stood before the closed doors, waiting for the word. A new photographer had just entered and was quickly acknowledged by the officiator who was still studying the script. Everything was set and everything would be the same, down to the last measure of Tchaikovsky's familiar music. For even in marriage there is this Soviet sameness, this ideological conformity.

But after observing the traditional laying of the nuptial flowers at one of the monuments which commemorate Russia's "Great Patriotic War," the sense of equality will begin to fade. The customary wedding receptions that follow the ceremony differ in their elegance and cost. Some will take place in the private banquet rooms of Russia's best hotels and restaurants, while others will be celebrated in more modest surroundings, perhaps in the one-room communal flat of one of the newlyweds' parents.

With all the heavy emphasis on humanitarianism in Soviet thinking, you would expect that in the joy of a marriage ceremony there would be a greater sense of emotion. And yet it is the very lack of human sensitivity and expression that creates the comedy. So much official attention is devoted to the great political virtues of peace, friendship, and equality. In the form of slogans that exhort the masses from readied rooftops, greetings of peace and friendship go forth to all the peoples of the world. But as for love, it just doesn't make it as an advertising technique. It's not a part of the propaganda trade, nor, as we just saw, an integral part of the Soviet view of marriage.

But it really shouldn't come as a shock to us that the Soviet architects left the apolitical quality of love out of the communist equation. For God, who Himself is love, has been denied a place, any place, in the revolutionary society.

As I recalled my day in the palace, my thoughts were quickly drawn to the sacred marriage rite I witnessed in Moscow's only registered Baptist Church. A visiting British minister performed the church wedding following the 10:00 A.M. Sunday service. The preacher's words were translated into Russian before an absolutely overflowing congregation. It was from the Book of Ecclesiastes that the English minister drew his text:

> Two are better than one; because they have a good reward for their labor.
> For if they fall, the one will lift up his fellow . . . .
> And if one prevail against him, two shall withstand him; and a threefold cord is not quickly broken.[1]

Smiling quietly at the bride and groom, the minister began with some words of counsel, scripturally-grounded and naturally royally British. "And if you should fall," he said, "your partner will be there to pick you up. And if it should happen that you both should stumble, you need not fear. Remember, you will be a threefold cord and Jesus will be there to lift you back up again." When I get married, I thought to myself, these are just the words of encouragement that I would find so meaningful. The Body of Christ prayed for the

---

[1] Ecclesiastes 4:9, 10, 12 KJV

Mushrooms, Marriages and Metros

Lord's blessing on the union He would now ordain. Spontaneous prayer and spirit-filled countenances revealed that the Lord was here among His people.

In Soviet marriages, husband and wife become legally united under the authority of the state, and they begin to live out their lives together subject to the state. But in the Baptist marriage, husband and wife pledged mutual subjection to each other out of reverence for Christ, the cord that made their union indissoluble. In the bond that the Lord had established, two would become one in a mysterious and supernatural way. For Soviet Power too, a bond was secured, and evidence of it was contained in the official record books in the palace lobby.

There is still a third distinction here, one that separates Christianity and communism even more profoundly. The ceremonies that take place in the palaces are set, however inconspicuously, in the context of the coming of a new age, the sinless age of communism. Here, in this radical state of human nature, state-regulated weddings will likewise drop into the great garbage bin of history. Soviet husbands and wives will be completely capable of dealing with all that marriage entails. In the Christian wedding, there is also a sense of expectancy; it is spiritual and biblical. The marriage relationship between husband and wife is compared in the Scriptures to the relationship between Christ and His church, a bride that is now being clothed in matrimonial array to meet her bridegroom.

Skipping from marriages to metros doesn't necessarily involve taking a giant step. Both themes find their peculiarity in their focus on an even bigger theme that also begins with the letter "m." And it is *man!* The achievement, ingenuity, and perhaps even glory of man is what Soviet metros and marriages have in common.

For the foreigner visiting Russia, a visit to the metro in

either Moscow or Leningrad is a time to be impressed. Descending the metro escalator is like being transported down into the depths of a diagonal, cylindrical tunnel. Science fiction fantasies of entering into the refuge of an underground world tend to come to mind. Although the escalators move at a pace about three or four times the speed of their American counterparts, the trek deep into the earth can take more than two minutes. Impatient Russians will often sprint past their more complacent comrades, using the left-hand side of the fast-moving stairs which is kept free for that purpose. Some Russians will use the occasion for some soft touching and holding, with the one short step that separates the couple making the display of affection here seem almost natural.

There are few conveniences in Russia to make life easier and more enjoyable, and the relatively quiet metro has to rank right on top. Automatic money-changing machines which accept ten, fifteen, and twenty kopeck pieces instantly clang out the appropriate number of five kopeck coins like a Las Vegas slot machine. In many stations, there are maps which will light up the route you need to follow to reach your destination. The Moscow underground, in particular, is a remarkable example of artistic excellence. Nearly each and every stop is decorated with mosaics, murals, chandeliers and ceramics. The palatial atmosphere makes commuting a royal experience.

More impressive than the decorative splendor of the metro is the cleanliness that is beyond description. No one smokes here, more a Russian tradition than a government regulation. There can be no doubt that the Bolshevik Revolution is responsible in some way for the spotless, graffiti-free subway. In Soviet socialist society, carelessly discarding paper wrappers and cigarette butts is regarded as positively *net kulturno,* uncultured, although, of course, it does happen.

Mushrooms, Marriages and Metros

Littering in the free Western world may be legally prohibited, but culturally speaking, it's almost regarded as doing your own thing in some countries. But on the revolutionary side of the East-West frontier, at least as far as littering in the metro is concerned, the "I-me-my" mentality has been nearly completely removed from natural man.

The phenomenon of the metro is another of the many contradictions in the Russian world. Not only does it contrast with the general grayness of the Russian world, but the pace of life underground creates a sensation that time is of the essence, a notion that is confounded by the streams of lines on Russia's surface. The Russian metro, speeding along at up to nearly sixty miles per hour, is an escape from the tedious world of endless waiting.

The Russian people are enormously proud of their subway system and display their pride openly. A conversation with a Russian in the metro is apt to produce the rather leading question, "And how do you like our metro?"

"Showoffmanship," (or *pokazukha*, as the Russians call it), cannot by itself fully explain the underground palace wonders. The subway serves a more practical purpose as a civil defense shelter, which is in fact what the Moscow subway became during World War II. The depth of the metro is not published anywhere and is regarded as a military secret even though, as a bold Muscovite guide playfully teased, "Anyone could simply find out by measuring it." But then again, stringing a measurement tape along the metro tunnel is just something one would not do in Russia, especially if you happen to fall under the category of *"inostranets,* (foreigner)."

For nearly every experience in Russia, there is a difficult lesson to be learned. When the doors of the metro open to disgorge their human cargo, the waiting crowds outside take up their positions along the sides of the doors, allowing the outgoing travellers sufficient room to struggle among themselves. Each Russian knows that the opening and closing of the train doors are automatically timed and wait for no man, woman, or child. As the surge into the train car erupts, a recording of a stern, confident voice announces, *"Ostorozhno! Dveri zakryvayutsya!* (Look out! The doors are closing!)"* This bit of timely advice can often lead to a good shove forward to be given or received depending on one's position near the doors. All Russians learn through experience, either their own or someone else's, that the fast-moving doors don't bounce back after catching hold of an unlucky passenger's limb. Punishment is an effective teacher, a lesson that I more than once learned the hard way.

To finish in an alliterative fashion, I would have to heap bundles of praise on the great Soviet subway. It is magnifique, majestic, and a little mind-boggling. But although its glory will not fade like the flowers nor wither like the grass, the unquestionably great Soviet metro will not stand forever.

8

Under the Revolutionary Law

But if ye be led of the Spirit, ye are not under the law.
(Galatians 5:18 KJV)

Riding along in a crowded metro train, I decided to pass the time by reading the three columns of rules that were posted in front of me. Rule #1: "Each citizen must observe social order." My days in Russia had taught me that this was not only the main rule for subway travellers but was also the foundation of all of Soviet society. Engaging in my theatrical antics once again, I turned to the middle-aged soldier crushed against me. "Excuse me, please," I said, pointing to the Soviet law of order, "could you please tell me what is meant by social order?" The soldier, a little confused by being asked such a philosophical question deep beneath the earth's surface, answered in perhaps the only way possible. "To us Russians," he smiled self-assuredly, "it's completely understandable." And how right he was!

The principle of *poryadok,* or order, in Soviet society may be compared to some form of secular morality to which the Russians become conditioned from birth. What is acceptable and unacceptable behavior is a matter of culture and even politics. According to the Soviet Constitution, Article 65, citizens are expected "to be intolerant of antisocial acts, and to assist in every way in the safeguarding of public order." This observance of *poryadok*, in many ways a national neurosis, creates the pressures for social conformity and restraint, which are so important in the Soviet state.

In the context of the totality of the great Soviet mission, Soviet morality is all of this, and more. It is man's wisest idea for forming Soviet community, a unified Marxist-Leninist collective. It is a law that defines and governs the societal view of what is right and what is wrong, proper and improper, good and evil. It is a prescription on how man is to view his fellow man, how comrade is to relate to fellow comrade. Indeed, Soviet order, revolutionary order, is the gateway through which the new sinless society is supposed to emerge.

The virtue of order is one of the greatest of Soviet virtues. In the revolutionary scheme of things, it towers high above almost everything else as the sure and perfect way to the visionary society. Here Christianity and communism again stand as polar opposites. In Marxist dialectical terms, the conflict between the two is a contradiction between opposing world views.

For the Christian, love is the greatest virtue, the foundation of all that is good. In the two greatest commandments—to love God and thy neighbor—the Old Testament laws and the writings of the prophets are perfectly summarized. Love comes from God and is the very nature of God. Only in sharing in His Divine Spirit are any of us able to love at all.

Conversely, order, revolutionary order, comes from man; it is the fruit of human thinking and ingenuity, of a peculiar ideology. Revolutionary order is a kind of radical consciousness that looks forward to a new, improved world where Soviet men and women will live a brand new kind of life.

What happens to a society that makes order the sole "moral motivator," the supreme law of human behavior, indeed the greatest commandment? Let us for a moment step inside the revolutionary conscience. Let us examine man's wisest precepts ordaining that which is moral and immoral, right and wrong. Let us explore the way to revolutionary happiness.

Taking off my shirt and sprawling out on a park bench to soak up the summer sun are two violations I learned which could net me a fine from a vigilant police officer. "We don't do this sort of thing," I am told in a snobbish way by more than a few offended Russians, who expected me to immediately mend my foreign ways. Once, as the lights went out at the Moscow Circus, I moved from my assigned seat to one that was a little closer to ringside. Not far behind, however, was an explodingly mad czarina who pretended to be selling circus programs. The self-ordained guardian of Soviet discipline gave me a thorough tongue-lashing for my un-Soviet endeavor and ordered me back whence I came.

While pushing themselves forward into an overflowing bus, passengers might occasionally utter a few choice Russian words to those impatient comrades who push too hard or cut ahead. Yet self-control and endurance in such situations is the Soviet norm. A Russian stewardess may instruct her passengers in the proper use of the life vest and explain how order will be maintained in case of an emergency over water. "Do not inflate the vest until outside of the aircraft and until you have received the permission of the crew." And if I hand my coat to be checked and the pensioner-attendant mumbles under his breath, what could be wrong? Oh, of course. My torn coat loop makes his job that much more difficult and breaks the ritualistic order of the monotonous chore.

"Comrades, everybody into his *kupé* [French for train compartment]," a conductor might command her passengers who are staring out the window as the train slowly rolls up to the last stop on the Soviet frontier. Customs and passport officials will soon be processing outgoing passengers, and a little Russian discipline will be an appropriate farewell as they leave the restraint of Russia for the warmer environs of Poland. A metro *dezhurnaya* (the subway escalator monitor), might calmly watch an overflowing crowd endure the unnecessary inconvenience of long lines, but refuse to start up the other available escalators—par for the Russian course.

"Four kopecks more," I am informed by a saleswoman who has awarded me with a kilogram of imported lemons.

"Do I have to?" I teased.

I could have predicted the reply, for the Soviet script is everywhere the same.

"Yes, you must pay, for the sake of order."

Playing hooky one day from classes at Leningrad State University, I slept until mid-morning and woke up famished for, of all things, Bulgarian stuffed peppers. I remembered the canned goods display of the imported delicacy at a nearby *gastronom* and decided to spare myself the unappetizing greasy meat and potato fare at the university cafeteria. I set out for the grocery store hoping that my culinary fantasy wouldn't be *rasprodano*, sold out.

I found that the Bulgarian stuffed peppers were still there, unimaginatively piled one on another, though this, I knew, was far from proof that the delicacy would be for sale. I had already learned the lesson that Russian window dressing doesn't always advertise what's in stock. It's often simply window dressing, the implementation, one might say, of the art for art's sake idea with a Soviet twist.

Entering the *gastronom* I prepared myself to put up a stink if I was cruelly told that I couldn't have my delicious stuffed peppers, that they were sold out. In that event I'd try the common sense approach, asking if I could take two cans off their "attractive" display in the window. But after only a few steps inside the store, abrupt hollering cued me in that I would be aggravated before I might aggravate. "Go back out and come in the entrance," the Russian cashier ordered. "That's the exit."

I turned around and realized that indeed she could have been right. There were two doors separated by a wall about five feet long. Of course there was no identification which was the *vkhod* and which the *vykhod*. It was difficult enough to try to speak this Slavic tongue, but reading Russian minds was not my forte, at least not just yet.

"I'm already inside," I nonchalantly answered. "What's the use of going out and coming back in?" I asked, a not-so-dumb question I thought.

"For the sake of order," the young matron dressed in virgin pure white snarled, obviously taken aback by my disobedient attitude. I ignored her with impunity and went after my stuffed peppers.

Minutes later the entire scenario was repeated, but this time a Russian actress was playing the protagonist, or do I mean antagonist? A middle-aged Russian woman fell into the same trap I did by entering the store via the exit door. But now the script was slightly modified. The same hollering spontaneously exploded from behind the cash register, but the reaction to it was now typically Russian. The hopeful shopper made an immediate about-face and obeyed the command with the speed of a Red Army recruit. As she re-entered the state shop, the dejected woman hung her head remorsefully; she had been punished and her countenance showed she was contrite.

Back in the safety of my dormitory room, I ate the cold green peppers from the can, contemplating the depths of that great Russian trait—passivity.

Again we find the revolutionary way fidgeting in the darkness, dealing with things which it considers of paramount importance. Confusing entrances and exits hardly seems to me like sin, but for Revolutionary Russia, it's a leopard spot, and it has to go. And again we can't but sit back and have a chuckle or two as man tries to spell out his unusual program for saving himself and his revolutionary society. But unfortunately, the victims of such ordered madness are the poor Soviet people.

Human wisdom dictates that healthy helpings of order and discipline are essential ingredients in the making of a harmonious society. Indeed, the Word of the Lord also underscores the importance or order, for example, in the conduct of a prayer service. But revolutionary order still doesn't succeed in creating a congenial socialist atmosphere where comrades can come together in peace and joy. For a mere five kopecks subway riders stoically suffer through the rigors of riding the Soviet metro, and in the pursuit of Bulgarian stuffed peppers, confused Russian shoppers heed the shouted commands of unyielding cashiers. How well do we sense there is no peace in it all! Obviously, something went very wrong somewhere. Revolutionary order is everywhere observed in Russia, but there is no communist utopia. Why not?

The Christian can offer some answers, specifically, an answer. It may not satisfy the constraints of Marxist thinking, but it will ring a familiar bell with anyone who has tried to live under the Old Testament law. Those who have sought to live out the Gospel teachings without being led by the Spirit will know exactly what went wrong with the Soviet-ordered plan. Anyone who has endured the vanity and futility of trying to perform good and noble deeds on his own will power will know precisely what I'm getting at.

The whole of the New Testament reveals there are two ways of living, both diametrically, dialectically opposed to the other. There is the way of the law, by which a man might try to better himself. And then, there is the way of Jesus Christ, the divine pathway by which we find our righteousness in

Under the Revolutionary Law

Him. When we allow Jesus to become our Master and Lord, we allow Him, we invite Him, to live His perfect life in us. This is the great mystery hidden so long "from ages and from generations" that Paul so gloriously revels in: "Christ in you, the hope of glory."[1] And this too is why we rejoice as Christians. He has done it *all* for us!

It is clear. Looking to the law alone for justification and salvation is to separate ourselves from Christ and His grace. The Scriptures teach that on our own we can never conquer sin. Trusting in our own power, all our good works will inevitably, assuredly wind up falling short of the good we would like to do.

I think what the Soviet Union needs most of all today is another Apostle Paul, someone who will go one on one with the leadership and call a spade a spade. Imagine for a moment what kind of epistle Paul would write to the revolutionary Soviets. It might go something like this:

"Grace and peace be to all of you from God the Father and from our Lord Jesus Christ. I also send my warmest greetings to your fellow citizens of the Soviet Union.

"Word has reached me of the revolutionary vision that seems to inspire you and your cohorts to go forth laboring for a better tomorrow. If you would permit me, gentlemen, I have some thoughts on this, and would like to share them with you. Please do not be offended, but I shall make my point without reserve.

"Your radical revolutionary creed can never in God's world, in the twentieth century, succeed. The experience of man through the ages, since the coming of the Son of God, the Messiah, Jesus, proves this beyond a doubt.

"By decree you have set up a society governed by law, a revolutionary law of *poryadok,* as you call it. But what fruit has

---

[1] Colossians 1:26-27 KJV

127

it produced in your lifetime? Has it yielded the fruits of peace, joy, love, gentleness, and trustfulness? No, the sad fact is, gentlemen, that the fruits of your revolutionary law are self-indulgence, feuding, wrangling, being hot-tempered and disagreeable, seeking and lusting after power and the like. These are the fruits of the flesh, whether that flesh is socialist, communist, or capitalist. We are all sinners despite our political inclination—to say otherwise is to call God a liar.

"Gentlemen, I know of the Communist Party's atheistic platform and it is here that your program fails. In your rejection of God and the record of eternal life found in His crucified Son, you place yourself under the law. And not just your man-made revolutionary law, but the divine law of God. Your revolutionary vision is helpless under this law. It cannot save you from your sin.

"Without yielding to the Spirit of the Living God, the selfish flesh is always, time and again, going to win out over the loftiest of humanitarian and humanistic goals. Gentlemen, you need to put love not only in your slogans and banners, but in your entire program as well. Without it, revolutionary propaganda can become nothing more than mere chatter, 'a sounding brass, a tinkling cymbal.' In a word, all of your efforts are in vain, as were those who sought to erect the Tower of Babel in ancient days.

"I pray that you and your compatriots will at last accept the grace of our Lord Jesus Christ and free yourselves from the burden of bondage. Now unto God our Father be glory without end. Amen."

Perhaps Paul would word his message a bit differently, but the simplicity of the Gospel message of love would certainly be there. For Paul, and for us, the extent and fullness of Christ's love was revealed on the blood-stained cross of Calvary. And even in Soviet Russia today, it is possible to turn to the crosses that crown the ancient churches and be amazed. This is how much He loved us!

How inescapably true it is, love often means dying, dying to our selfish desires and vain ambitions. What great enduring truth there is in the Master's words: "Verily, verily, I say unto you, Except a corn of wheat fall into the ground and die, it abideth alone: but if it die, it bringeth forth much fruit."[1] Praise the Lord! Salvation, yours and mine, is the fruit of Jesus' passion and death and His glorious Resurrection on Easter morn.

This is the only code of conduct, if you will, that is going to bring peace on earth and true good will toward men. These scriptural truths are the only sure way to create Christian community, the Kingdom of God on earth. But before any of us can have the desire to share our talents and wealth with others, we must be willing to share our love. It's unavoidable, wonderfully so. We need the Lord so very, very much.

Coming from a society that elevated freedom from tyranny as a fundamental right of the governed, I did not easily grasp this Russian fetish for control and being controlled. I had grown up with the great political theories of John Locke and Montesquieu, which advised the separation of the legislative, executive and judicial branches of government. For me, absolute power was anathema; it just wasn't the American way.

But wait a minute! I was no longer in America. I was among a people who display a deeply ingrained respect for power, even when it is used against them. I was looking at a nation whose ancestors knew only an impoverished peasant life, while the czar lived in a fairy tale world of palaces and imperial ceremony. Yet he was not just the incarnation of absolute power, he was their *batyushka,* their father. As the divinely appointed representative of the Lord on earth, he

---

[1] John 12:24 KJV

reigned as the first among Russian Orthodox believers. In their subjection to him, Russian believers were submitting themselves to Christ Himself.

Certainly to some degree, Russian history helps account for the Russian inclination, perhaps even desire, to be controlled. But it is only partly true to say that the obsession of Soviet order is merely the continuation of czarist rule. It misses an important point for it overlooks the spiritual goal to which Soviet Russia is so jealously committed. If man is to kneel before the revolutionary Golden Calf, if Soviet man is to draw his very life-blood from the communist philosophy, then the very spirit in man must be destroyed. That spirit does not seek to be bound up, neither does it cherish conformity or thrive on atheism. No, the revolutionary way, if it is to succeed in its spiritual aim, it must somehow extinguish that which is divine in every man.

If it means anything, and I believe it does, examples of Russian passivity sprinkle the pages of my diary from the Bulgarian stuffed pepper caper to more common everyday occurrences. The mosaic of revolutionary passivity show the Russians to be the meekest people on all the earth. Some examples:

Across from a Leningrad department store, a group of silent Russians watched the summer pedestrian traffic as the city gardener, in the person of a stocky fiftyish year old woman, aimed her water hose at the sprouting shrubs, showering them and the nearby Leningradians with healthy squirts of cool, refreshing water. Everyone automatically jumped up and scuttled away like timid little animals. Almost as if they were dumb, no one spoke. A noisy street-sweeping truck, while washing Moscow's sidewalk curbing, sprayed some unsuspecting pedestrians. They should have been more attentive to the constant street-cleaning going on in the capital.

Under the Revolutionary Law

V chasy pik, at rush hour, all public transportation systems are overflowing with their human cargo, setting new records for the *Guinness Book of World Records*. Shoving and being shoved, stepping on your comrades' toes and having yours stepped on in return—these are the pains and pleasures that the Russians experience going to and coming from their communism-building labors. For those fatefully packed in the middle of the subway car only an enduring physical struggle will lead to liberation.

In Spartan-like Russia, however, the adrenalin flow is not accompanied by groaning or even sighing. "*Vy vykhodite* (Are you getting out)?" are often the only human sounds that can be heard as Russians strategically position themselves near the doors in order to be discharged from their collective at the appropriate stop. Experiencing Russia from the vantage point of my American culture, I had to conclude that Russians are no more than state-conditioned human animals. They make the word passive seem somehow weak and ineffectual in describing their behavior during the Soviet rush hour.

As I was being chauffeured by taxi to a business meeting at the Intourist headquarters in Leningrad, my driver speedily swerved off of Nevsky Prospekt onto a side street. His maneuver forced an elderly woman, already in the middle of the street, to try to run for safety. Instead, she fell onto the hard pavement and was helped to her feet by two charitable Russian men who displayed no anger toward the young taxi driver who merely waited for the human obstacle to be cleared from his path. Perhaps this woman had no right to be crossing where she did. At least this is one way to explain away the passivity that everyone displayed—that is if you want to ignore the systematic pattern of utter passivity that infects the Russian people.

My date and I had arranged to have dinner at a small out-of-the-way restaurant in the capital. We arrived to find it closed.

A CHRISTIAN VIEW OF RUSSIA

"They must have closed it down because of a fight," Vera concluded.

"When do you think they'll open it?"

The attractive brunette, who was looking for a quick way out of Russia, raised her shoulders and shook her head. "Who knows, maybe never!" she grinned.

A heavy fog had stranded my adventuresome group of Americans in the central-Siberian city of Novosibirsk, almost three-quarters of the way between Moscow and our destination, Lake Baikal, the blue gem of Siberia. Waiting inside the terminal for the bus that would take us to the airport hotel, we saw hundreds of our fellow travellers slouched over a few chairs and lying in an orderly way on the floor. The nearly six hours my tourist troops spent in large communal rooms was more like a slumber party than a rest.

The fog finally lifted and the call came that we would fly. In the cool air of a Siberian summer morning, we paraded with our handgear a short distance to the now bustling airport terminal. Lines had formed everywhere as passengers queued up to board their waiting aircraft. But for the privileged foreigners, there would be no waiting. In Russian tradition we were escorted to the front of a long line, as exhausted-looking Slavic faces looked on in angelic silence. There was no anger, no sign of disgruntlement, just pure unadulterated passivity. Where else on planet earth would or could a crowd contain itself as did these inhumanly patient Russian souls?

We boarded the plane first, plopped into our seats and waited for the second-class Russian citizens who would now be permitted to enter. A steady stream of submissive Russians, burdened down with their cumbersome packages and bundles, made their way along the narrow aisle of the Aeroflot jet, fumbling about and bumping into one another. After a sleepless night this additional aggravation could only have elevated their frustration tolerance level.

Under the Revolutionary Law

For the czarist disciplinarian, disguised in a navy and white stewardess uniform, the Russian passengers were still moving too slowly. *"Bystrò! Bystro!"* the young Russian woman snapped, scolding everyone to take their seats. Silent obedience was the group's collective response. Many of the tourists were exhaustedly dozing off, oblivious to what seemed definitive evidence that the Soviet experiment was succeeding, and succeeding magnificently.

Russians could complain about the conditions of their lives, but almost always with resignation. Russians could be disgruntled by having to wait in long lines for staple groceries, but there always seemed to be more passivity in the expression than disgust. In everything the attitude was *Chto delat?* What can you do?

On the few occasions that I watched Russians confront authority, I must confess I found it most heart-warming. I once saw a wiry girl in her mid-twenties standing in line outside of the Uzbekistan Restaurant in Moscow try to maneuver past the doorman each time the doors were opened to let guests leave. And each time the muscular arms of the *shveytsar* checked the assault of this determined little girl. But such a dramatic resolve to confront official uniformed authority is too rare a strategy in Russia to meet with defeat. On the fourth try the Russian *shveytsar* withdrew from the confrontation, conceding defeat. He let the girl in. Russians instinctively respect the powerful and dominate the weak.

Certainly Russians could be angry with Moscow, but at least for my friends, the bottle often seemed to supply the courage. "How much do you pay for jeans?" Dmitry asked me. "Fifteen to twenty-five dollars, right? But here they're sold only on the black market and for 180 rubles and more. And what are jeans? They're simply for workers, and what are we? We're workers, and they still won't give them to us."

Nadezhda tried to calm her husband's ranting and raving as

he paced about the small living room. "Look," Dmitry said loudly as he pointed to the television news report on the Soviet leadership. "They're a bunch of senile old men in power who can barely talk. They mumble jumble, and yet they still tell us what to do." Darya, the Jewish couple's three-year-old daughter was upset as she watched her father pour himself another straight vodka. I was watching what seemed to be a destructive pattern.

For most Russians, I found, laughter is the usual means used for coping with frustration and hostility. "Russians laugh when we would cry," was one of the first observations I entered in my diary. The following experience illustrates this.

I had taken my safari slides of Africa to show some of my Leningrad friends. They had rented a projector for the weekend from the *prokat*, Russia's equipment rental store, and we got together for a viewing. But Soviet fate, or rather the system, was obviously out to do us in. After showing the first slide, the projector broke down. No one was upset, only disappointed. And everyone was roaring with laughter. But what else could be done? You couldn't stride angrily down to the state rental store and demand another projector immediately. It wouldn't do any good. No one is responsible for anything in the Soviet Union. It's all the system, impersonal, external, unreachable, out there somewhere, but controlling all. Passing it off to fate, laughing it off, is the only sane way to deal with it, that is, if you're sane. I wasn't always.

At this particular stage in my Soviet experience I was rather stubborn, or maybe just plain downright stubborn. The American fight that I still had inside me hadn't yet surrendered to the realization that in the Soviet Union there is nowhere to take the battle. The broken projector was the straw that broke my back. I could no longer restrain my impatience and frenetic energy. I had spent hours the evening before arranging those slides chronologically, all three-hundred of them. And for what? To see slide #1, appropriately titled "Welcome to Kenya!"

There is a time for everything, a time to keep silent and a time to say your piece. There was absolutely no question in my mind what season it was. Grigory, his brother, Pavel, and their friends just sat back, grinning expectantly, waiting for the American dramatic comedy to begin. Had Voice of America and their own domestic broadcasts prepared them for this moment? That I can't answer, but as the Russian proverb says, "It is better to see once than hear a hundred times."

I launched full force into an accented soliloquy about the frustrating experiences that confronted me everywhere in Leningrad, the endless queues, the waiters and waitresses who ignore your very existence, the taxis that drive head-on into scattering crowds of hapless pedestrians—I raged on, limited only by my sense of diplomacy, or what was now left of it. "It's a *sumasshedshy dom*," I shouted, using the colloquial slang expression meaning "madhouse." My friends just listened, enjoying my American insanity and perhaps even expressing themselves vicariously through it. "Americans just wouldn't put up with all this nonsense," I continued, explaining how notoriously impatient Americans are, though it surely wasn't necessary. My friends could see for themselves.

It took an outsider, a foreigner in every sense of the word, to present their life in such a fresh and unlikely way. Their laughter was a collectively unifying one—we're all in this mess together. Human comradeship had superseded the political kind.

As one among us looked for a disconnected wire in the uncooperative projector, Pavel came up to me and asked what kind of projector it was. Everyone began to snicker and soon began roaring with laughter as I tried to come up with the different Russian adjectives I knew; the university had not prepared me for real Soviet life. Finally, I gave up. *"Sdelano v SSSR,* Made in the USSR," Pavel quipped, commenting wryly on the quality of Soviet consumer goods.

Two and a half hours later, we saw the slides. The manual tray for pushing and pulling the slides proved too cumbersome to use, so each and every one of the three-hundred slides had to be hand-fitted into place and the light in the room put on between slides. For my friends the added inconvenience was amusing; for me it was nerve-wracking. But I was learning. I went back to the dormitory that evening realizing how different I was from my Leningrad friends. I'm sure they couldn't have agreed more.

For Russians, anecdotes are a way of life, a way of pungently commenting on everything that official Moscow holds dear. They are the quiet, ever so subtle, signs that the Russian spirit is still breathing inside the privacy and protective domain of the Russian home. An example:

"Who has the happiest children in the world?" a kindergarten teacher asks her class. "Kids in the USSR," everyone answers in unison. "And who has the finest toys in the world?" "Kids in the USSR," is again the chorussed reply. "Fine, children," the teacher congratulates her pupils. Little Sergey sits at his desk with his head bent over. Tears are streaming down his cheeks. "What is the matter, Sergey?" asks the teacher in surprise. Sergey raises his unhappy face to the teacher, "I want to go to the USSR."

Passivity is a conditioned reflex; it is a response to power that Russian children learn from their parents. Passivity is the fruit of years of societal-political conditioning. And in a broader, historical context, contemporary passivity is the reaction to the totalitarian power that governs every aspect of Russian life.

For the psychologist, Russian passivity may be viewed as

the inevitable result of Soviet society's conditioning of rewards and punishment. Punishments like the forceful slam of the metro train doors may painfully encourage the sluggish and disobedient passenger to be less sluggish and more obedient. Well-trained, Russian circus animals are turned into docile, spiritless creatures that seem to have been deprived of their instinctive wild nature. Horses, for instance, are taught to perform the most intricate types of choreographic patterns. They are rewarded with a hunk of sugar for success; for failure, they taste the whip. Is this a subconscious device to signal to the Soviet audience that "this goes for you too"?

There is yet another variant here, the most obvious one. As I concluded on more than one frustrating occasion, Soviet passivity is the epitome of Russian sanity.

However the observer approaches the problem one thing is for sure. The dignity, creativity and self-worth of the human person is on the revolutionary chopping block. Russian patience has evolved into a senseless kind of passivity, a pitiful helplessness. The design of the Soviet mold is to create a fleet of revolutionary soldiers who will march to the beat of the communist drum. There is only one way to describe this phenomenon: spiritual bondage. Applied to Soviet communism, Jesus' words about the true nature of the enemy take on new meaning: "The thief cometh not, but for to steal, and to kill, and to destroy. . . ." It was to destroy the works of Satan, to overcome the powers of darkness that Jesus Christ came into this world. "I am come that they might have life, and that they might have it more abundantly."[1]

The prophetic words that Isaiah spoke of the coming Messiah is a message of freedom that must be proclaimed to the captive Russian nation:

---

[1] John 10:10 KJV

A CHRISTIAN VIEW OF RUSSIA

The spirit of the Lord God is upon me; because the Lord hath anointed me to preach good tidings unto the meek; he hath sent me to bind up the brokenhearted, to proclaim liberty to the captives, and the opening of the prison to them that are bound . . . .[1]

In trying to form a spiritless, spotless leopard called Soviet Man, Soviet Russia is waging a battle against God Himself. And how very foolish are they that believe that communism can be victorious. Throughout the Psalms, David gladly proclaims that the Lord is King over *all* the earth. Despite the present political power of Revolutionary Babylon, we too must join in the Psalmist's proclamation, clap our hands, and sing praises unto the Creator of all, the Sovereign King. It is as true today as it was centuries ago: "Yea, all kings shall fall down before him: all nations shall serve him."[2]

---

[1] Isaiah 61:1 KJV
[2] Psalm 72:11 KJV

9

Under the Boot

Every kingdom divided against itself is heading for ruin . . . .
(Matthew 12:25 TJB)

In the America of the sixties, screen writers went wild portraying what they thought life was like in mysterious, faraway Russia. The comedy was often hilarious, especially for America's war babies like myself, who spent the afternoons glued to their television sets watching the famous cartoon series *Rocky and Bullwinkle.* Rocky, a witty squirrel, and his dumb sidekick, Bullwinkle the moose, were the good guys. Set in the context of Soviet-American relations of that period, the villains of the series were Russia's illustrious duo, Boris Badanov and his slinky accomplice, Natasha. Though unrelenting in their effort to do evil, these "bad guys" would always in the final scenes end up being outsmarted by the animal heroes of the great American city, Frostbite Falls.

There was another character in the program who made few appearances, but you always knew he was there somewhere. Known only by the name Fearless Leader, he was Russia's Big Brother who masterminded Boris's and Natasha's sinister plots. Whenever Fearless Leader summoned his two lieutenants for a little chat, Boris and Natasha would shiver in their Russian boots, terrified by this awesome character. For those of us who grew up with such political cartoonery, the *Rocky and Bullwinkle* show was entertaining and truly great comedy. Undoubtedly it subconsciously conditioned us to see Boris and Natasha as a caricature of all Russian men and women.

But comedy and paranoia are one thing: reality, Soviet reality, is another. The behavior of today's true-to-life Russians certainly shows that Big Brother is more than some fictitious concept in the heads of American screen writers.

Anyone who spends time on Russia's protected soil cannot but be impressed by the fact that Russians simply, obviously, don't trust each other. Instinctively, Russians are tight-lipped about things that in most open societies would be discussed without a second thought. But in the Soviet Union, everything, from what you thought about the propaganda film last night on television, to whether you caught the evening broadcast of Voice of America, has sensitive, political ramifications. There are two Russian worlds; like nearly everything else in the Soviet Union, they are part of the great Marxist dialectic. There is the real world of how a person perceives his life and the things about him, and the very unreal world, where everyone must to some degree play the role of being a fervent supporter of the regime's revolutionary goals.

It would invariably happen that whenever I gave someone on the hotel staff one of my American novels, it would be returned with some type of paper covering. The added protection was partly to protect the book's cover, and partly to protect the Russian's privacy. It just wasn't necessary for others to see what they are reading.

Russians also have a habit of whispering to one another when they are in a group. To an American it may seem rude and impolite; for Russians, it's simply being careful. I can remember innumerable times one particular Intourist guide

taking me aside whenever she wanted to ask me a favor or tell
me something she thought was personal. (I usually didn't.) In
Russia, politics has a strange way of constraining the tongue.
For Anna, our conversation was only between her and me.
So, why let others in?

Other guides besides Anna would also confide in me that I
tended to be too open and careless with my words. "You don't
realize how dangerous some guides can be. They will report
everything you say and do." Reporting on others seems to be
very much a part of today's Soviet life. Informing the higher-
ups of what a colleague said or did is a convenient way of
getting in tight with those in control, and a way to progress in
one's career.

A hotel waiter, Viktor, claimed that one of his co-workers,
he didn't know who, squealed on him for accepting illegal
foreign currency tips from tourists. "Some people just squeal
because they feel that they may be implicated by association
when someone is caught doing something wrong," he
explained. Nadezhda and Dmitry just assumed that in my
university student group there just had to be a few American
informers, despite the fact that I categorically denied that this
could be true.

In a Moscow restaurant I was seated across from a rather
inebriated middle-aged Russian who refused to believe that I
was an American. "You speak Russian like my son," he lauded
me undeservingly, revealing how much liquor he had
consumed. "You must be an *obmanshchik*," he accused, "we
have lots of people like that." It seemed significant, I thought,
that even though at that time my Russian vocabulary was
very basic, I already knew the Russian word for deceiver, for
it was so frequently used.

Two prostitutes outside of Moscow's famous National
Hotel invited me to their den. Declining in Russian, they
immediately became suspicious, joking nervously between

themselves that I was a plant. Even innocent Russian children could become suspicious when I pried into their little Russian world. "Are you looking forward to the Pioneer Day Celebration?" I asked a group of ten- and twelve-year-olds rehearsing on Leningrad's Palace Square on the eve of the children's extravaganza. I overheard one boy giddily telling his school chums that I was Andropov, the former head of the Soviet secret police, now the chief Soviet boss.

Travelling abroad, especially to a capitalist country, is a cherished hope for many Russians. After all, much of the content of the Soviet media is directed to events that take place beyond the limits of the Soviet world. The barrage of political propaganda which seeks to demonstrate that Soviet citizens live better than anyone else whets the Russian appetite to see the "decaying" Western world. Few Russians however will ever receive the privilege of judging for themselves which political system is better. Russian *kapusta*, cabbage, the Russian slang word for money, will not by itself get you an airline ticket on an Aeroflot jet bound for an exotic destination beyond the Soviet frontier. Not only do you need a visa, but also a foreign travel passport. Both are difficult to get. The internal passport, which must be carried while travelling inside the country, just won't do.

If you're interested in a round-trip to the West, a group tour organized by your trade union is in most cases your only realistic hope. And if you're a student, you might have a chance by applying to *Sputnik*, the Soviet travel agency for young people. But by and large, only an elect few, mostly select Communist Party members and Komsomol activists get the opportunity. The usual procedure is that spouses and children remain at home and keep an eye on things; and of course, that is also a good incentive for the lucky traveller to hurry on home. Many of these tours are within the East European Communist bloc, and therefore do not deplete the

Under the Boot

Soviet Union's limited reserve of foreign currency. And if you're fortunate enough to be able to go somewhere else, there is a good chance it might be to India, a country which is friendly to the Soviet Union and where poverty is everywhere evident. It's the kind of eye-opener that Soviet authorities wholeheartedly approve of.

If you're interested in a one-way trip out of the country, your options are also limited, basically to two. The first is to marry a foreigner. It's almost a sure bet you'll make it out, the only question is when. But then again, there is no such thing as a "sure thing" inside Russia. Nonetheless, "fictitious marriages," Russians marrying foreigners simply to get out of the country, are not that unusual.

The other alternative is to show that you or your spouse are Jewish, or at least have some Jewish blood.* Since your standard internal passport contains all vital statistics, like name, place, date of birth *and nationality,* the first part is easy. It's easy because the Soviets conveniently look upon Jews as a nationality, not as members of a religion. Although Jews in the U.S.S.R. have an autonomous republic, you have to receive an official invitation from your Jewish kinsfolk abroad. Only an invitation from an immediate relative, like a mother, a sister or a brother, is worth its weight in gold, particularly since tighter restrictions on Jewish emigration came into force following the 1980 Moscow Olympics. The real hurdle to overcome is to actually receive the document in hand. Censors can and do weed out such mail, an effective Soviet means of hindering easy emigration.

Instinctively, Russians know that there is a tight web of security and bureaucracy that surrounds the process of applying for travel abroad.

---

* Armenians and ethnic Germans seeking to be reunited with their families living abroad also have a chance to emigrate.

A CHRISTIAN VIEW OF RUSSIA

"If I want to go abroad," Andrey, a train technician, said with a big grin, "the security people would probably start with my grandmother and ask her all kinds of questions about me."

"Your grandmother!" I exclaimed.

"Yes," he continued, "my grandmother. They'd need to know what I said when I was a little boy, what my favorite foods were, and—"

I broke up laughing, finally catching the wisdom of his wit. It reminded me of the great Russian truism that the only Soviet organization that works effectively is the secret police.

Most Russians simply resign themselves to the fact that they'll never ever travel outside of their homeland. Perhaps in some distorted way, their confinement at home makes them feel wanted by their government. Undoubtedly however, it creates the feeling that someone is in control, ordering their existence. The protective wall that confines the Russian people can only thicken, whether Russians like it or not.

One of the most, if not the most, agonizing decision anyone in the Soviet Union can be faced with, is whether to formally petition for a visa to leave the country. Everyone knows only too well that Revolutionary Russia is a possessive protectress who will spare no effort to keep her multi-national flock together. A young Lithuanian mother talked about the apprehension and anxiety that she and her husband deal with as they grapple with the ultimate question, "to apply or not to apply."

"If we make application to leave," Sofya began, "we're so afraid that our lives will become much worse. They won't give us the visa we want. They'll say 'no one wants you, all Western countries have problems of their own, like unemployment.' Maybe after we apply, they'll never let us leave Vilnius, our capital, or they'll exile us to Siberia. We'll lose our jobs immediately and our co-workers will be forced to publicly ostracize us. They tell us, 'We shot traitors like you during the war.' And who knows what else the authorities will do? And my little son, what will happen to him?" Her face became contorted by the anguish that had overwhelmed her. "But," she concluded, "we'll have to try to leave. We must."

And even if permission to emigrate is given, there is always the consideration of the family and relatives that would be left behind. Revenge could be taken on them. Saying good-bye to family and friends can also have a haunting finality to it. For any number of "good" reasons, or for no apparent reason, even correspondence may not be possible. Russia's totalitarian control has effectively covered all the bases. The final decision could be psychologically devastating.

There is also the testimony of Galina, the born-again Pentecostal in Kiev. Like some fifty-thousand other Christians, she has applied to emigrate to the West for purely religious reasons. But each year, for four years in a row, she has been repeatedly denied an exit visa, allegedly because no one in the Western world had invited her.

"Each day that goes by," Galina explained, "my aunt and I wait for a knock at the door, for the police to come and take us away. Some believers who are not on the list to emigrate are being taken and given sentences. But for those of us who are trying to leave, it won't just be a few years. One brother in the community with sixteen children added his name to those who want to emigrate. And already now for two years, he's been in a 'psychiatric hospital.' But we're ready for that too."

I must confess that these words simultaneously strengthened my inner spirit and scared the living daylights out of me. This was my first experience with a persecuted believer in Jesus. True, Jesus had made it plain that persecution and following Him go hand in hand, but these had been just words. I had to give the Soviet authorities credit for teaching me biblical lessons I really couldn't learn at home. Following

A CHRISTIAN VIEW OF RUSSIA

Jesus in Russia involved a heavy cost—and if you weren't careful, it could cost you everything. The man with sixteen children inside a Soviet "hospital," was paying the price. Despite the heaviness of the experience, I had to thank Russia for revealing to me its domestic policies, policies that Jesus had foretold.

Galina went on to describe the situation for believers since the Olympics ended in the summer of 1980. She used a word that I was not familiar with, so out came a pencil and pad. The picture of a stick of dynamite with a burning fuse needed no translation; it was fearfully unmistakable. "So far," she stressed, "so far Soviet Power has been patient with us, but the fuse grows shorter with each day. In a year or so, many, many more of us will be taken away." Her aunt, who had remained silent and solemn during our talk, nodded in agreement, showing that she too was ready to go all the way for her Redeemer. "So we just wait," Galina continued, "and never know when they may come for us."

I felt led to ask Galina why she wanted to leave Russia, as if what I had just heard was not reason enough. Like all Russians, she was well accustomed to such no-nonsense, right-to-the-point kind of questions. Her equally direct reply testified to the working of the Holy Spirit both in her life, and in her nation. "There is only one reason," she said, "because Our Lord has told us through prophecy to do so. And not just our church, but brothers and sisters throughout the country. Sure, not everyone will leave, but some will. And if the Lord has chosen me to go, no one will stop His will."

Now these two testimonies do not square with the official view, as any foreigner who has attended a Soviet Round Table Discussion knows so well. Tourism to Russia involves a great deal more than sightseeing. Often it involves coming to the negotiating table where some honest talk and powerful therapy take place.

Under the Boot

The Round Table on the Soviet side usually consisted of three officially unofficial Russians. For example, a typical delegation might be made up of a member of the Soviet Academy of Sciences, a journalist, and a specialist on American affairs. Such a professional team is rather impressive and usually a little overwhelming for the average American tour group. The lively "exchange of views" that would occur would always, absolutely always, include a question on emigration.

The answer, to be sure, was always the same official one. Statistics would be cited to show that a phenomenal 98 plus percent of all applicants who sought exit visas received them within a reasonable period of time. This official propaganda always made my Americans anxious and upset, and sometimes quite angry.

When one official quoted the almost 100 percent figure, and added insult to injury by claiming that the statistics came from *The New York Times,* an elderly man sitting in the front row of the auditorium jumped to his feet. "Now wait one minute!" he protested. "You say that *The New York Times* printed that, but you know damn well that the *Times* was simply quoting your own sources." The speaker did not reply.

Now as to the less than two percent of the applicants who are denied visas, they are said to fall into one of three categories. First, individuals who have been associated with the military-industrial field. As a matter of security, it was explained, these citizens must change their jobs to a non-scientific area and wait two to three years until what they know becomes obsolete. The second category of citizens who temporarily may be refused a visa are children of parents who need their support, not necessarily financially, but psychologically and morally as well. And finally, individuals about to stand trial would also be detained. As one panelist put it, "We don't export our criminals."

A CHRISTIAN VIEW OF RUSSIA

If these three categories are in fact all-inclusive, then why is Sofya, the girl from Lithuania, and Galina, the Ukrainian Pentecostal, still in Russia? I never asked.

"Criticism to improve our country is welcome," a Soviet official once lectured to his audience at another Round Table Discussion. "But," he pointed out, "any attempt to condemn or defame the fundamentals for which our society stands is slanderous and criminal." This vague formula, defining what Soviet Power will allow and what is strictly forbidden, caused a wave of tense energy to sweep through the auditorium. We all sensed what Russia's dissidents must be up against. Sighs of anxiety, heads shaking negatively and perhaps defiantly, and the creaking sounds of bodies nervously squirming in their chairs seemed to unify everyone in a sense of angry anticipation.

Acknowledged by the chairman of the question-and-answer symposium, a young man took the floor. He was visibly charged with emotion and asked the question that needed no answer. "Who decides what is criticism and what is defamation?" All the Americans present realized that the Soviet authorities were the final arbiters of all such questions.

Propaganda comes in two varieties: good and bad. When my American clients were treated to the good propaganda, they wondered if perhaps they had been wrong all these years about Russia. Maybe the American news media hadn't been fair in describing what the Soviet state is all about; Russia just didn't seem all that bad. But when they endured the bad propaganda (for instance, this nonsense about being free to emigrate and criticize), everyone began to feel what it must be like to live under the Revolutionary Boot.

The question of reforming totalitarian Russia was a line of inquiry that I usually dared not pursue with Russians. "To reform or not to reform" was the ultimate of questions. The times that I did brazenly pose the question to those whom I trusted, I met with caution and genuine uneasiness. The instinctive reflex was to move to a less sensitive set of problems. *"Ochen slozhno,* it's very complicated," was Grigory's way to slough off the question.

"Sure we're dissatisfied with the system," said Viktor, the hotel waiter who had been reported to the authorities for taking foreign currency tips. "But you know what stops us from actively trying to change things? Fear. We're still afraid of the camps. Sure, we'll accept a changed system, but only if we don't have to do anything about it. We're afraid to get involved and support the dissidents. My friend, he got seven years for self-publishing, and I've seen the camp, from the outside, of course. They work them nine, ten hours a day and allow them less than fifty kopecks for food per day. We're afraid. I can still remember when the the KGB came to my flat and searched the place. They found the foreign money. And you know what happened? They took me to the Big House, KGB headquarters, and questioned me for hours. Finally, they let me go. It was a nightmare!"

"Sure, we can demonstrate," he jested. "We can demonstrate on May Day and Revolution Day. Other than that— jail, if you dare. We have this saying, criticism that comes from the top is medicine to those below. But the criticism from below to those on top? That's poison."

A psychiatrist talked about what goes on inside the psychiatric hospitals, distinguishing between normal psychiatry and the political kind. A former psychiatric patient, who had recovered from a nervous breakdown, told me he thought there were perhaps five legitimate cases like himself in the hospital where he was interned. The rest were political and religious dissidents who were tortured, beaten, and drugged into submission. The few isolated pieces of the puzzle were revealing a terrifying scene, one that I knew little about firsthand.

A CHRISTIAN VIEW OF RUSSIA

Only during my last few visits to Russia in 1982-1983 did I make contact with the Christian underground. Each new experience made me more painfully aware of what Soviet believers must do to remain faithful to the Gospel.

After making plans to go to an illegal prayer meeting, I was counseled to follow my friend to the bus stop from a safe distance. Being seen with her could mean serious trouble. This particular unregistered Pentecostal church we were to go to moved from one location to another to keep ahead of the KGB. When this endeavor failed, it could result in the believers being arrested, but the most common punishment is a fine. Just before entering the apartment where the prayer gathering was taking place, I was again cautioned that one of the "believers" was thought to be an "informer"; there was obviously some risk involved. As fervent prayer to the Lord went up from the believers, it was easy to spot the "imposter." His lips seemed to move, but he was obviously not a genuine believer.

This too simultaneously built up my faith and tested it. It seemed as though I was walking among spiritual giants who had all it takes to walk through the waters of the turbulent revolutionary Red Sea. No one seemed distracted or tempted in accepting Jesus' call. But this was not so. Each and every new day involved new trials and fresh fiery testings. One day at a time, the persecuted flock had to draw anew from the Lord's spiritual reserves. Enduring purification like this demanded an overflow of His grace—and it was there, ready and available for the asking.

"I'm afraid," I sincerely confided to a sister in the Lord who exuded the presence and humility of Jesus. "What happens if they come?"

The young believer, my peer, only smiled courageously, her "face of faith" precious enough for the canvas of another Da Vinci. "That's the way we feel every day of our lives,"

Under the Boot

I was plainly told. "Our hearts want to follow Him, but our flesh is afraid."

The truth of this testimony is the abiding truth of the Scriptures. I pray that I shall never forget that day, her face, such courage, those words—

My rather limited contact with the Soviet Union's multinational people was mostly with the inhabitants of Transcaucasia and the Soviet Baltic Republics. The former inhabit the Republics of Armenia, Azerbaijan, and Georgia. The latter, the Latvians, Lithuanians, and Estonians, became incorporated into the Soviet Union only in 1940; their memory of freedom is still very much alive. These nationalities share the Soviet Union with their more numerous Russian brethren, but if they had their choice, according to the few I met, they would immediately dissolve their status as Soviet Republics. Georgians, Armenians, Estonians—they all referred to their birthplace as their country, not as one of the fifteen Union Republics, as they are officially called.

The story was always the same. The Russians had imposed themselves on the nationalities and ruled them with an iron hand. In Estonia, the anti-Russian sentiment revealed itself in what can only be described as an outward antipathy at the sound of the Russian language. Russians seem to enjoy spending their vacations and holidays in the charming Estonian capital of Tallinn. Affectionately nicknamed, "Little Europe," it is well known for its many quaint little sit-down cafés, elegant restaurants, and cozy bars. But for the Russian tourist who seeks to find a harbor of comfort from the ideological rigors of building communism, his native tongue might very well ruin his holidays. *"Svobodnykh mest nyet,* no vacant places," is likely to be the response to even the most polite of Russian questions.

"The Russians are our masters," said Sofya, the Lithuanian girl who so longed for freedom in the West. "The Russians, they understand our language, and could speak it if they tried, but they refuse to learn. If you go into a shop in Vilnius and speak Lithuanian, they'll tell you, 'speak Russian, it's the language of the country.' "

Boris, a Georgian doctor living in Moscow, spoke sympathetically of the Russian people, but referred to those in power with disgust. "They're just swine. They control us so completely, and we can't do a thing about it. Maybe," he continued, "maybe the Russians want communism, but not the other nationalities. Our life here is so empty, nothing to do, nowhere to go. And they are always playing that stupid Russian folk music in the restaurants and on the radio. We're fed up with it all."

By their very nature, totalitarian systems are absolute, controlling everything and everyone that fall within the domain of their power. In the Soviet system, this includes the unlucky foreigner, whether he be a tourist, a student, or a business man. No one is exempt.

For the foreigner, the punishment is one of imposed isolation, to forever remain with other unwanted foreigners. Strangely enough, it is the Russians themselves that are supposed to enforce these punitive sanctions. They have been instructed, not by decree, but through the process of acculturation, to stay clear from the tempting, but unclean, *inostranets.*

When you ask Russians, why promoting international friendship, a constitutional duty of every citizen, is a big *nyet* in practice, you do get a few concrete answers. Fear of black market business, spying and even drugs are the reasons most commonly given. But as always, many curious Russians seem as bewildered by the political no-no as the suspected foreigner, which, ironically, creates a bond where there isn't supposed to be one.

Russians may not fully comprehend the ways of their

government, but they are often fearfully obedient to its
revolutionary will. At times, however, the temptation of the
forbidden foreigner from the exotic, "decadent" West
becomes too great to resist. It only goes to show that Soviet
leopard spots run deep. Some examples:

A casual conversation with a young taxi driver about
American jazz prompted the cabbie to invite his American
passenger to a Leningrad jazz concert. An English-speaking
Russian came up to me as I was crossing a bridge. "I thought
you were an American," he grinned. "Would you like to join
me in a bar? I'd like to practice my English with you." Love
Russian style was what a romantically cold Dr. Zhivago
February brought for an American high school girl and a
Russian sailor. They found each other in the train's restaurant car, an hour outside of the snow-covered capital. A
museum guide, after taking my group through a Moscow art
gallery, crumpled a piece of paper with her address into my
hand, and whispered to me to write to her from America.

Yet this eagerness to partake of the forbidden fruit is
usually modified by a careful, cautious approach, making
meetings with foreigners somewhat secretive. The rendez-
vous would usually take place a healthy distance away from
Intourist hotels, which are constantly patrolled by the militia
whose duty it is to prevent Soviet citizens from meeting
foreign tourists. Russians would generally be more ready to
meet outside of a student dormitory, but as far as venturing
to go inside is concerned, their political intuition tells them *ne
nado,* you shouldn't.

cRussians can be as suspicious that hotel and dorm phones
where foreigners reside are bugged, almost as much as
neurotic foreigners themselves. The preference, though far
from an obsession with Russians, is that all telephoning be
done from public booths on the street.

Taking a foreigner back to your flat is another matter that

is often approached with due caution. The curiosity of a snooping tenant might be aroused by the unfamiliar sounds of a foreign language, or even a heavily accented, ungrammatical Russian like my own. This is why some Russians may prefer silence in their apartment building until you are inside the safety of their flat. But once inside, out of the reach of Big Brother, complete freedom and openness reign untrammelled.

Tanya, a young Muscovite kindergarten teacher, who seemed to have quite a few foreign friends, told me that her neighbor across the hall threatened to report her the next time she had foreign guests.

"Is he just an average guy?" I asked.

"Of course," she answered. "Everyone in Moscow knows that associating with foreigners is forbidden."

Intourist hotels, where primarily foreigners reside, make for good "quarantine" centers. A *propusk,* an admission card, distributed by the hotel administration, must be shown to cranky doormen who guard the premises around the clock. These Intourist hotels are in a very real sense located in a dimension of space far removed from the local environs. They become impenetrable bastions which seal out the Russian world and seal in the foreign one. The isolation is total. Hotel policy prohibits giving out over the telephone a foreign guest's room number to a Russian-speaking caller. All attempts at communication with the taboo foreign world have been dealt with, and dealt with most effectively. Intourist hotels may not be surrounded by protective moats, but the presence of patrolling militiamen, undercover agents, and even student detachments, form an effective cordon sanitaire.

Russia's chosen fate is to remain a lonely island unto itself. All ties with the outside world are to be severed as efficiently as possible. Even the written word, in the form of an innocent letter abroad, may never reach its destination. And so Russians are forced to give their letters to sailors going overseas, or even to a foreign tourist; they understand only too well that their fate is to be that of an estranged people.

Nowhere is the fear of foreign contamination more evident than at the customs arrival halls at the international airports in Moscow and Leningrad. Security consciousness is reflected in the sometimes rather intense inspection of luggage, where it is not uncommon to see every piece of clothing taken out one by one. Loose pieces of paper quickly draw attention, and letters and local addresses would at least be temporarily confiscated, and perhaps reproduced and filed.

But there is a lighter side even to paranoia. Customs, for instance, once tried to confiscate a slip of paper from an old Russian emigré. It contained a series of numbers which the customs official believed to be telephone numbers. He was right. "But you don't understand," Sonya protested in a New York Jewish accent, "that's the number of my girlfriend in the Bronx."

Officials are inclined to inspect nearly all reading material that enters the country, especially popular magazines like *Time* and *Newsweek.* Thumbing through the pages, they look for anything which might deflect the Soviet citizen from the labor of building communism. There is also an official listing of books considered to be anti-Soviet and authors who have become "enemies of the Soviet State." These books are immediately exchanged for an official looking *spravka*, a receipt, simply indicating that the Russians now have your book.

Information inside Russia is a highly political commodity. The right words and ideas can make attractive, or at least try to, the whole notion of building a communist world; the wrong ones can jeopardize the stability of the Soviet political structure. It is no surprise then, that Western literature is looked upon suspiciously because it tempts and tantalizes the potential Soviet reader with democratic or "decadent" bourgeois ideas.

Foreign books which are officially translated into Russian often negatively treat some aspect of life in the West. These kinds of books lend confirmation to the official propaganda line that Soviets live better than anyone else. It is no coincidence that both John Steinbeck and Theodore Dreiser are among the handful of American novelists that have been translated itno Russian. Steinbeck's portrayal of mistreated migrant workers in *The Grapes of Wrath*, and Dreiser's condemnation of the materialistic American society in *An American Tragedy* are regarded by Soviet authorities as classical lessons in politics as well as literature.

Only once was I lucky enough to get a hold of a copy of Canada's *The Globe and Mail*, one of the few capitalist English newspapers available, at least theoretically, to information-starved tourists. Hotel saleswomen usually hide the few month-old copies they have under the counter and sell them only to bona fide foreigners. Russians who have access to duplicating machines are forbidden to reproduce any unauthorized material. Even Western music, according to a college professor, is considered a threat by the Soviet government. "They feel that through the words in the songs, the poison of Western propaganda is seeping through."

Airport customs may be regarded as a basic introduction into Russian security, but a Soviet border crossing by train is an advanced lesson in Russian paranoia. My first adventure travelling by train beyond the Soviet frontier is unforgettable. On a sunny Sunday afternoon, unseasonably warm for mid-February in Moscow, I took a taxi out to the Belorussia Railway Station. Placing my luggage into a convenient cart, I was escorted by a muscular porter to Train #61, which, I was confidently told, would take me from the Soviet capital to Warsaw.

Under the Boot

Once inside my assigned *kupé,* a compartment with room for four, I introduced myself to my two *poputchiki,* my travelling companions, who were assigned the upper and lower bunks across from me. Since Soviet compartment assignments are made regardless of sex, I wasn't surprised to learn that I would be travelling with two women. The middle-aged mothers and I had quite a time of it, chatting, playing cards, and just reflectively gazing out the window as afternoon turned to dusk. As we sped westward into White Russia, the two lucky women, I learned were, like myself, travelling to visit relatives in Poland.

The last member of our little family, a Red Army officer, joined us about an hour outside of the capital. He had little to say except *spokoynoy nochi,* which was his crafty way of telling us we should turn out the lights and bed down, which we did about ten thirty that evening. In the morning when we woke, he was gone, off to duty I supposed.

At about four in the morning the train conductor just casually stopped by to let us know that we were approaching the Soviet border at Brest, and that we should begin preparing ourselves for *Kontrol.* It was all very efficient, and orderly, as one would expect, but I was not used to getting up before dawn for inspection. When the train pulled into Brest I was still half dozing, though I noticed that my two *poputchiki* were obediently ready to be processed out of Russia. Without so much as a knock, the swinging doors opened, flooding the compartment with unwanted light. I jumped up to see what the intrusion was all about.

A young soldier with an absolutely expressionless, mimed look stood in the doorway, symbolically saluting us as if we were soldiers too. We were greeted with an unemotional, rapidly-spoken, "*Zdravstvuyte! Pasporta pozhaluysta.* (Good morning! Passports, please.)" I jumped down from the bunk in my non-Russian, flannel-looking p.j.'s, and fumbled through

157

my briefcase which lay on the small table near the window, soon producing my American passport. By the time I had handed it to the young man, I was wide awake, almost as if I had dived into a pool of ice water.

Each passport was carefully examined, checked, and double checked, in an effort to make 100 percent certain that the passport photos and our wretched-looking morning faces resembled each other. It must be an art, I thought, to be able to glean a resemblance between the two.

Our precious passports and visas, our only authorization to continue on Train #61, were placed into a small rectangular box. Straps were fastened to the wooden container which was hung like a primitive medallion around the rather thick muscular neck of the athletic-looking soldier. The receptacle was carefully handed to the conductor who stood in the aisle, prepared to assist as the remainder of the inspection ritual was performed.

Politely, but sternly, we were asked to leave our *kupé* and stand outside in the aisle. Armed with only a flashlight, the soldier lifted the mattresses of each of the four bunks and went through the motions of running his hand along the padding below. The area for luggage storage below the lower bunks and above the top ones was also examined.

Custom officials followed soon after to complete the registration formalities. Then we waited. It took two hours for workers to change the wheels of the train to fit the narrower gauge of the track in Poland. It was yet another unexpected and unwanted opportunity to acquire the kind of patience that the Russian people possess.

After spending a week in the beautiful village of Lincut, the birthplace of my grandfather, I returned to Russia, this time to Leningrad, to meet my next group of adventuresome Americans. Crossing over from the Polish city of Kuznica onto Soviet soil at the village town of Grodno, I could see in the sunlight of mid-afternoon what the darkness had concealed at Brest. Barbed wire fencing was strung along the immediate border through the dense forests, and two watchtowers peaked above the trees, giving the soldiers on duty a good view of their socialist brotherland to the west. What looked like furrowed beach sand designs, twelve to fifteen feet wide, formed paths through the forests, a readily available way to detect both animal and human footprints.

My *poputchiki* this time consisted of three Lithuanian women who were returning to their Baltic republic after family reunions in Poland. While they were waiting in our berth to be checked out, I was, as usual, trying to learn more of Soviet Russia's mysterious ways. Standing in the train corridor, I pulled down the window to get a better look around.

On either end of the train, soldiers were walking along the tracks, opening the little compartments beneath each car. They worked quickly and efficiently, perhaps because this was their routine duty. It didn't take long for one of them to notice that I was poking my head where it shouldn't have been. *"Zakroyte okno!* (Shut the window!)" he yelled out, breaking the peaceful solemnity that seemed to rest over the expansive, snow-covered forests. I obeyed the command, shut the window, and returned to my cozy *kupé* to tell my Lithuanian *poputchiki* what was going on outside of our little world.

"What do you think they're looking for?" I asked.

Shrugging her shoulders, one woman explained what the paranoia was probably about.

"Maybe they're looking for weapons?" Perhaps weapons which could help bring a revolution against Soviet rule, I thought. Most likely we were all thinking the same thing, but the heavy atmosphere about us wasn't really conducive to such talk. As we waited in an articulate silence for the internal search to begin, the eerie sound of footsteps walking on top of the train made us all the more aware that once again we were under the Soviet Boot, literally as well as figuratively.

The tactics of Soviet rule—revenge and retribution, the labor camps and the frontier towers, an imposed isolation and the imposition of a foreign language—are designed to maintain absolute power. And that power is harnessed toward achieving one ultimate end: the final realization of communism and all that that entails.

The Scriptures, I think, would have something to say about the dynamics of totalitarian power. Jesus said it in response to the Pharisees saying among themselves that He cast out devils by the power of Beelzebub. "Every kingdom divided against itself is heading for ruin; and no town, no household divided against itself can stand."[1]

If Soviet Marxists choose to ignore scriptural truth, they need only to learn from the lessons of history. While the reasons for the decline and fall of the Western Roman Empire are complex and many, it does raise an interesting question. Why was the Eastern Roman Empire able to survive for almost one thousand years after the West's demise? Historian Michael Grant argues that the barbarian invasions by themselves, although a greater problem for the Western than the Byzantine Empire, do not offer a complete answer to the question. Both empires were attacked from the outside, but the West caved in because its internal divisions were greater, divisions, for instance, which alienated the people from the emperor, pitted the German people against the Romans, and created enmity between the Christian and pagan faiths. According to Grant, true resistance against the foreign enemy never materialized because of these and other "disunities."

---

[1] Matthew 12:25-26 TJB

Under the Boot

A group of young Russian Orthodox believers, some of whom are now in prison, not long ago wrote an open letter addressed to American youth. In it they explained that for them, freedom from the oppression of Soviet Power can be found only in Christ. "We know that Christ is a liberator, not a legislator, and no one can be a barrier between our hearts and Him. But," they continued, "we gratefully accept the help of those servants of His who help unite us to Him."

In the concluding lines of their letter, they make an appeal to us to grow closer to them. "We appeal to the people with an open soul. Open your hearts to us, as we have opened ours to yours." Their plea for unity and fellowship is a challenge that each one of us must answer.

10

The Victorious Russians

I will sing unto the Lord, for he hath triumphed gloriously: the horse and his rider hath he thrown into the sea.

(Exodus 15:1 KJV)

The Russian character, like the society that produces it, is complex, confusing, and royally contradictory. In public the Russian countenance appears almost expressionless. An unnatural sense of order and silence seems to make the Russian human spirit whimper. Spontaneity and individualism have been strangled by a repressive state that has executed its goals remarkably well. Under the Soviet Boot, the freedoms set forth in the Soviet Constitution have become empty and serve only the purposes of revolutionary rhetoric. The powers of government are used not to protect man, but to imprison him, mentally, spiritually, and sometimes physically.

But even totalitarian power is not without limits. It may isolate, manipulate, restrain, reeducate, but it cannot destroy. In many ways the Russian spirit has been crushed, but there are many signs that it has not been buried. There is another chapter, often ignored, to the story of the meek Russians. It is about a spirited people who live a robust life full of gusto and spark. It is a story about a form of freedom that is neither political nor social, but spiritual. It is a story of the victory of the human spirit over man's insatiable lust for power, his quest to control and stifle what refuses to be contained. It is an inspiring story of a people who can be as warm and compassionate toward each other as they can be cruel and sadistic. It is the story of the victorious Russians.

But the real victor of the story is not really man. It is the same God of Jacob that made a way through the Red Sea where there was no way, saving Israel and casting Pharaoh's hosts into the sea. The Russians may have no human armor to defend themselves against the onslaught of a superior enemy, but it doesn't matter; the Lord has already given them their defense. Created in the image and likeness of an Almighty God, the oppressed Russian people are adorned in triumphant battle array. Beaten down, molded and re-molded, silenced for a time, exiled and alienated, the great Russians, the meek of the earth, shall not be moved. For the breath of the Almighty has given them life, and His Spirit shall live forever.

Foreigners who visit Russia live in a tourist shell. They become acquainted with only one side of the Russian character, the public one. Bank clerks, saleswomen, waiters and waitresses, floor attendants and maids—these are the service people that abide with foreign tourists in their well-protected world. Politer and more helpful than the service staff on the street, this contingent of Russians can often be impersonal, rude, hot-headed, and impatient. Guardians of Soviet order in their respective domain, each is a legitimate czar or czarina. They decree and ordain how things must be done, indeed how things *will* be done. They do not use the smiles and sweet talk that we in the West have grown so accustomed to.

I always regretted that there was never enough time for my Americans to learn that what they considered being insen-

The Victorious Russians

sitive was, to be quite blunt, the Soviet character of the public Russian. But sadder still, most of my flock never got that chance to penetrate beyond the superficial facade to the interior of the Russian soul. Like the many contradictions that make Russia the paradox that it is, the openness and freedom of the Russian soul contradicts the often downright ugly ways of the public Russian. Together, they synthesize in perfect dialectic fashion the essence of contemporary Russianness. There are indeed few Americans, few foreigners, who in the short period of a few weeks can obtain the insight and experience to draw such a conclusion. But for those who managed to see but a faint glimmer, what they saw was usually fascinating and faith-enriching.

Americans had the greatest difficulty with the idea that there could be happy Russians in "communist" Russia.

The perfect example of the near trauma that scenes of happy Russians create for the American tourist took place in the village setting of Kalinin along the mysterious Volga River. Here in the restaurant of our cozy Motel Tver, a few of my tourists and I had just pulled up our chairs to a table full of merrymaking Russians. Immediately our glasses were filled to the brim with sparkling Soviet champagne from a newly-opened bottle. I was busy interpreting the greetings and long-winded toasts to peace and friendship. After one of the toasts was proposed to the sounds of clicking glasses and much hoopla and hobnobbing, this charming elderly Southern belle seated on my right bent over my shoulder. Obviously perplexed by this free-spirited encounter, she whispered to me, "But what about Stalin?" This classical one-liner so magnificently expressed the idea, "can this be the real thing?" For Americans, happy Russians are a contradiction in terms.

Somewhere along the line, my fellow countrymen, even fellow Christians, got a little misguided. Russians too have the same Creator who has shared his life-giving Spirit equally with all His creatures, capitalist and socialist alike. If the Lord is not a respecter of persons, He certainly doesn't care about political ideologies, even if their color is revolutionary red.

From the elevation of their coaches, foreign visitors surveying the Russian landscape will find little evidence of the happy Russians. Gloomy-looking pedestrians complement the lifeless institutionalization of Soviet apartment complexes and the dreary surroundings of the cities that all seem painted in shades of depressing gray. The Russian people, at times dressed colorlessly and with little imagination, go about their business oblivious to, and alienated from, everything and everyone about them.

But foreigners need not be frustrated in their pursuit of the happy Russians. Although almost everywhere the happy Russians appear as an extinct species, there is one place in the public domain that is like a sanctuary where Russians freely let it all hang out. It is in the restaurant that the Russian soul emerges, resurrected from the doldrums of Soviet society. Here, restraint gives way to a free-wheeling spirit that is often electrifying and contagious.

Bottles of fine Armenian cognac, sweet and dry Georgian and Moldavian wines, Russia's own bitter vodka, and sparkling Soviet champagne, the pride of the Union, are spread on tables creating a banquet atmosphere. Russians can be seen generously partaking of the fruits of the various republics, raising glasses in an unending litany of toasts that gives everyone an opportunity to become a part of the Slavic ritual. Revolutionary Russia's decree restricting the public display of human spontaneity does not seem to apply to the sanctuary of the restaurant. Here, partying Russians often rhythmically sway together at their tables joyously singing national songs.

Anyone who dares doubt that the Russians are free need only watch these Slavic people trip the light fantastic on the crowded dance floor. Happy pairs of Russian partners, the young attired in their chic Western jeans, and the not-so-young less stylishly dressed, express themselves by frolicking to the loud sounds of Russia's nationalistic music interspersed with popular Western selections. Women dance with women, girls with girls. In terms of style and grace, the Russians just don't have it. But in terms of self-expression, the shaking, jumping, and bouncing that Russians call dancing is doing your own thing in its purest and finest form.

At the first blare of music bachelors anxiously jump up from behind their tables and head for a partner often much younger or older than themselves. All facades vanish, for nothing really matters except being free. The band too is rather free, traditionally taking leisurely fifteen- to twenty-minute breaks regularly. So when the melody begins it's time to rock. Not a second is wasted. The food gets cold and unappetizing, but Russians have come to unloose their spirit, not fill their stomachs.

I noticed that the spirit of the Russian people could break through the rigidity of their Soviet society with just a little gentle prodding. And my antics often seemed to provide that gentle release. Besides my political teasing in the classroom and informative street-side chats, I could also be an accomplished practical joker. It was yet another way of dealing with an uptight society that was so different from the social and political freedom of America. "Playing games" in revolutionary Russia kept me sane and healthy, even if it didn't do anything for my impatience.

One of my most imaginative pranks was during a bus ride through downtown Leningrad. Getting on the bus I placed an uncounted handful of kopecks into the fare box and took myself maybe a dozen receipts or so. Naturally the socially responsible Russians who watched my foreign behavior were quick to point out that only one ticket was really necessary.

A CHRISTIAN VIEW OF RUSSIA

Even before I could launch into my Las Vegas act, I joyfully watched an array of Slavic grins and smiles poke through the ordered Soviet scene. Oh, the wayward ways of the crazy foreigner; that was the expression that I could read on the embarrassed faces of my almost captive audience. American vaudeville comedy had at last come to Russia.

I was compassionately instructed to take the seat beside the fare box and hand out receipts to the boarding passengers. I would get rid of the excess tickets, collect my five kopecks, and everything would be *po poryadku*, according to order, that marvelous Russian fixation.

Well, my approach to the contrived dilemma was basically as these well-meaning civic citizens had suggested. I took my place in front of the fare box and greeted each passenger with a big smile and a heavily accented *zdravstvuyte*, the word for hello in Russian that takes a slippery tongue and more than a modicum of effort to pronounce. I showed each new passenger the receipts, they immediately produced a five kopeck piece, and I was in business. No one asked what I was doing, perhaps because they just assumed that it was all perfectly kosher, and of course, orderly. After all, no one else on the bus was especially curious or inquisitive.

But there was just a slight twist in the script I had written, an American variation. Before any of my paying customers could take their seat, I came up with their change of one kopeck. "I know the government charges five kopecks," I explained with a straight face, "but I only charge four. You see, I'm just a kopeck cheaper than what you normally pay." I spoke loud enough so that my audience to the rear of the bus could also get in on this comical bit of disorder.

In just minutes my ad-libbing was producing wonders. Alienated-looking faces vanished as smiles and nervous laughter filled the bus. The idea of competing with the government selling cheaper bus tickets was slightly irreverent,

The Victorious Russians

tickling the socialist funny bone. It was one of my best performances anywhere.

Although being insensitive and just plain cruel to one's fellow comrades tends to be a part of public Soviet life, Russians at the same time are immensely capable of communicating a great sense of intimacy. Deprived the right to express themselves politically and socially, Russians seem to compensate in their demonstrative way of expressing "the inner man." Baring the soul and spirit comes easy to the meek of the earth.

As we have seen, Soviet Power prefers not to talk about love; it is of little pragmatic value in building a communist society. But it matters little, for although Russians are told how to live, work, and think, and everything else that happens to fall in the middle, Russians just seem to be able to love on their own. Loving is natural; and more than that, it is spiritual and very biblical.

In the beautiful Song of Solomon, King Solomon poetically portrays love as eternal, all-enduring, and ever-abiding. "Many waters cannot quench love, neither can the floods drown it . . . ."[1] It is wonderfully true; love is the flame of God Himself. Despite whatever may befall Soviet Man on the drawing board, it is comforting to know that as long as God is on the throne, man will always, somehow, someway, find a way to love.

Some of my American tourists seemed to carry around a score card on which they listed all the signs that pointed to the Russians as a people withdrawn and alienated from one another. For them the evidence was conclusive, perhaps as conclusive as the evidence of my previous chapters. But several days in Russia is hardly long enough, figuratively speaking, to put one's ear to the Russian earth. Yet a mere

---

[1] Song of Solomon 8:7 KJV

169

week was often long enough to confirm the preconceived American notion that Russians just have to be a thoroughly cowed, estranged people.

But it just isn't true at all. Praise the Lord! Even in the vicious dog-eat-dog Soviet world, there are the wonderful signs that King Jesus reigns.

As a people, Russians just seem to love to touch one another; often they have no choice. Jammed public transportation systems, tiny apartments and hotel elevators, the tight configuration of tables in restaurants and cafeterias, the "very cozy" seating arrangements on Russia's fleet of Aeroflot jets, and congested communal living—they all bring Russians up close to one another. Sharing the socialist tight quarters which their society affords can be uncomfortable and a real nuisance. But for Russians, sharing space is a way of life.

For my Americans however, who got a warm "touching" welcome during their subway tour in a packed train car, it was all a little too touchy, too intimate, and all too funny. At least in America, lots of touching in public just isn't called for, which goes to show that we all have our own peculiar cultural inhibitions.

All over Russia women and girls can be seen walking arm in arm. Traditionally, strolling together in this way has a real practical value. Along crowded city boulevards a pair of locked arms prevents oncoming pedestrians from plowing through you. Intimacy and insensitivity clash in a great dialectic bang. Touching is as Russian as *bliny* and *balalayki*, and as commonplace as somber-looking Russian countenances.

The generous display of affection that Russians are capable of lavishing on one another isn't something that is reserved to the privacy of the home. It's up front for all to see; it's a perfectly legitimate form of creativity. And it is one of the few

The Victorious Russians

ways of doing your own thing that isn't considered uncultured or offensive.

Taking hold of the hand of your *priyatel* or *drug*, your pal or
best friend, is a natural gesture among Russians. Such
spontaneity among Russia's littlest Pioneer citizens is
certainly to be expected. But how would you react to the sight
of two Russian soldiers, one loosely hanging onto the thumb
of the other as they parade at the tail end of a military
contingent led by a fluttering red flag. Yes, even Red Army
recruits are great lovers.

Gently patting a friend on the arm or head is a popular
Russian way to show affection. Such physical exchanges even
between friends of the same sex are not that uncommon and
carry no sexual connotations. My notes are full of examples
of this Russian custom.

In the service bureau of a Siberian hotel I couldn't help
staring at two young girls in their early twenties seated on
the edge of a large desk. One was softly stroking the hair of
the other as they busily chatted. It seemed so strange to me,
especially when the pretty girl receiving all the affection
responded by momentarily laying her head on the breasts of
her girl friend.

Outside of a metro stop in the capital I once saw four
teenage Muscovites who were enjoying the fresh air of a
balmy summer afternoon. One of the youngsters was
sprawled out with his head resting on the lap of his pal. His
shirt was wide open and one of the other boys was nonchalantly rubbing his stomach and mischievously untidying
his hair. This too is Russia of the revolutionary yoke.

It was one thing to observe the Russian concept of space
and touching; it was quite another to experience it. I was
always a little leery about having the Gala Farewell Dinner
with my tourists at Moscow's Arbat Restaurant because of a
waiter named Eduard. It always happened that when he

hadn't seen me for several weeks he would greet me with an unrestrained kiss smack on the lips. Such a display of affection certainly wasn't good for my public image.

My male friends liked getting up real close when they spoke, creating an intimacy that I was just not accustomed to observing or experiencing. I recall helping Grigory bone up for an upcoming exam on American idioms. We were sitting on his couch comfortably propped up against pillows that Grigory had arranged á la Russe. Each time we took our eyes off the textbook and turned towards one another to try to iron out a sticky point of American word usage, we were staring at each other from a distance I felt was best reserved for looking into the eyes of a pretty Tanya or Kira.

Russians are also free with their words, very free. They say exactly what's on their mind, and often with a bluntness that takes a bit of getting used to. When Jesus told his disciples that their "Yes" should mean "Yes" and their "No" "No," I always thought that He left a little room for diplomacy and, certainly, charity. Unknowingly, the undiplomatic Russians have perfectly put into practice Jesus' teaching on telling it like it is. Their uncanny knack for straightforwardness can be befuddling and amusing. It can immediately put you on the defensive. It may seem unexplainably vindictive, perhaps even cruel. But chances are you'll go away impressed with a people who don't seem to have any hang-ups about expressing themselves.

For those of us being Russianized at the university, absorbing Russian culture was stimulating and great fun; there were times, however, when we had to pay a dear price, which wasn't fun at all. Our test scores were often announced in class which let everyone know who were the *otlichniki*, Russia's A students, and those who were far from it. Zoya Sergeevna, for instance, would make public evaluations of all of us, getting right to the point with a sense of honesty that

The Victorious Russians

could hurt. She didn't mince words; she let her "Yeas" be resounding "Yeas" and her "Nays" unqualified "Nays." No one had to try to read between the Cyrillic lines; it was all out front.

"John, you're really making very little progress. Your grammar is poor, Peter, but you communicate well. Susan, any Russian would have great difficulty understanding your pronunciation, and your Russian in general. And David, you need to spend a lot more attention on your verb endings as well as your homework." At least as far as I was concerned, Zoya was right on target. But her cute little smile made it all very worthwhile.

On a few public occasions I found that Russians dared to be themselves and let their spirits run wild. For me it was always a time to rekindle my belief in the indestructibility of the soul of man.

Earlier, I mentioned the holiday of *Alye Parusa*, Scarlet Sails, which Leningradians celebrate each year. It is indeed an unusual day, a day when a fairy tale takes precedence over a revolutionary tale. The celebration recalls a popular novel written by the Soviet writer Aleksandr Grin a few years after the revolution. According to the fable, an old man calling himself the good wizard prophesies to a little girl that when she is older she will meet a daring prince on a certain ship which is to dock at the local port. The sign she is to look for is a ship hoisting scarlet sails.

One day, many years later, a young handsome captain sails into the port on his ship called "The Secret." He was a true romantic who sailed only for the adventure that the sea could offer. Walking along the shore, he comes upon a maiden who is fast asleep. Immediately, the young captain falls in love with the beautiful damsel. After slipping a ring on her finger, he mysteriously departs. At a nearby tavern the captain is told by the local villagers that this sleeping beauty is just that crazy girl who is forever watching the ships come in. When the captain learns of the wizard's prophecy, he quickly sails away and dramatically returns with the radiant scarlet sails, fulfilling the prophecy and opening the way to a beautiful love story.

Toward the end of June when romantic White Nights reach their peak, mystically covering Leningrad's darkness with an illuminating dusk-like light, crowds of Leningradians, mostly adolescent, celebrate *Alye Parusa*. Strolling along the streets strumming guitars and joyously singing national tunes, Leningradians are as wild and uninhibited as you'll find public Russians anywhere. Compared to the frightening solitude that grips Soviet nights in Russian cities, both big and small, Leningrad is in the throes of anarchy. On this fairy tale night, Leningradians are much more than ideological revolutionaries; they are out to create a new order by unleashing their spirits which have been pent up inside their Soviet bodies. Everyone enjoys each other's company, relishing the collective freedom of the moment.

The focal point of the festivities is the historic Neva River. Throngs of excited young people crowd along the river embankment hopefully waiting to gaze at the shimmering scarlet sails, the romantic symbol of the destiny of every fair maiden and handsome prince. But even fate in Soviet Russia falls under the boot; it too stands in awesome submission to the will of the revolutionary state. When Russian grandmothers correctly predict the coming of the *Alye Parusa*, it is a truly magnificent sight to behold.

Crimson masks rippling in a gentle northerly breeze magically unveil the *Alye Parusa*. Moored across from the baroque Winter Palace of the czars, she becomes triumphantly illuminated by midnight fireworks. These fireworks shot off along the banks of the Neva sporadically shower Leningrad's White Nights with a dazzling, multiple rainbow of fiery lights.

All of Leningrad seems a stage on which grand Russian theatrics are superbly executed. But there are always a host of Russian actors who serve as a reminder that the spectacular production is taking place in a well-ordered society. All along the Neva, in full view of the *Alye Parusa*, the sidewalks are cordoned off, preventing the crowd from standing along the embankment wall. Red Army soldiers take up their positions every fifteen to twenty feet behind a rope barrier. The few Leningradians around me who seemed curious enough to wonder why they were being forbidden to get a closer view, seemed to think it was to keep the more active celebrants out of the dark Neva. As always, the holiday is celebrated with a wide assortment of half-liter bottles.

With each colored display of light that ricochets against the unusually pale blue Leningrad sky, melodious cries, *"Ura! Ura!"* echo from one side of the Neva to the other. The two-syllable Slavic sounds seem to emerge from deep within the Russian soul. A fairy tale was being relived, but fantasizing was not the only collective experience. The masses were participating in a great primal therapy encounter, getting rid of the great Russian passivity that overwhelms their lives. It was a catharsis, a way of letting it all hang out, a temporary remedy for what ails you.

For now, we may close the books on the victorious Russians. They have managed to find a way to be happy in a society that offers them little to be happy about. Within the context of their Slavic culture, assaulted as it is by a spiritual form of totalitarianism, the Russians have discovered a way to remain human.

In the end, divine providence sees to it that all things balance out. Man, with all his clever designs and ingenious programs, remains but mere man, a creature of the Almighty. God, permitting evil and injustice to go on, works His divine will in spite of both. Divine perspective has a wonderful way of reducing everything, including man, to basics. It is a biblical fact. Before the Lord, the "Great October Socialist Revolution" amounts to very little, a drop in the bucket, a speck of dust on the scales of time.

11

The War: Pathway to the Cross

Behold, I stand at the door, and knock: if any man hear my voice, and open the door, I will come in to him, and will sup with him, and he with me.

(Revelation 3:20 KJV)

Arriving at Pulkovo International Airport, foreign guests excitedly make their way into the former czarist city of St. Petersburg, named after its founder Peter the Great. But before the troops of tourists can be dazzled by this city of unparalled beauty and splendor, they must first be reminded that this is also the city that during World War II sacrificially endured the 900-day blockade.

Dramatically defining the approach to the outskirts of the city stands a towering slab of crimson granite some 150 feet in height. A circular wall of granite forms a ring at the base of the obelisk. It is a broken ring, symbolically showing that the blockade too was finally broken in January, 1944. The central sculpture, "The Victors," is of massive men whose bronze faces conjure up a nightmarish feeling of the horrors of war. They hold high rifles and flags, symbolic of the might and patriotism which led to the triumphant defense of the Russian motherland. An aura of power seems to radiate about the grand architectural masterpiece, which was

A CHRISTIAN VIEW OF RUSSIA

unveiled in 1975 to commemorate the thirtieth anniversary of the victory in the "Great Patriotic War."

Forty years ago, the German Luftwaffe rained tons of incendiary and high explosive bombs on the beleaguered city that majestically served as the capital of the Russian empire for more than two centuries. Those who managed to survive the brutal assault lived to witness a miracle. A city once reduced to heaps and heaps of charcoaled rubble was resurrected to again become "the Venice of the North." Today, Leningrad, its revolutionary name,* looks like it could have leaped out of one of Pushkin's fairy tales. Consisting of many quaint and narrow rivers and canals, symmetrically encircling dozens of islands, the revolutionary city is a testimony to the courage of man, the power of God.

In the city proper there are two authentic physical vestiges of World War II which eloquently speak of Leningrad's war history. The first are the conspicuously gun-riddled marble columns which surround the outer facade of the magnificent St. Issac's Cathedral, once the principal church of old St. Petersburg. It does seem ironic that this, the third highest single-domed cathedral in the world, now a government museum, has been selected by an atheistic government to serve as a war monument to testify to one of the greatest military defenses in the face of overwhelming odds. And yet how fitting it is that such a grand symbol of the might and power of Almighty God, should be chosen to represent the very source of the Leningradian victory.

Just after the war broke out in 1941, Stalin temporarily put aside his vicious persecution of the church. There was a war to be won! Religion was no longer a Soviet scapegoat, the whipping boy, Marx's "opium of the people." Now it suddenly

---

* St. Petersburg was renamed Petrograd in 1914. And with the death of Lenin, in 1924, the city was called Leningrad.

The War: Pathway to the Cross

became a source of hope, a pillar of strength, and a symbol of triumph. Russian heroes and saints came marching out of the closets. Church doors were open again and prayers were offered for national victory. The League of Militant Atheists was suspended and officials of the church were appointed to investigate Nazi war crimes. Even the harsh rules regarding religious instruction of children were eased. And in 1943—perhaps the most far-reaching concession of all—the Holy Synod was permitted to convene and elect a Russian Orthodox patriarch. One by one, the old Bolshevik policies toward believers fell by the revolutionary wayside. There was a great war to be won!

Only the Lord knows of the countless men, women and children, who, in the privacy of their homes, in the shelter of foxholes, prayed fervently for the joyous peace that finally came on May 7, 1945. Leonid Brezhnev could boast that the Communist Party's "vast ideological and political effort was our powerful weapon during the war." The columns of St. Issac's, however, silently speak a simple message that few dare to shout. "God is our refuge and strength, a very present help in trouble."[1]

The second remaining remnant of the "Great Patriotic War" is not far away from the massive columns of St. Issac's. Located on Nevsky Prospekt in downtown Leningrad, there still remains on the wall of House #14 a small painted sign: "Citizens! In the event of artillery fire, this side of the street is the most dangerous!" Apparently, more artillery shells fell on this side of the street than the other. But this is not important, for the words are no longer of strategic value; they are symbolic, and for many, spiritually so.

Without exception, each time I passed this inconspicuous war memorial there were always flowers lying on the tiny

---

[1] Psalm 46:1 KJV

179

metal holder just below the words. Sometimes in winter, only one or two strewn flowers were visible, lightly snow-covered and closed, a natural defense against the winter cold. Somehow wilted flowers seemed more appropriate than a glorious bouquet. The films I had seen of the blockade showed bodies lying in the snow, the victims of mass starvation, unbearable winters, and fatal epidemics.* People pulling sleds of corpses and coffins across the snow for burial are sights not easy to forget. For me, the dying flowers did not so much pay tribute to the city's defenders as they symbolized, perhaps in an unconscious way, the manner of their deaths.

Each time I returned to Russia after being away anywhere from a few days to a few months, I had to readjust to being in a country in which the memories of the "Great Patriotic War" are always kept fresh. Each ride in from the airport, whether it was in Leningrad or Moscow, was like my first. The experience was always new, there was always something different that struck me, a dimension that I hadn't seen before, or which I had forgotten about. The shock effect of it all never wore off.

Most vivid in my mind as I now write is a very large poster attached to a high fence on the outskirts of the capital. The portrait of a Russian woman dressed in a flowing red robe magnetically drew my attention as I drove into the capital from Sheremetevo Airport. In the background, she was flanked by an array of bayonetted rifles and in her outstretched hand she held the words of a military oath. In her courageous face, I saw the physical embodiment of maternal power and military patriotism.

The descriptive caption was only of three short words, but

---

* According to the *Great Soviet Encyclopedia*, Vol. 14, p. 383, more than 600,000 people died of starvation during the blockade, compared to about 17,000 casualties from bombings and shellings.

The War: Pathway to the Cross

it captured the spirit of the portrait perfectly, *"Rodina-mat zovyot.* Mother Russia Is Calling You." I had only seconds to glimpse this most famous of all World War II posters as I sped by in a chauffeured Volga to my hotel. Waiting to catch sight of the inspiring face became a ritual for me each and every time I drove into Moscow.

The totality of the war memory elevates the antagonistic poles of war and peace as the supreme dialectical battle of life. Everything else becomes secondary. All other aspects of existence take a lesser role in Soviet society. In addition to the media, literature too differentiates between the two polar opposites. In the official Russian world, happiness is solely in peace and its preservation. The antithesis of happiness is pain, agony, and suffering in war. Russians live in peace, but with the always ever-present awareness that life could be transformed into its contradiction—death and dying.

Russian youth are not less patriotic than the generation that bore them. Many seem to have accepted the belief that Russia herself saved the world from becoming a mass concentration camp of the Third Reich. Nadya, for instance, Anna Aleksandrovna's teenage daughter who led me on my first mushroom safari, held to the official Soviet view. She responded to my observation that the Poles despise the Russians for enslaving them with a burst of flag-waving patriotism. "Yes, I know, but what would they have done without us? How many hundreds of thousands of our soldiers perished liberating Poland?" Her friends nodded in agreement.

But this is not to say that Russia's generation of war babies approve of their government's all-pervasive campaign to propagandize peace and war as the only factors of existence that deserve attention. Many are totally turned off by the inescapable war propaganda barrage. Like all young people, they have personal problems that desperately need to be dealt

A CHRISTIAN VIEW OF RUSSIA

with and aired in the open. Films and books about themes other than the great war cannot only be stimulating, but a way to escape from the pressures of daily living into the wilds of imagination and fantasy. But for young Russians there is only one world, a highly political and spiritual one. It is a world where the tenets and ideals of communism and the memory of the "Great Patriotic War" reign supreme. Perhaps this fact alone partially accounts for the alcoholism epidemic among Russian youth.

Those who visit Leningrad conclude their city tour with a trip to the suburbs and an unforgettable visit to Piskarevskoe Memorial Cemetery. Here an estimated 470,000 mainly civilian Leningradians are buried, many by their own friends and relatives, and some by strangers, who pulled the wrapped corpses on sleds during the brutalizing winter months. In the cemetery, solemn music captures the visitor and almost instantly creates an emotion of sadness and heartfelt sympathy for the courageously tragic Russian people. As one walks along the huge mass graves, adorned with single strewn flowers, toward the statue ahead, an indescribable sense of sorrow silently speaks on numbed Slavic faces.

Quietly, reverentially, they walk deeper into the memories that are their only union with their beloved war dead. At the end of the central avenue stands an enormous bronze sculpture of a mourning woman, symbolic of Mother Russia, and the flesh and blood mothers of Russia. In her outstretched hands she holds a wreath of oak leaves, symbolizing the eternal glory that only she can somehow bestow upon her heroic chidren. At the base of the figure, floral bouquets pay tribute to the nameless Leningradians who surrendered their lives for their Mother Russia.

Just beyond the statue stands another tribute in the words of the Leningrad poetess, Olga Berggolts, who survived the 900-day siege. Carved on a huge granite wall are these words:

182

The War: Pathway to the Cross

Here lie Leningraders
Side by side—men,
*   women and children.*
Red Army soldiers lie next
*   to them.*
They gave up their lives
In defence of you, Leningrad,
The Cradle of the Revolution.
We are unable to give you their
*   noble names—*
There are too many of them,
*   forever protected by granite.*
But remember you who are
*   hearkening to these tombstones—*
Nothing and no one have been
*   forgotten.*

These solemn words effectively make use of the emotions of a sorrowful, mourning people. They seek to gain political mileage by playing on man's greatest capacity, his desire to love forever. Defending the motherland and embracing communism become indivisible. The cry for peace, the exhortation to embrace a revolutionary way of life become one. Nowhere is the government more out of step with its people, more insensitive, more manipulative, than here at the graveside.

Yet the flowing power of this verse is not what draws bereaved Leningradians to this beloved site. The sons and daughters, brothers and sisters, and friends and relatives who have come here, have come out of love, a love that is forever enshrined in their hearts, a love that goes much deeper than the appealing words that are chiseled into the hard granite. No one really needs to be encouraged to remember what has happened; love does not forget. It never fails.

A CHRISTIAN VIEW OF RUSSIA

I always felt that the Russians' search for the Lord was intense here, here in the remembrance of the great sacrificial war. Certainly nowhere are the Russian people closer to Calvary than here, surrounded by the memory of a modern-day Golgotha. And nowhere do the heavy beams of the cross so naturally, so symmetrically, fit into the Russian landscape than here.

Just as the Saviour calls each of us in a unique way, using our particular life experiences and respecting our very individuality, so too, He must call nations in a wonderfully special way. Nearly all of Europe was devastated in one way or another by Hitler's war. And yet, only one nation, an officially atheistic one, chooses to publicly live out the war memory in such a dramatic way. Sure, it's good propaganda, but there is another question here, a profound one: Is the war Russia's pathway to the cross?

World War II was Russia's greatest cross, a collective cross borne by every Russian. Indeed, nearly every Russian family living today has given up someone—brother, uncle, father, sister—to the evils of war. Twenty million citizens perished in the course of four crucial years when peace was a cherished hope, a repeated prayer for the great Russian people. How many died a martyr's death, giving their lives for family, country, and the beloved mother earth? Only the Lord knows. More than the poetic words on a piece of granite, the memory of World War II is for all Russians a testimony to life and love, a life that once was, a love that will forever remain.

"Greater love hath no man than this, that a man lay down his life for his friends."[1] To surrender life and breath for another, even a good and worthy man is not easy, the Scriptures teach. And yet how infinitely greater was the Father's supreme sacrifice, for "God commendeth his love

---

[1] John 15:13 KJV

184

The War: Pathway to the Cross

toward us, in that, while we were yet sinners, Christ died for us."[1] Is this the message that is the way to the Russian heart?

The war experience, as it is relived today, has transformed the Russian people totally, absolutely, irreversibly. There are no words, verses, or historical accounts that can begin to explain what has happened to an entire people. Even the tremendous power of the revolutionary Boot, with all its mental and physical might, has been unable to touch man in the transforming way that the war has. The ultimate in earthly power stands virtually powerless when compared with the invisible, eternal will of the soul to love and not forget. The conflict between the human and the divine again reveals that, much more than a political animal, man is first and foremost a great lover.

Perhaps the best way I know to describe how the war has changed a people is with the assertion that the Russians want peace as much as life itself. For the war veteran, whether soldier or civilian, there is no distinction between the two. The words always on the tip of his tongue are of peace and friendship with all people. True, no people want war, but for the Russians the theme of peace is communicated with such an intensity of emotion and sincerity of heart that it is prayerful.

Emotionally wounded by Soviet propaganda that portrays President Reagan as a man of war, Russians of all ages would ask me to carry home the same simple message: "Don't tell your friends and relatives about the Kremlin or about our museums and beautiful churches. Tell them only one thing. That we don't want war. We know too well what war is all about."

Soviet Power may forbid public prayer, but its revolutionary decree is all in vain. Its sphere of influence, it hasn't yet

---

[1]Romans 5:8 KJV

185

A CHRISTIAN VIEW OF RUSSIA

learned, is limited to the things of this world—kindergartens, the marketplace, wedding palaces—but in the end God will always have His way. In the remembrance of the great war, draped as it is with a holy shroud, the Russian heart soars upward unrestrained. Amid the confusion of evil and the anguish of a bitter memory, there is a searching for the meaning of death, the meaning of life. In the cry for peace that rises from deep within the Russian soul, a people, a blessed people, are turned toward the Prince of Peace.

As an overnight patient in a Russian hospital where I was being treated for a minor stomach ailment, I again came face to face with the drama of how the war has recreated the Russian people. After the customary registration procedure at the hospital, an orderly led me to my *boks,* the appropriate Russian word for the isolation cubicle where I was quarantined. Here, a youthful-looking nurse, who looked much younger than her fifty-four years, attended to me. She had a gentle bedside manner and seemed genuinely interested in talking with me. Perhaps because it was rather rare to have Russian-speaking foreigners in the hospital.

"I've been a nurse here for thirty years," she told me.

"Why didn't you become a doctor?" I asked.

"The war interrupted my studies," she explained in a soft-spoken way. "I was sent to the front to work in a hospital, this very one," she continued reflectively. "Life was a nightmare then." Her eyes began to moisten. "I lost my father and others. That was a long time ago, and I don't like to think about it."

That night she dropped by again to give me a sleeping pill and the war, in some unexplainable, haunting way, again became the subject of our conversation. The memory of the war was one that just wouldn't go away. It seemed like no matter what Russians said about trying to avoid the *koshmar* the nightmare, it always surfaced. The war ended more than

The War: Pathway to the Cross

thirty-five years ago, and when it did, time stood still in Russia.

Taking a seat on the bed adjacent to mine, she continued to talk about those unforgettable years. "I've been in this hospital for a long time," she smiled as she looked up at the ceiling. "I lost my father, brother, and two younger sisters during the blockade. Bombs were dropping everywhere. You'd be on the street and hear the siren which signaled to everyone that Nazi war planes would soon be overhead." Her still-compassionate eyes descended on me as her voice became stern.

"The young people today, your age, they see and hear of the war only in films and books, completely different from living through it. They don't know what it was like. They hear us talking about war, but they don't understand, they can't, I guess." There was a silent pause. "And it's good," she concluded, slowly nodding her head in deep thought. "It's good that they don't know what a war is like, and I hope they never will."

She got up from the bed and picked up a slab of uneaten bread, which together with a bowl of plain macaroni had been my supper. "Imagine this for a whole day, 125 grams (4½ oz.) and 250 grams (9 oz.) for workers. We ate bread made of flour, cellulose and wallpaper paste. That's the way it was back in the winter of 1941. Many, many died of hunger and we buried them even without registration."

I had already taken the sleeping pill and my eyes were quickly growing heavy. And although it took an effort to keep my eyes open, my senses weren't dulled to her stirring words. She got up and put out the light. *"Spokoynoy nochi,"* she whispered, and left me to a peaceful sleep.

I would often spend a lot of time in the quiet parks and gardens of Aleksandr Nevsky Monastery where young men were studying to become Russian Orthodox priests. Referred to as the *lavra*, the name given to the principal monasteries of the Russian Orthodox Church, it was a place of retreat and solitude from the madness of the American tourist world and the needs and demands of my clients. Russians too seem drawn here, especially on Sunday, when it became a sanctuary from the busy Leningrad city life.

On a balmy afternoon I was sitting on one of the benches in the monastery, admiring the beautiful flower gardens which adorned the grounds in all the colors of the rainbow. Sitting nearby were two *babushki* and a woman in her mid-fifties sandwiched in between. Her strategic position could not but draw her into the grandmothers' conversation.

One of the old women in particular caught my eye. She was most assertive and dramatic in her mannerisms and gestures. Although she sat on the edge of the bench closest to me, she continually would turn her head away from my direction as she spoke, (or perhaps preached is the better description). I was becoming more curious to find out what was being said and decided to try to move into the conversation.

It appeared that they were talking about the pigeons that were busily pecking away nearby, so I used this as my cue. "*Nado kormit*, you've got to feed them," I said in a loud voice, making my accented Russian quite obvious. The dramatically gesturing *babushka* turned to acknowledge my comment. I slowly got up and walked over, continuing my small talk for a few more minutes before plopping down on their bench.

In some mysterious way I turned the conversation from pigeons to the Lord. As strange and unrelated as the transition may seem, it then appeared very natural in the setting of this Garden of Eden, where the Lord had thought to bring together such an unlikely quartet. We learned that the younger woman wasn't a *veruyushchaya*, which led to quite a scene. The spirited grandmother took to scolding her.

'You're not a believer! You know that you can go to church

anytime and be baptized a Christian. Just lately one of our believers, eighty years old, got baptized."

"She must have been ashamed," replied the non-believer, laughing at what must have been an unusual ceremony.

"Didn't your mother and father teach you about Christ?"

"No, my father, well, he wouldn't allow it. He had his goal of communism," the woman answered slowly, staring into the pale blue sky, a rare sight for Leningradians. "But, it happens that sometimes I go to church and light a candle."

It was now my turn to get in the free-for-all that I had apparently instigated. "You're not a believer, but you go to church and light candles?"

"Well, what do you mean by being a believer?" she responded.

The talkative *babushka* interrupted, becoming more theatrical in her style. Her evangelical approach was fire and brimstone pure and simple.

"Now listen, you must become baptized. At the end of the world when God comes, each person will have to explain what they've done, good and bad. Your mother is the guilty one for not baptizing you as a baby, but now you can go to church yourself."

"I'm a Party member," the non-believer answered softly.

"So what! That makes no difference."

"I know," the woman said, looking down defensively. A few minutes passed in silence and both *babushki* got up and were about to leave. The old believer gave one last shot to try to win over a convert. "If you don't do as I'm telling you, it's going to be real bad for you at the end of the world. Believe me! It's true." The woman looked up at the octogenarian who could have been her mother and respectfully thanked her for her concern.

The two of us sat silently together on the bench for a few moments. I really didn't know what to say to this stranger who shared with me the comedy and profundity of what had just taken place. While I was trying to think of something to say, the woman turned toward me with her own thoughts to fill the vacuum that Russia's fiery evangelist had left. Her words were of the scarred memories that the great war had left. She told how she had lost her brother and sister in the 900-day siege. "I have a picture at home of my sister," she went on, with an indescribably intense look on her face. "She was only nineteen years old." There was a pause. "But I can't look at her."

At first I couldn't understand how this grandmother's old-time preaching had led to the war memory and her sister. But as I thought about it, it seemed so fitting that the Russian war, with its deep sacrificial spirituality, should be associated with the Lord. Again, the Lord had revealed to me a little more of His special plan for His beloved Russian flock.

When you cut away all the politics and revisionist history, what were the war and the death camps but another Golgotha, another bitter crucifixion. When the Lord slowly enlightened me to this mystery, it was all but overwhelming. In the faces of the scarred Slavic people—the compassionate, loving nurse, the grieving woman still mourning the loss of her brother and sister—I saw the bloodied, bruised face of Jesus. If only the suffering Russians could re-focus for just a split second. If only they could take their minds off what the horrible war did to them and onto what He did for us, Revolutionary Russia would never be the same again. There were so many broken hearts, broken spirits that needed to be touched by the Great Healer. How they needed to know how much He loved them, I often wondered in prayer. How they needed to know!

In the memory of World War II, the Russian people confront head-on the unsettling matter of evil and death. Unholy Russia chooses fundamentally to ignore these

The War: Pathway to the Cross

questions. Communism is only for the here and now, not the hereafter. The explanation as to the whys and wherefores of suffering and war are carefully limited to political and dialectical phenomena, the Marxist view of the violent antagonisms that rage within all capitalist societies. Placing the burden of guilt on perverted economics and the greedy military-industrial complex of the Western nations is ideologically sound in the Marxist-Leninist world view. Doubtless, to a certain extent, Russians have been conditioned from birth to glean some truth from Soviet Marxism. It all goes back to the first formula children learn in school: World communism equals world peace.

But by themselves, world history and theories of radical economics cannot convincingly answer the great eternal questions of life. The Lord just didn't make us that way. Along with our mortal bodies, He gave us an immortal soul. This biblical truth alone suggests that communism and "the inner man" are incompatible. Communism can feed the mind, and it tries to do a good job at it. But who takes care of the spirit? It doesn't exist! Matter alone is the sole basis of our universe.

In denying the existence of spiritual things, Marxism weakens the power of its own revolutionary propaganda. It deals with only half of man, his weaker side. Even to those who are basically unspiritual, the desolate, God-forsaken scenes of 1941-1945—Leningrad, Auschwitz, Babi Yar—suggest that man alone is incapable of such unspeakable brutality. Man can hate, but the reign of terror in the death camps in Auschwitz (Oswiecim), Poland, and Babi Yar, in the Soviet Ukraine, where millions were systematically exterminated—such a demonic hatred is beyond even man himself. The search for truth leads man—Russian man, American man, indeed, all men—beyond the vicissitudes of human logic and neat, explanatory philosophies into another realm, the realm of the supernatural.

"Why do people die if they live right? And why do people suffer if there is a God?" In Russian society these are pretty heavy questions that have nothing to do with philosophy. Rather, they raise the sensitive issue of the "Great Patriotic War." For many, these are provocative questions that are confusing and painful. For still others, they are questions that can lead to a great deal of anger and resentment.

For the captain of the cruise boat that took me and my group along the Moskva River one hot and humid summer evening, the war seemed evidence enough that Soviet atheism was totally accurate. You will remember that I had engaged the young mate in a lively dialogue on the existence of God and the principles and proofs of St. Thomas Aquinas. Through it all, the captain remained silent, only watching his instrument panel and navigating his craft through the pitch darkness. He just listened to my foreign ideas—that is, until the conversation drifted toward war.

"Look," he interrupted, in more of a hurtful than an angry tone, "I've witnessed victims of terrible war suffering. There is no God! Would a God have allowed men to kill each other, men killing their brothers? Would a God have permitted brothers, mothers, sisters, fathers to perish? No, there's no God. I'm certain of it. Do you think this God would have allowed Hitler to invade our motherland?"

The captain had raised questions that all Russians must in their own way struggle with as they try to place the war in perspective. Perhaps he was an avowed atheist as he emphatically professed, but even in his despair, I could sense something religious, something very spiritual. Throughout the Psalms, indeed, running throughout the whole Word, man in moments of great desperation, cries out to God for help and deliverance. Was this war veteran, within the confines of his atheistic society, pleading the same words that

The War: Pathway to the Cross

Job, David, and Jeremiah had already set forth in the Bible? "Why standest thou afar off, O Lord? Why hidest thou thyself in times of trouble?"[1]

Even official propaganda cannot conceal the emotional anger and bitterness of those who survived the war years. Towering high above multi-storied apartment buildings and sweeping across broad city streets are propaganda slogans that tell of Russia's great desire for peace: "PEACE IS NECESSARY FOR EVERYONE"; "THE RIGHT TO PEACE MUST BE GIVEN TO ALL PEOPLE"; "THE SOVIET UNION HAS FOUGHT AND IS FIGHTING FOR PEACE FOR ALL THE PEOPLES OF THE WORLD." In more ways than one "nothing and no one have been forgotten." One poster, for example, is of an angry woman whose mouth is open as if she is violently shouting and her hand is raised in a clenched fist. The three words, "Peace, Friendship, and Solidarity," are the title caption. But below the tight fist the real meaning comes through, "Not Fascism."

Young Russians have also inherited some of the disdain and bitterness toward both East and West Germany. "When I see a German tourist," nineteen-year-old Tanya admitted, "I get this strange feeling in my stomach. My grandmother told me what they did during the blockade. We'll never be able to take them to our hearts."

"I was born in 1942," Sergey, a young heart surgeon, told me during dinner in his Moscow apartment. "Naturally, I don't remember the war, but I have a deep feeling inside me about it. I lost relatives. My people perished, twenty million of them. Sometimes I just look at my little daughter and know that ones like her were mercilessly murdered. Why?" It was getting dark so Sergey's wife closed the curtain and lit a candle.

As Servey talked about the war, his wife remained silent.

---

[1] Psalm 10:1 KJV

A CHRISTIAN VIEW OF RUSSIA

As she stared into the quivering flame which cast a soft light on her unimposing, but attractive countenance, the tightened, drawn muscles of her face stood in bold relief. "Maybe part of it is that I'm a doctor. I want to cure suffering," Sergey continued. "I keep asking myself, why such slaughter? Why was this suffering necessary? That is why I can never forgive the Germans, never."

Both Sergey and Tanya were right. Alone, they are incapable of forgiving the Germans for what certain members of a previous generation had done. Even Soviet Russia, in the totality of its state power, could not proclaim forgiveness to the German people. Only at the mount of Calvary can the Russians, along with all the other mistreated peoples of the world, find the power to forgive their enemies, as He forgave us. "Father, forgive them; for they know not what they do."[1]

For the Russian people, and for us, there is a wondrous mystery to be grasped at the foot of the Cross. It is the one place where all the perplexing questions of life find an answer, and where we find the courage to go on. Let us never forget that Jesus too knew what it was like to suffer and hurt as He agonized in the Garden of Gethsemane. " 'My Father,' he said, 'if it is possible, let this cup pass me by. Nevertheless, let it be as you, not I, would have it.' "[2] He too knew the wracking pains of loneliness when he felt so utterly abandoned by everyone. "My God, my God," He prayed, "why have you deserted me?"[3] But "for the joy that was set before him,"[4] He endured it all, gloriously winning our redemption. Following Him, we too must ascend to Calvary and then rise to Resurrection.

---

[1] Luke 23:34 KJV
[2] Matthew 26:39-40 TJB
[3] Matthew 27:47 TJB
[4] Hebrews 12:2 KJV

12

Living Signs of Christ Alive!

Let the nations praise you, O God, let all the nations praise you!
(Psalm 67:3 TJB)

Officially, God died in Russia in October, 1917 with the events surrounding the Bolshevik coup d'etat. The Soviet government, however, has proved powerless to expunge from the Leninist society, the mystical manifestations that silently, though eloquently, speak of a living divine power. On the surface, the new society has successfully fashioned a great atheistic state, but many of the pre-revolutionary vestiges of Russian Christianity have been untouched by the assault on religion. They gloriously symbolize the turning to the Messiah that has marked the centuries of recorded Russian history. They are the fulfillment of His promise never to leave nor forsake His people. They are living signs of Christ alive!

For nearly a millennium, Russia lived a deeply spiritual life. It all began along the shores of the Dnieper River in Kiev, "the Jerusalem of Russia." Here in 988, according to an ancient chronicle, the Kievan Prince Vladimir was baptized a Christian; there followed a mass baptismal rite for his subjects. By this single act, Christianity officially became the religion of the first Russian state.

A CHRISTIAN VIEW OF RUSSIA

What is historically significant is that Prince Vladimir chose the way of Orthodox Christianity which came from Byzantium. The influence of nearby Constantinople, the capital of the Byzantine Empire, had a profound impact on Kievan cultural and religious life. With the advent of Christianity came the Cyrillic alphabet and the Church Slavonic language, the works of two Greek missionary brothers, Cyril and Methodius. Books of the Bible, both Old and New Testaments, were among the first works to be translated into Old Church Slavonic. Nearly a thousand years later, with the emergence of the new radical Soviet regime, the Russian language would be used for a far different purpose—to spread atheism.

The Byzantine inspiration could clearly be seen in the ornate, spiritual beauty of the great Kievan cathedrals. Monasteries sprang up and became important factors in shaping early Russian religious life. It was here in the seclusion and isolation of the monastic life that the ancient Russian tradition of spirituality evolved. In seeking to imitate the humility of Christ, the Russian monks led lives of penance and poverty At times these ascetic practices went to unhealthy extremes, but in their zealous desire to grow closer to the Lord, the early fathers of the Russian Church inspired the peasantry to greater holiness. This practice of purifying the soul through suffering still seems popular among the Russian people today.

Sacred paintings called icons or images also came from the East and quickly became popular with the poor peasant people. They expressed in a visual way Byzantine theology and the Russian religious experience. Certainly the most famous of all icons in Russia today is the Miraculous Virgin of Vladimir. Brought from Constantinople to Kiev in the 12th century, this compassionate, mystical representation of the Madonna and Child is believed to have protected Moscow from foreign invasion three different times. Following the

Living Signs of Christ Alive!

Russian Revolution, this holiest of Russian icons was removed from the Kremlin Cathedral of the Assumption and placed on exhibit in the Tretyakov Gallery in Moscow.

Kievan Russia also inherited the Eastern Greek tradition of Caesaropapism by which the secular ruler also became the high priest. As the Lord's divinely appointed representative on earth, the czar exercised supreme control in all religious affairs. By the early 1300s four stone cathedrals were under construction within the Kremlin walls, signifying the deepening faith of Holy Russia. With the fall of Constantinople to the Ottoman Turks in the 15th century, Moscow was well on her way to becoming "the Third Rome." This was the messianic belief propagated by a Russian monk that Muscovite Russia was the legitimate heir of the Roman and Byzantine Empires. Both Rome and Constantinople had fallen because they lost the true faith. Only Russia, now and forever, knew the way to the Lord.

Some of the great giants in Russian literature come to mind as we recall the days of Holy Russia. Fyodor Dostoevsky, perhaps best known for his novel, *Crime and Punishment*, was profoundly influenced by the person of Jesus. In *The Brothers Karamazov*, still popular among Russians today, Dostoevsky shows that there is freedom and redemption only in Christ, the only source of all human love. Calling himself, "a child of the age, a child of unbelief and scepticism," Dostoevsky once wrote of his unshakeable faith in Christ:

> . . . if anyone proved to me that Christ was not the truth, and it really was a fact that the truth was not in Christ, I would rather be with Christ than with the truth.

Nineteenth century Russia also gave birth to another world-famous novelist, Count Leo Tolstoy. His novel *War and Peace* is regarded as one of the great classics, but there is another side to Tolstoy, one that is not universally known.

A CHRISTIAN VIEW OF RUSSIA

Before finishing *Anna Karenina*, Tolstoy experienced a spiritual and moral crisis which brought him to the Scriptures. In Jesus' teachings, he found the answers to life's perplexing questions. Brotherly love and the resistance of evil without violence was for him the way to human perfection. Greatly beloved by the Russian peasants to whom he preached, Tolstoy died at a rural railway station. At the ripe old age of 82, he was secretly running away from home to find a distant sanctuary where he could grow closer to the Lord.

The peculiar faith of the great Russian people never died. The Revolution changed some names and brought about some new institutions, but, as we shall now see, God made a way through the Revolutionary Red Sea.

Before the Revolution, the phrase, *Slava Bogu!* (Thank God!) was colloquially popular. Today, decades later, it's still in use. The Soviet slogan industry seized on the idea in an effort to sell communism. Now institutionalized slogans exhort Russian workers to praise work and even themselves. Perhaps the idea is that work should be praised since it is necessary for building a communist society, and Soviet people are worthy of praise because they work. Well, I admit, the logic may seem a little strange, but as we well know, the Russians are a patient bunch. They just go on living, letting their advertising people get as much mileage as they can out of praising work and those who like to work.

The Good Lord still remains a part of the world of Russian colloquialisms. *Gospodi!* Lord! *Bozhe moy!* My God! *Ne day Bog!* God forbid! *Bog s nim!* God be with him! (Let it pass! Forget about him!) and *Radi Boga!* For God's sake! are frequently used expressions that gloriously spice up even the most boring of Soviet conversations. For God's sake, the most popular of the expressions, is often used to mean "go right ahead."

"May I have another cup of tea?"

"*Radi Boga!*"

Living Signs of Christ Alive!

What a testimony to the Lord's marvelous ways! And there is something very humorous about it. A nation of would-be atheists mouthing the praises of their God. Perhaps few Russians realize that in their daily conversations they are rejoicing and praising God, but nonetheless, Soviet Russia cannot reverse the divine plan. Every day inside the U.S.S.R., the Scriptures are being fulfilled. Like the stones that Jesus said would cry out if men were to hold their peace, the Russian people cannot be silenced. The message to Moscow is a mighty one: "Be still, and know that I am God: I will be exalted among the heathen, I will be exalted in the earth."[1]

The irony of atheists giving glory to the King, is matched only by the sight of "unbelievers" proclaiming the power of the cross. Although crucifixes worn around the neck can be purchased only at kiosks inside Russian Orthodox churches, the wearing of crosses seemed to be becoming increasingly in vogue during the late seventies. Clearly, the meaning that Russians associate with the crucifix, Christ or style, is more significant. But for one black marketeer who wanted to change money with me on busy Nevsky Prospekt, the cross at least had some kind of spiritual value. When I prodded the young Russian that I saw his offer as a KGB setup, he quickly unbuttoned his shirt exhibiting the crucifix underneath. Would a true communist agent wear a cross?

For me, experiences such as these were both welcome and uplifting. I could sense the hand of the Lord tugging me up by my bootstraps and closer to Himself. He seemed to know just when I needed to be ministered to, and His timing was, as His timing always is, incredibly perfect. When my spirit was heavy, when the void of Soviet communism was pressing in all about me, when it appeared that "he that is in the world" was turning the Russian world upside down and inside out, it

---

[1] Psalm 46:10 KJV

199

was time again to have my spirit renewed.

The Lord had this divine knack for confirming the truth of His Word in the most unusual ways. Remember when St. Paul said that the Lord chooses the foolish things of the world to confound the wise? Well, during one of my last sojourns in Russia, He chose a "foolish" Soviet guide to confound the revolutionary wisdom of Soviet Power.

In the lobby of the hotel where I was staying, my concentration on an irritating tourist problem was gently and welcomingly broken by an extraordinary sight. It was Tanya passing by. But not just Tanya, the Russian girl, but Tanya the Intourist guide, the one wearing a bold green Russian Orthodox cross around her neck. "Praise you, Jesus!" was all that I could say under my breath. "Thank you, Lord, I needed that!"

The set of contradictions that come together inside Russia are not only woven into the fabric of society and developed in the character of the Russian people, they also clash in the real physical world.

The majesty of Red Square juxtaposes in a splendid way the polar opposites of God and communism. On one side of the square stands the solemnity of St. Basil's Cathedral, with its inspiring multi-colored cupolas that dazzle the viewer with a storybook sense of wonderment. No longer serving the spiritual purpose for which it was built, this grand architectural masterpiece now operates as a branch of the State Historical Museum. The Cathedral, however, commissioned by the notorious Ivan the Terrible in the sixteenth century, stands as much more than an empty pre-revolutionary symbol. Each man, woman, and child, atheist or believer, who raises his or her eyes toward the heavens to try to visually capture the power radiating from the psychedelic "onion domes," cannot avoid the shiny silver Russian Orthodox cross that towers high in glory.

Living Signs of Christ Alive!

Confronting this centuries-old cathedral, stands a contemporary-looking monument constructed to house the corpse of the man Russian officialdom in many ways claims to be immortal. The ritualistic changing of the guard at Lenin's tomb, which goes on around the clock as the Spasskaya (Saviour) Tower chimes the hour, always draws crowds.

Perhaps less than 300 feet apart, two diametrically opposed sources of power clash in much more than a poetic sense in the minds and imaginations of the perceptive observer. Both compete for the undivided allegiance of man's mind and soul, one through the use of an extensive campaign of mind-bending techniques, the other relying on the power of the cross. Two monuments stand side by side. One rises in inexpressible beauty to the sky. The other offers the promise of a perfect world on earth. It is up to each individual to decide where lies the truth that will set him free.

Like the prophet Habakkuk, at times I too was anxious for the Lord to act, to restore Russia to its pre-revolutionary past. The conflict between the cross of St. Basil's and the remains of V.I. Lenin caused me to wonder. "Lord, why do you allow it? Why do you permit revolutionary atheism to have the upper hand? Hurry up, Lord! It's time to act! What's happening?" As I stood on my watchtower, surveying the Soviet landscape, the Lord, in His time, answered me. "The vision is yet for an appointed time." Although it may tarry, or at least seem to, "it will surely come."[1]

Maybe I'm still just a bit impatient and a few paces ahead of the Lord, but I believe the appointed time is near. I can see how the eyes of a nationalistic, proud leadership have been totally blinded as the Lord works His will in the Russian earth. I can sense how the Soviet Union is now being prepared for a not-too-distant age of revival when Christ will once

---

[1] Habakkuk 2:3 KJV

again reign as the Divine Czar and Lord of All. It seems to me quite unmistakable. The Holy Spirit is renewing the face of Russia.

In every Russian city, almost everywhere you look, stand non-functioning Russian cathedrals and churches of old, symbols that must remind the local people of the days of Holy Russia. The names of churches themselves speak of a time and a faith so different, so radically different, from the politics of the present day. There are Churches of the Annunciation, the Nativity, and the Holy Spirit, Churches of the Transfiguration, the Crucifixion and the Resurrection, and Churches of Mary Magdalene, St. Lazarus and the Twelve Apostles.

Indeed, there is a lot in a name, much more than might appear on the surface. Take, for instance, Leningrad's Church of the Saviour on the Blood. Historically, it is important, for it was here in 1881 that Czar Aleksandr II was shot and murdered. Resembling from a distance Moscow's famous St. Basil's Cathedral, the Church of the Saviour on the Blood is shut up tight and surrounded on all sides by a rather symbolic scaffolding. "Eek," one of my tourists nearly grimaced in pain when I told her another of the Church's gory-sounding names. "Church of the Spilt Blood! Couldn't they have chosen a more pleasant name, like Church of the Precious Blood?" And yet, how much closer to the living truth, the brutal reality of the blood-smeared cross, does the Russian translation come. The blood of Jesus was *shed* in a violent way for the remission of our sins.

Most Leningradians know the original name of the imprisoned church. But did they know the scriptural meaning of the name, that it represented the saving power of the blood of Jesus? For Natasha, an Intourist guide, the unusual title did have some kind of significance. She explained it this way. "Well, in an allegorical way, I guess you might say that the

Living Signs of Christ Alive!

Czar gave his blood for the Russian people, just as Christ is said to have given His life for all men. Now I'm really not sure if that's right, but anyway, that's as I understand it."

The scales were slowly beginning to fall from my eyes. Through the old names of Russia's great churches, the Gospel message was being proclaimed. A nation was being prepared to hear the Good News of salvation!

I shall never forget the concert of Moscow University's Academic Choir which performed inside the small Znamensky Cathedral in Moscow. The church commemorates an apparition of Mary to the people of Novgorod in the twelfth century. The concert took place in a small hall, perhaps once a sanctuary, which seated an audience of less than 200 people. A few small restored frescos, depicting scenes of the angelic Annunciation to Mary, are portrayed on the walls of the "theatre" which were painted in light shades of blue and white.

Without instrumental accompaniment, the choir of men and women, led by a stately white-haired conductor who resembled the late Arthur Fiedler, produced unquestionably the most soul-captivating music that I have ever heard. Their rendering of choral music of the seventeenth and eighteenth centuries brought tears to the eyes of many. A few of the chants and canticles were unmistakably religious in content and expression, which seemed to make the meaning of the frescos gloriously come alive. The faces of the choir were glowing, their voices full of rapture and swift-moving power.

This time Revolutionary Russia had certainly outdone itself. With all its ingenuity to create a godless man, it had been mysteriously drawn to use the pre-revolutionary setting of a former Russian Orthodox church. The musical performance was for many slowly transformed into a spiritual awakening. The religious rites of the past were not dead; only the form had changed.

A CHRISTIAN VIEW OF RUSSIA

Such a performance was by no means a Soviet aberration, an extraordinary coincidence. Soviet wisdom has mastered the art of showmanship, political and otherwise. Revolutionary Russia seeks perfection, precision, and, most importantly, authenticity, even when it conflicts with the values of communism. In the ancient city of Suzdal, bespeckled with golden domes and cupolas of various shades, Soviet Russia was again, unknowingly, pointing the way to God.

Like most other Russian Orthodox churches, the Cathedral of the Nativity in Suzdal has also been irreverently transformed into a museum piece. It too must serve, however externally, as one of the Revolution's greatest trophies. Inside, the cathedral is breathtaking, indescribably so. Expansive walls are painted with ancient frescos that have withstood the tests of time and Soviet might. Many are completely restored, others still remain faded, but majestic nonetheless. The real beauty of the scene, however, comes not from the masterful handiwork of man, but from the truth of God, a portrait which the Spirit has imprinted in the soul of every believer.

My little family of thirty or so art lovers had already been dazzled by the magnificence of Russian art in the cities of Moscow, Leningrad, and Novgorod. And there was more to come. But this walk back through the ages into Russia's holy past would not be like the others; Revolutionary Russia had already seen to that.

Inside the grand cathedral the stage was set for the performance to begin. The laconic sounds of church bells began to ring out, at first slowly and methodically, then gently giving way to a quicker, more lively rhythm. In the background, choral voices, soft and serene, intoned the melody of the Russian folk song, "Evening Bells." It was perfectly spectacular, spiritually so. Eyes became moist and spirits free.

Living Signs of Christ Alive!

Gradually, mysteriously, in couples or one by one, my Americans drifted away from our Soviet guide, free to wander with the Slavic spectators that were also there. Finally, our guide, Natasha, was also free, free to wander, free to pray.

When the tape recording was over, no one spoke a single word. Everyone seemed for the moment to freeze in his or her place, each alone with his thoughts, perhaps alone with the Lord. We each gazed about the cathedral, at the frescos, at each other, and at the historic Russian people, together absorbing the impact of what had just taken place. And then, collecting ourselves outside of the museum, once the Cathedral of the Nativity in the ancient city of Suzdal, we continued our tour.

Almost sixty-five years of uncontested Soviet rule have passed, but the Russian Orthodox crosses still tower as steeples above the contrived atheistic state. And perhaps one of the greatest ironies inside Russia today is that these monuments to Russian Orthodox Christianity are being restored with a great sense of pride and earnestness that preserves the spiritual legacy of centuries of Russian history. Not only is attention being given to the outer facade, as domes are re-gilded and cupolas are re-touched, but inside, wall frescos, like those in Suzdal, are being restored.

Old Russian and Byzantine icons are also being preserved in art galleries like the world famous Tretyakov Gallery in Moscow. Here on exhibition are some of the works of Russia's greatest icon painter of the Middle Ages, Andrey Rublyov. In addition to his spectacular icon, "The Old Testament Trinity," one can find other Rublyov masterpieces, such as "The Apostle Paul" and "The Savior." Tours are conducted by Intourist guides, well-versed in biblical history and pre-revolutionary religious life.

Before the Revolution, these icons were placed in the

corner of the large room where peasants ate and slept. Flickering before the image of Jesus, Mary, or one of the Russian Orthodox saints, was a small icon lamp called a *lampadka*. This corner of the peasant hut came to be called the *krasny ugol*, the place of honor. These colorful remnants of pre-revolutionary days can still be found in many Russian homes, though the candles are usually missing and the spiritual significance muted.

In the small living room of Nadezhda and Dmitry hangs a worn, cracked icon depicting the Transfiguration of Jesus, perhaps one of the most popular themes among the old Russian masters. For my Jewish friends, it is art, religious art, Christian art, but nonetheless, fundamentally just art. But in the context of the unsearchable ways of the Lord, the face of their Messiah is art and more. It is the unfolding of a vision that will surely come in its appointed time.

Paintings with biblical motifs hang in art galleries and in the ornate rooms of the former czarist palaces, expressing in a visual way the Christian faith of Russia's holy past. Through the medium of art, the rupture between then and now is vividly conveyed. To the foreigner, the sense of beauty and awe seems so unnatural in the Leninist state, but in pictures and portraits, big and small, His truth is marching on.

Only in my final days in the Soviet Union did I begin to grasp the enormous potential and power that lay hidden, perhaps untapped, inside Russia's myriad of art galleries. Like the crucifixes that quietly preach Christ crucified, religious art, the achievements of both Russian and old world masters, is a dynamic, visual kind of evangelization. The whole Gospel messge is there in pictures and portraits, Rembrandts and Rublayovs, icons and images. And what's more, Soviet officialdom, aware of the propaganda potential of the museum, encourages its citizens to reap the benefits of the

Living Signs of Christ Alive!

Revolution and pay but twenty to forty kopecks to be thoroughly entertained.

Unlike the museums about Lenin and his Revolution, the art galleries are the real winners with the culturally oriented Russian people. The boredom of Soviet life makes the trip to the museum an uplifting and inspiring experience. There may be few Bibles in Russia to read, but in nearly every Soviet city and town, residents can see at least some part of the story of Jesus portrayed in pictures.

The Hermitage Museum in Leningrad has a superb collection of 26 Rembrandts including such works as "Abraham's Sacrifice," "Parable of the Labourers in the Vineyard," and "Descent From the Cross." There are also some fine pieces of the Dutch master on display at the Pushkin Fine Arts Museum in Moscow. I particularly like Rembrandt's masterpiece called "The Incredulity of St. Thomas" painted in 1634. The Soviet state has appropriately displayed it along with other religious works that reveal Jesus' public ministry. For those who have trouble believing that Jesus healed the sick and multiplied the loaves, this Rembrandt is just for them.

There is still another powerful sign of the Russia that once was. Less majestic than cathedrals and icons, but nonetheless a beacon of spiritual light in the cold, gray, communist world is the Russian *babushka*. Recognizable by the colored kerchiefs they wear, they are the link with a world long gone. On any day of the week, these avowed witnesses to Christ can be seen making their way to working Russian Orthodox churches, seeming to ignore the fact that they are living in revolutionary days. But then again, maybe they never forgot it.

Only on church grounds can you find Russian beggars, mostly bundled up *babushki*, barely holding out their hands or just looking humble and pitiful. Muttering prayers, they hope for a passerby's spare kopecks. Those charitable souls who are moved to compassion at the sight of sad, dog-like, drooping faces, are blessed by the old believers as they bless themselves, repeatedly thanking the Lord for the fate He has ordained. An unselfish handful of Soviet change will often produce an outpouring of emotion, releasing a stream of tears rolling down the stretched, grooved lines of an old believer's face. "What's your name, sonny? I want to pray for you, that God will keep you in good health," is likely to be the grateful reception a generous donor might receive.

In the early morning hours, I would often become a part of the procession of believers who sought to escape from the dark and dreary Soviet world into the light of the Lord's temple. I came to accept as a cultural oddity the almost total absence of men, and, for the most part, the younger generation. The war had claimed the lives of many of the men, and the Soviet government was seeking to claim the lives of all of its young people. I would praise the Lord and seek His face in a congregation composed almost exclusively of Russian *babushki*.

Church doors would usually open about a half hour before the service was formally to begin. Traditionally, the members of the local community would bless themselves repeatedly as they approached and departed from the church. This public witnessing to faith in Christ served as an evangelical reminder of His supreme sacrifice. To the unacquainted it may seem unusual, certainly unexpected, and maybe even shocking, though still impressive. It just isn't what you expect to see in "communist" Russia.

Copying these old-timers, Russia's war babies, I found, knew how to make the sign of the cross in Russian style. Maybe they still have a good way to go before accepting Jesus as their personal Lord and Saviour. Maybe the full meaning of the gesture is partially lost in the observance of Orthodox

Living Signs of Christ Alive!

ritualism. But let's not forget that this is not the United States or Great Britain, it's the U.S.S.R., where atheism, state atheism has become the official rule. The Lord deals with all of us where we are in our walk with Him. And this also happens to include where we happen to be geographically. The sign of the cross represents the crucified Christ. Whatever else a person may associate with that gesture, is something that is between him and the Lord.

Inside the church, ritualism and faith continue, as candles sold in small kiosks, are placed in candleholders and lit to illuminate the icons that seem to be everywhere. When smaller churches become filled to capacity, candles are passed along in relay fashion from one member of the community to another until they reach an available candleholder. But the more passionate and determined believers simply jostle and shove their way in traditional Russian fashion, making their way to the front to perform the prayerful ritual themselves. Zealously, these old Russian survivors methodically move about the church bowing, making the sign of the cross, and reverentially kissing the protective glass covering that shields the icons.

Women, church custodians, energetically removing dried wax from the candleholders, and occasionally wiping the glass covering of the icons, are sometimes dressed in black habits, tied back with a cincture, and wear a black kerchief-like veil. Together with the monastic nuns who live predominantly in convents in the Ukraine, they are a holy heritage from centuries past.

In my favorite Russian Orthodox church in Moscow, the Church of the Resurrection, just blocks from Red Square, quiet bells would sometimes ring out the beginning of the ceremony. Silence, however, was more the norm. Russian priests, attired in ornate vestments, would enter unannounced from behind the iconostasis, a partition decorated with icons that separates the holy sanctuary from the central part of the church. Throughout the service, kerchiefed heads would unrhythmically bob, while worshipers would repeatedly make the sign of the cross, also out of unison. Believers were often busy writing lists of names of their loved ones, living and deceased, and leaving them on a designated table close by the offering box.

Here among this faithful community of mainly seventy- and eighty-year-old Christians, I always felt the Spirit of the Lord moving. The beautiful choral singing of only five or six aged resonant voices chanting *Gospodi pomiluy,* (Lord have mercy!)* is something I have never before experienced and will probably never forget. I often saw in the countenances of their dry, wrinkled faces an inescapable sadness, some outwardly crying, perhaps reflecting on an inner loneliness or hardship. For them the church was a place to let it all hang out. Somehow I always felt that some of those tears were shed in anguish for the state atheism that quietly gripped Russia almost three-quarters of a century ago. Perhaps it may seem a bit far-fetched; after all, 1917 was a long time ago. But the soul does not forget.

Signs of humility were everywere in the impressive sight of old believers bent on both knees with their heads touching the floor in worship. They often appeared paralyzed as they held the uncomfortable position for minutes on end. With hearts full of contrition they humbled themselves before the exalted Creator of the universe who, they believe, is wonderfully present behind the closed doors of the icon- ostasis. Repentance was always in evidence.

Repentance is not a word that can be found in the Soviet

---

* *The Way of a Pilgrim* (New York: Image Books, 1978) is a timeless classic that will introduce the reader to the beautiful "Jesus Prayer" that Russians have been praying for centuries.

Living Signs of Christ Alive!

political lexicon. Oh yes, criminals and thieves have the need to reform themselves and return to the path of socialist righteousness. But beyond that, there is no need to repent, for, according to the revolutionary conscience, man is good; it's the class system that needs to repent, to be changed, and radically so.

Russia's *babushki* are not a part of the self-righteous Soviet world. For these "fools for Christ," the darkness of sin in their own lives is recognized for the evil that it is. It is this penitential acknowledgment that leads them to realize their own desperate plight, their need for salvation, and for a Saviour. These holy grandmas seek an inner transformation and healing. No ideology, no matter what kind or how good, can perform such a miracle. Only the Lord can convict, regenerate, and save, and they know it.

I was young enough to be almost any believer's grandson, or great-grandson, and my presence was sometimes misunderstood. Not only did I have the liability of being a foreigner, but I was also a young intruder in the community's spiritual world. Perhaps some thought that I was part of Soviet Russia's younger generation who had come to stare at a bunch of religious fools taking part in a meaningless rite. The Russian *babushka* seems to be everybody's mother; they do not hesitate to be instructive or give advice, and they can be reproving when the situation warrants. I had already learned a few choice lessons from these wise old teachers. "Put your hands to your side." "Stand up, seats are for the old, not the young." "Why do you look at us like that?"

On Sundays, there always seemed to be more young people attending worship services, especially in the larger churches and cathedrals. I recall one cold, bleak, November Sunday watching a devout grandmother lead her little granddaughter through St. Nicholas' Cathedral in Leningrad. The old believer would kiss the different icons and stand a few seconds in prayerful reflection. The little girl, no more than five or six, paid little attention to what was happening. Coming to a life-size crucifix, the grandmother fell to her knees, praying her petitions aloud while her granddaughter looked about. Close by, two adolescent girls, arm in arm, began whispering to each other, trying to contain the giggles that the"foolish" scene had triggered.

Are Russia's *babushki* keeping the Gospel story alive among the younger generation? How will the Russian church survive when these old believers pass on to their eternal reward? Will the younger generation be ready to accept the torch of faith and continue a thousand-year-old tradition? These are the thoughts that often distracted my prayers inside Russia.

Publicly less visible than these Orthodox octogenarians are Russia's Baptist believers. In the Soviet arena their presence is much less spectacular than that of Russia's grandmothers, and there is good reason for it. First of all, historically speaking, Russian Christianity over the centuries has found its national expression in Eastern Orthodoxy. On the other hand, the Baptist church in Russia, which was planted by German missionaries, was not well established until the end of the nineteenth century.

History can explain why Russia is predominantly Orthodox and not Protestant. But to find out why the word "Baptist" can evoke mixed emotions among the Soviet-educated, we must again turn to the nature of Soviet Power.

Uneducated and unorganized, Russia's "denomination" of grandmothers is also untouchable, impervious or nearly so, to the designs of the committed atheistic state. The Baptists, however, are not so privileged. These Bible-believing fundamentalists are organized, organized to live out the spirit of the Scriptures in a way that contradicts every letter of the unwritten Soviet law.

Living Signs of Christ Alive!

There are registered and unregistered Baptist Prayer Houses, as they are called, the latter refusing to submit to the state's control of that which they believe belongs to God alone. Many believers have found Soviet regulations and restrictions so unbearable that they have left the registered churches. Other congregations have been so thoroughly intimidated and persecuted by the zealous revolutionary order that they have had no choice but to go off on their own.

A few of the Soviet rules and regulations which apply to registered churches include the following: Religious associations are forbidden to organize Sunday schools, Bible studies and prayer groups; all church leaders must be approved by the government; organized charitable activities are not permitted; special permission is required to conduct religious ceremonies outdoors as well as in the homes and apartments of believers; religious rites may be performed in hospitals for "dying or seriously ill persons" only if "specially isolated rooms" are available.

Today, there are more than 350 Soviet Christians who are in prison because of their activities in seeking to spread the gospel of Jesus Christ. Some believers have been sent to psychiatric hospitals to be "cured" of their faith in Christ. Parents who have been deemed unfit to bring up their children to become "worthy members of a socialist society" have had their children taken from them and placed in state orphanages. And it is not uncommon for fervent believers to be the victims of harassment and beatings, as well as all kinds of educational and employment discrimination.

Indeed, the accounts of persecution and retribution that find their way beyond Soviet frontiers are stories of another world and time. They are stories reminiscent of the first days of the early church, a church that Jesus said would suffer persecution. This too must be counted as one of the living signs of Christ alive.

A CHRISTIAN VIEW OF RUSSIA

My contact with Russia's official Baptist community was limited mainly to the single registered Baptist church in Moscow. It is a congregation made up largely of women, mostly in their sixties and older, yet there seemed to be more young and middle-aged believers here than in the Orthodox assemblies. Anyone from the Western world who is so blessed to worship with this loving community will not quickly forget the experience.

More than in a figurative way, these God-fearing people draw their very life-blood from the Scriptures; it is their spiritual food and drink. When the Word is being taught, Slavic countenances look fresh and alive, eyes radiate with an eagerness and vitality born of a desire to be filled with the fullness and power of His Spirit. Many take notes, some voraciously copying as many words and ideas as their nimble and not so nimble fingers will allow. Perhaps these truths will be savored when they return into the darkness of the outer world. Maybe a pastor's insight will be joyfully shared with brothers and sisters from a distant community. Whatever the reason, the scene of persecuted believers feasting on the Word makes Jesus' words jump right off the page. "It is written, Man shall not live by bread alone, but by every word that proceedeth out of the mouth of God."[1]

For Moscow's population of eight million residents, Soviet wisdom has decreed that one Baptist assembly is enough, or maybe even too much. The praying that goes on among the overflowing congregation turns a temple into a spiritual powerhouse. Prayers and supplications before the Father are punctuated by a sporadic chorus of heartfelt pleading and groaning that comes from within. Strong crying and tears, and at times profuse wailing, reveal the desolation and infirmities of suffering souls. They are free expressions of

---

[1] Matthew 4:4 KJV

anguish and joy that for a blessed moment liberate the soul from the prison of the body, the prison of the state.

The communion service exemplifies the reverence and awe that is given to the remembrance of the Lord's Last Supper. After the reading of the account of the sacrificial Passover meal, the deacons of the church pass through the assembly with platefuls of broken bread and chalices of symbolic wine. Tears and sobbing, faces full of remorse and contrition create a spirit of wonder and thanksgiving that fills this upper room. Again, love remembers and cannot forget. As each makes his or her way off the Lord's protected island back into the Red Sea of raging winds and pelting rain, smiles and holy kisses are beautiful signs that it is true. Alleluia! Christ has truly risen!

Russia's Pentecostals too are living signs of His Kingdom among us for those of us who have been blessed by their presence. In both Russia and the Ukraine I had the opportunity to meet with Pentecostals of unregistered churches. Their tremendous testimonies witness to the fact that the miracles from the Book of Acts continue to this present generation. The Holy Spirit is at work among His Soviet people.

A believer in a Siberian village spoke joyously about her bout with cancer. The diagnosis was made by a Jewish physician who prescribed the required treatment. But Tatyana knew a much better way. She went out to the nearby forests where her brothers and sisters met for prayer. Falling down before the Lord, she prayed, waiting for the loving touch of the Divine Healer. "I felt the sickness drain from my body," she beamed. "When I stood up, I was completely well and made strong again. Oh, how the doctor was amazed when I told her about Jesus!"

Prayer communities throughout the world have received prophecies about the soon return of Our Lord and Saviour

Jesus Christ. Russia's Pentecostals have also received this word.

There is one final sign of Christ alive in Russia that I must mention. It is the four-syllable tongue twister, *Voskresenie*, the Russian word which means both Sunday and resurrection. This linguistic tradition of referring to Sunday as "Resurrection Day" has remained unbroken with the new radical Soviet regime. Every day, every week, indeed literally every time the Russian people talk about Sunday, they are speaking about Jesus' rising from the dead. Perhaps, I thought, this was more than coincidental. Maybe it was in some way symbolic of the state of contemporary Russian Christianity. Or at least it answered the question that Soviet Power totally ignores: What happens after death? Or maybe I was desperately looking for something to hold onto at Easter, the most glorious time of the year for all Christians.

It was Easter Eve in the capital. Outside of Yelokhovskaya Cathedral a huge crowd of maybe a thousand people had gathered for the midnight celebration. There seemed to be an awareness that something extraordinary was about to take place. An electrifying anticipation swept through the assembly. All age groups were represented, the young, the middle-aged, the old, and the very old. How many were believers and how many were spectators was a question that only each individual could answer. Some were undoubtedly looking forward to the mangificence of the Byzantine rite. But there must also have been those waiting to meet the Resurrected Christ.

The New Testament speaks of the crowds that followed Jesus everywhere. There were the sick and the infirm, the believers and the doubters, and those who were just plain curious and wanted to find out firsthand. Even the Samaritans made haste "to come and see" at the behest of the woman who had met her Saviour there at the well.

Living Signs of Christ Alive!

The Russians excitedly milling about outside of Yelokh-ovskaya Cathedral were hardly all believers. Except for the *babushki*, perhaps there were only a handful that could have prayed, "Lord, I believe, help my unbelief." But there were skeptics on Calvary too. And wasn't Russia now enduring a spiritual crucifixion of its own in the form of imposed Soviet atheism? No doubt there were those here who were looking for a sign, just like certain of the scribes and Pharisees of Jesus' day. But regardless of how much or how little each knew about the historical Jesus, each was looking, watching, and maybe even hearing.

In the period of the last two-thousand years, things haven't really changed that much.

13

Revolutionary Man
on the Drawing Board

King Nebuchadnezzar had a golden statue made, . . . The herald then made this proclamation: "Men of all peoples, nations, languages! This is required of you: the moment you hear the sound of the horn, pipe, lyre, trigon, harp, bagpipe, or any other instrument, you must prostrate yourselves and worship the golden statue erected by King Nebuchadnezzar. . . . ."

(Daniel 3:1-6 TJB)

The crimson red stars which magnificently shine above the towers of the ancient Kremlin illuminate Moscow's nights with rays of theatrical splendor. On any romantic evening, when a deep pitch blackness consumes the capital, the glowing ruby-red stars, which can be seen from a distance, seem to be suspended in time and space, creating a mystic wonderment that evokes a childhood feeling of walking through a fairy tale. A bright red Soviet flag flies atop the central dome of the Kremlin's former Senate building, mysteriously fluttering both day and night. When gusts are strong and violent, the Soviet flag ripples incessantly, spectacularly. And when there is no wind, no breeze at all, the flag still salutes the Revolution. In some supernatural way, it is almost as if the political tremors of October 1917 reversed the laws of nature, bringing them into subjection to man himself.

The "Great October Socialist Revolution" is officially heralded as "the main event of the twentieth century." It is only fitting then that Revolution Day should become the Soviet holiday supreme, commemorating as it does the death of the old political order and the joyous birth of a brand new era. According to the script, Russians celebrate the momentous day when all earthly power, and then some, was given to the working people. On this day of days, all Soviet cities are drenched in red, the color of life and blood. Countless banners and flags, many of enormous dimensions, almost seem to paint the facades of two- and three-story buildings. Street lamps are decorated with light-filled scarlet stars, but the illuminated crimson hammer and sickle somehow seems more appropriate for the festivities.

Revolution Day is set aside to honor the Revolution, and of course, man, notably Lenin, the ruling Communist Party chief, and a handful of other elite. But every day, every Soviet day, is set aside to honor today's Soviet people. Continuing in their forefathers' steps to labor to create a new world, they are also heroic and deserving of honor and praise, as official slogans announce. Soviet media techniques convey in a subtly dramatic way that their people are not ordinary, but makers of history. Only they fully understand the historical process that will change the human complexion of the entire globe. Soviet people today are heroically marching past the onlooking spectators of the world, bearing the banner of peace, equality, brotherhood, and communism.

Revolutionary Russia, according to Soviet thinking, is destined to proclaim the news of a grand new political order which will wipe away the sins of discrimination and injustice that have so discolored the history of all governments. The message of communism has been brought to more than 100 different nationalities, from Armenians to Ukrainians, all who, along with their Russian brethren, inhabit the Union of Soviet Socialist Republics. And everywhere throughout the Union, the utopian drama is performed with nearly the same rigor and earnestness as it is on center stage, Russia.

In the sun-drenched Central Asian Republic of Uzbekistan, a sound and light show takes place on Registan Square before the exotic-looking madrasahas of ancient Samarkand. At one time they were Moslem schools; now they are used to teach a much different lesson. As changing colors create psychedelic images on the tiled buildings, a voice calling himself, "The Heart of Samarkand," tells the tragic story of cruel attacks in the city by such madmen as Genghis Khan and Tamerlane. Life was an endless hell in which souls were tormented with social and political injustice.

The dramatic musical overture, which surrealistically created sensations of a nation in the throes of agony and war, was visually enhanced by abrupt flashes of colored light. The taste of power and magnanimity exploded majestically throughout the presentation, sweeping the spectator into a theatrical world where scenes of ancient history rushed vividly through the mind. The narration reached its crescendo as "the Heart of Samarkand" spoke emotionally of the October Revolution. Sweeping like a purifying fire from Russia into Asia, it consumed the Uzbek political structure, heralding "a new age, a new life, a new century in communism, bringing peace and friendship to all men."

The drama of the Revolution, as it is portrayed on the Soviet stage, is much more than just an imaginative display of political theatrics. There is something else going on here, perhaps subtly, but unmistakably. The perversion of the revolutionary way is revealed for all that it is: an attempt to make gods of mere men. The October Revolution is lifted up, but it is man that is being glorified. Lenin engineered the coup; he is creator. And Soviet Man, in guiding "the laws of social development," becomes the sustainer of all things. Not content with trying to rob man of his spirit, Soviet Power seeks to possess the glory that belongs to God alone.

Subtlety is a genuine art form and one that Soviet Russia uses well. In the remembrance of the war years, the Soviet government has sought to twist powerful human emotions for self-glorification and the glorification of Soviet Man.

The "Great Patriotic War" is remembered not only by veterans but also by their children and grandchildren. They too must participate in the memory of what was. They are called upon to be forever vigilant so that the ferocity of war will never again be unleashed on their homeland.

Being taught to love one's nation and respect the memory of those who died defending it is natural and admirable. But beneath the disguise of Soviet patriotism, lurks a deeper, darker motivation. Russian children have been chosen not merely to carry the banner of the "Great Patriotic War," nor simply to pay their respects to those who died fighting in it. They have been summoned to stand before the altars of Soviet war memorials and pay homage to the Revolution and its defenders. They are summoned to worship man.

In Kiev, two teenage girls, no more than sixteen, marched symmetrically in goose-step fashion in front of the military graves which line both sides of the Park of Eternal Glory. The tomb of the unknown soldier in the center of the memorial complex is covered by bouquets of fresh flowers and a bronze wreath. An eternal flame burns at the base of a tall granite obelisk. Here another young honor guard of thirteen- and fourteen-year-olds stands in silence, while somber requiem music whispers across the weighty silence. The young girls bore red flags and the boys rifles.

Revolutionary Man on the Drawing Board

Three hundred miles away in Odessa, on the Avenue of Glory overlooking the Black Sea, a similar ceremony was being held at a war memorial erected to the memory of the unknown sailor. I watched as young Ukrainian and Russian boys, wearing Soviet navy shirts and bearing rifles, marched the goose step during the changing of the guard.

The Ukrainian requiem which is played every hour had just begun. The honor guard stood absolutely immobile. They appeared virtually paralyzed as their heads were reverently bowed. I glanced at the eternal flame burning nearby and the many flowers which paid tribute to Odessa's war dead. A voice spoke to the young defenders, telling them the story that led to the sacrifices of those whom they ritualistically protected. "People! As long as your hearts still beat, remember the price that was paid for your peaceful life." *"Pomnite! Pomnite!* Remember! Remember!" was the refrain which is slowly and melodiously intoned. *"Pomnite! Pomnite!"*

In the context of the atheistic vision, those who are buried here on the Avenue of Glory are not mere men or women. Nor are they heroes, the official Soviet title. No, they have been elevated to a supernatural level. Like Lenin, they have become like gods. As my group of Americans and I turned and walked back down the Avenue of Glory, we left behind not a physical monument but another world, a world that has pridefully created an idol, the revolutionary Golden Calf.

The Bible is very explicit on this matter of pride. Proverbs puts it in a nutshell: "He that exalteth his gate seeketh destruction."[1] God created all things for Himself, for His glory, and He will not share that glory with another. Men, nations, and kingdoms that have grown arrogant in their self-esteem and made idols to bow down before, have all met with the same inevitable fate. "Though thou exalt thyself as

---

[1] Proverbs 17:19 KJV

the eagle, and though thou set thy nest among the stars, thence will I bring thee down, saith the Lord."[1]

I believe that the Lord has a message for Moscow; it comes from the Bible, the Book of Daniel. The story of King Nebuchadnezzar is in many ways symbolically rich in parallels with the story of Revolutionary Russia. Let us begin from the beginning, with the sin of pride and the adoration of the golden effigy.

Historians regard Nebuchadnezzar II as the greatest king of the ancient Babylonian Empire. In his career of conquests, he reduced Jerusalem to ruins and led its people into the bondage of the long Babylonian Captivity. During his forty-three year reign, he transformed Babylon into one of the wonders of the world, its Hanging Gardens his crowning achievement.

The Book of Daniel records how Nebuchadnezzar, inspired by his kingly wisdom, erected a gigantic image of gold. At the dedication of the image the herald of the court cried out to all people, nations, and languages that they must bow down to the grand idol of the king.

The Soviet Union too has fashioned an idol. It is not made of gold nor does it take on real physical form. The glorious dream of communism—man becoming his own creator, re-creating himself, and giving birth to a super-natural society—has become the revolutionary idol. Like the temptation which befell the first man, the Soviet vision holds out before Soviet Man the possibility of becoming like a god.

Today, there are over a billion men, women and children living under communist regimes. Never-ending propaganda, secret police, labor camps—these are the methods that communist states have appropriated to bring man to his

---

[1] Obadiah 4 KJV

knees in submission and in adoration. Yet not everyone will fall prostrate at the Marxist command; there are many who refuse to even pretend to draw their life-blood from the radical ideology. Like Shadrach, Meshach, and Abednego, they are hurled into modern day furnaces and ridiculed, "Who is that God that shall deliver you out of my hands?"[1] The Pentecostal refugees who lived in the sanctuary of the American Embassy in Moscow for nearly five years were symbolically asked this very question by the presence of the militia that surrounded the embassy compound. It is the same timeless question that has the same godless meaning in all languages and cultures.

The frightful dream that confounded Nebuchadnezzar is rich in biblical wisdom. Pride, the seeking to usurp the glory that belongs to God alone, is sheer madness. It must be punished. In his vision, the king saw a great and powerful tree that ascended into the hevens itself and could even be seen from the ends of the earth. The tree was symbolic of the great Babylonian Empire, but it might well represent another kingdom, a kingdom which is also stretching into the sky. Geographically, the U.S.S.R. is not only the largest nation in the world, occupying one-sixth of the earth's total land surface, but its power also extends into nearly all of Eastern Europe.

In a moment's time, that which was magnificent becomes a scene of desolation. The mighty tree is to be hewed down, its branches severed, its leaves stripped away, its fruit scattered. It is up to Daniel, a member of the king's court, to interpret what the unsettling dream means. Being a prophet of doom is hardly an enviable position, but Daniel speaks the truth. The king has grown fat in his haughtiness and self-esteem. And now the Lord has chosen to punish and humiliate this

---

[1] Daniel 3:15 KJV

monarch of monarchs.

As Daniel foretold, Nebuchadnezzar endured a seven-year period of madness when he was exiled from human society and forced to live as a beast of the field. At the appropriate time, the Soviet Union too will be brought low. When the Lord has finished using the new Babylon to fulfill His eternal plan for mankind, another empire will come tumbling down. Stripped of its revolutionary regalia, a broken Soviet leadership will someday speak Nebuchadnezzar's humbling words: "Now I Nebuchadnezzar praise and extol and honor the King of heaven, all whose works are truth, and his ways judgment: and those that walk in pride he is able to abase."[1]

For Revolutionary Russia, the Book of Daniel, indeed the entire Bible, is regarded as an enormous obstacle to the realization of the communist vision. The Gospel message of salvation clashes inexorably with the revolutionary message of salvation. Throughout the Bible, the thrust of the Word of God is uncompromisingly clear. "Thou shalt love the Lord thy God with all thy heart, and with all thy soul, and with all thy mind, and with all thy strength . . . ."[2] Such a commandment is totally inconsistent with the goal of making communism the center and awe of every human movement and activity. In Russia then, the Bible is more political than religious. And it is a threat which will not be tolerated.

"You really don't need to bring Bibles with you into the country," a speaker at a Round Table panel told a large group of Americans. "Bibles may be obtained through the Russian Orthodox Patriarchate of Moscow for anyone who wants them." This official view, however, unfortunately doesn't jive with the supply and demand of the Soviet marketplace. On the black market, Russians hungry for the Word will

---

[1] Daniel 4:37 KJV
[2] Mark 12:30 KJV

easily pay more than a hundred rubles for a Bible, the equivalent of more than two weeks salary. Many believers will share their Bibles with others; the Scriptures are much too precious and all too scarce to keep for oneself.

Despite this famine for the saving Word, I was quite surprised to find that many Russians were familiar with at least some of the Scriptures. Thanks to Christian organizations abroad, new ways are being found to get Bibles into the Soviet Union. Foreign broadcasts proclaiming the Good News are reaching millions of starving Soviet people. Here are a few of these life-changing testimonies. From Siberia, a radio listener writes:

> I was brought up in an unbelieving home. My father is a Communist. At the age of 13 I was seeking a sense of purpose for my life. I hoped to find it in music, art and politics. My soul wanted real food. My family purchased a radio. I soon found your broadcasts. Through these programs the Lord brought me out of darkness into his glorious light. Oh, how happy I am! I am praying for my parents that God will reach their hearts.

Another recent letter shows that even Soviet soldiers are seeking after the truth:

> Greetings to all of you, our brothers and sisters in the Lord! I am a soldier in the Soviet Red Army, and therefore it is very difficult for me always to listen to you when I want. I am sending you this letter by special route. Many soldiers listen to you, yes, even officers, but always in secret. Please pray for us.

These lifelines from the West are how Russian believers survive the storms and tempests of the revolutionary Red Sea. The heartfelt message I was asked to carry back to believers at home is, "Thank you so much for the Gospel." The plea was conveyed through smiles, tears and a strengthened spirit.

A CHRISTIAN VIEW OF RUSSIA

The war on Bibles is very efficiently organized. On the outside, custom officials at airports and frontier stops thoroughly inspect luggage and parcels for biblical and other contraband. On the inside, the KGB does battle with the underground Bible "printing shops," where a primitive press might, incredibly enough, be composed of odds and ends from a washing machine.

Russia now has two Christian publishing houses, *Khristianin*, The Christian, and *Istina*, The Truth. These secret presses publish portions of Scripture, religious literature and even Christmas and Easter cards. The material needs to keep the operation going are great, and so are the prison sentences meted out to those who are apprehended. Nothing, remember, is supposed to be easy in Russia, especially something so threatening to Soviet Power. All the bases, all the avenues and alley ways, all the technical means—they've all been covered to prevent the proclamation of the printed Word. Even securing the paper to print on is no easy task since individuals in the Soviet Union cannot buy paper in bulk quantities. Money too is a problem, and one that we in the West can help with.

The Soviets have the manpower, and the power in general, to oppose the believers, to win decisively, resoundingly. But they don't, at least not always. The predictable ways of man and the unsearchable ways of God see to that.

There is the story, for example, of the two hundred or so Bibles that were confiscated at Moscow's Sheremetevo International Airport. Quite a lucrative find, and quite a job well done! The experienced customs people knew how much potential cash they were looking at. With spoils in hand, they flew out to a distant city and made their way to a nearby assembly of believers. Twenty rubles a shot was all they were asking for. Really, it was a bargain. The minister and the congregation agreed; it was a deal, that is, almost. The Big

Revolutionary Man on the Drawing Board

Brother assigned to keep tabs on the believers came out of the woodwork, blew the whistle, pulled rank, and ordered his colleagues back whence they came. But miraculously, the ranking KGB agent permitted the congregation to keep the contraband. God, greed, and the lust for power providentially came together to produce such an unbeatable miracle. And you can be sure, there have been others like it.

"*Domus Mea, Domus Orationis,* (My House Is a House of Prayer"), is the writing above the locked doors of St. Catherine's, a closed Roman Catholic church. Standing before the jailed temple on Nevsky Prospekt in Leningrad, Jesus' words seem so prophetic, so symbolic: ". . . but ye have made it a den of thieves."[1] There is no buying and selling going on here, but the inscription on the bronze tablet attached to the church suggests that another kind of robbery is taking place. "This is an architectural monument of the 18th century . . . . It is protected by the government." It is quite clear. It is man's ability to worship that is being taken away. It is the very spirit of man that Soviet Power jealously seeks to possess.

Another sign of the times is less than a block away. Since 1932 the former Cathedral of Our Lady of Kazan has served as Leningrad's Museum of the History of Religion and Atheism. The great number of inquisitive Russians who make their way through the state exhibit witness how their government would have them think about God. The intensive mind-forming attempt is boldly admitted in a quotation from Karl Marx which at one time greeted the museum visitor as he entered. "Religion will disappear to the extent that socialism develops. Its disappearance must take place as a result of social development, in which a major role belongs to education."

---

[1] Matthew 21:13 KJV

A CHRISTIAN VIEW OF RUSSIA

The two-story exhibit is designed to portray religion as exploitative, fanatical, hypocritical and decadent. And it does. For instance, a small gallery of nineteenth century paintings shows the ministers of God in the image of fat, bourgeois, cigar smokers, exorcising the possessed and lustfully scolding a beautiful girl. Religion as a capitalist tool to exploit the masses is the theme of a large poster depicting tuxedoed businessmen, rich peasants, and priests together hauling the wagon of capitalism.

A large map entitled "Financial Empire of the Vatican," shows the Pope ruling over predominantly Catholic nations. Statues of Christ and a display of gold chalices are mockingly exhibited. A large realistically-designed torture chamber with a spiked chair, red-hot branding irons, and whips demonstrates how heretics were tortured during the Inquisition. The contemporary religious scene in the West is presented in a series of photographs of young people who look drugged, freaked out, and frightened.

Nowhere is revolutionary propaganda more effective than here. The gallery of paintings, photographs and posters employs Satan's most subtle trick: *distraction*. Focusing our eyes on the foibles and failures of those who profess Christ is the surest way to be detoured, and sometimes derailed, in following the Lord. Admittedly, both men and nations have done condemnable and repulsive things in the name of the cross, in the name of Jesus. The Crusades and the Inquisition are prominent examples. Even the terror and savagery of Nazism came out of a Christian nation. But are we followers of Christianity or disciples of Christ? We in the free West have the Scriptures which point to Jesus as the Way, and we still fall into the temptation of distraction. What then can we expect from the spiritually disarmed? Unarmed, how shall they do battle?

It is noteworthy, however, that one Soviet guide, after

conducting a private tour through the museum confided to her American tourist that she always dreaded the experience. She said that she found the exhibits disgustingly misrepresentative of true Christianity and claimed she was not alone.

According to the Soviet Constitution, each citizen is guaranteed "freedom of conscience." However, since 1917, over two-thirds of all churches and places of worship have been closed down or transformed into museums, sports buildings or warehouses. Foreign guests are told that it isn't the government who decides to close a particular church, it's the people, the believers who decide. An Intourist guide explained that "the believers tell the government that they have enough churches, too many in fact, and so the unnecessary ones are closed." But somehow the Soviet argument was very unconvincing; it was another example of bad propaganda.

Church doors may be open to anyone, but attending a religious service goes against the grain of everything that Revolutionary Russia stands for. The Communist Party elect have an official responsibility to change the thinking of the believer.

"Yes, we have believers, young believers too," a Party enthusiast in his forties admitted in disgust. "These young kids, they just don't learn, that's their problem. They go to school and just sit. Their teachers instruct them in scientific materialism, but it doesn't sink in. Those of us in the Party try to correct this stupid, naive approach. And actually, this is not just the responsibility of Party people, but non-Party too. Everyone has the responsibility, but in reality only Party members are active in this respect. Our duty," he said proudly, "is to spread anti-religious propaganda everywhere."

I recall how frightened these words made me. I thought of the freakish muscular men and women on Soviet posters who were energetically doing the Revolution's work. Was I now seeing the caricature of these revolutionaries in the flesh? Russians had told me similar stories of Party types who proselytized atheism, but the impact couldn't be compared to what I was now experiencing firsthand.

According to the official line, not only do "the people" themselves close up the churches, but children fundamentally come to accept atheism on their own. One guide, however, offered a slightly different version. "Yes, parents and grandparents can influence their children into believing in God, but later when they go to school, their views change because of our atheistic propaganda."

"What do they teach you about God in school?" I once asked Nadya, my young mushrooming guide.

"That there's no God," she told me. "If we're reading a story which talks about angels or devils or saints or God, the teacher will just explain that no gods exist."

In the higher levels of education, in the institutes and universities, formal courses on religion and atheism begin. How a person views God is much too important a factor in the building of the communist world to be left to the prerogative of the individual. So, whether you're studying to be a doctor or a farmer, a teacher or an engineer, you can be sure that your standardized course work will always include "Fundamentals of Scientific Atheism."

The Soviet line of atheistic posters, which are sold in book stores, are yet another way to assault man's spirit. Especially in the countryside, where belief in God is still very much alive, posters that ridicule religion are frequently to be seen. "Without God The Road Is Wider," is the bit of Soviet wisdom that one poster proclaims. The revolutionary view is that religion is parochial, narrow-minded and confining. But the Scriptures also speak about a narrow way that is not confining at all, but the way to abundant, eternal life. The slogan industry has the facts right; it's the interpretation that they need help with.

Films too are another media tool used to disseminate atheism. "The Secret Monk," a cleverly anti-religious film, is a good example. The circumstances of the Russian civil war of 1918-1920 between the Red communist-inspired Bolsheviks and the White anti-communist forces provided the backdrop for the adventure-packed thriller. Partners with the White Guard forces working against the progressive achievements of 1917 were Russian Orthodox monks who hid "counter-revolutionaries" in their monastery sanctuary. The cowboy and indian drama, Russian style, which showed lots of killing on both sides, though little blood-letting, was, in terms of propaganda value, a rather innocuous film. Nevertheless, consistent with Soviet thinking, the church was one of the bad guys.

The great anti-religious campaign to form a godless man is not merely a tactical plan or a well-thought-out strategy. It has a definite spiritual and scriptural basis. "No servant can serve two masters: for either he will hate the one, and love the other; or else he will hold to the one, and despise the other."[1] If man's innate spirituality can be nullified, a new creature called Soviet Man may be molded, and communism will become the new secular religion. It really seems more than coincidental that a number of Russians who told me that they were not believers immediately added that they believed in communism. Deep below the Russian earth on a metro train, a young Russian put it this way. "There is Russian Orthodoxy, Catholicism, Protestantism and then communism. I believe in communism."

In Russia's great experiment in mind control, propaganda slogans take on an undisguised psalmodic quality. "GIVE GLORY TO THE COMMUNIST PARTY OF THE SOVIET UNION." "PRAISE THE

---

[1] Luke 16:13 KJV

A CHRISTIAN VIEW OF RUSSIA

OCTOBER REVOLUTION." "LONG LIVE THE COMMUNIST PARTY, THE SOURCE OF OUR STRENGTH AND THE FOUNDATION OF ALL OUR VICTORIES." "LONG LIVE COMMUNISM WHICH BRINGS TO THE EARTH, PEACE, WORK, HAPPINESS AND BROTHERHOOD FOR ALL." Reading official Soviet ideology in this way makes communism seem less like a political system and more like a religious cult.

"THE NAME AND DEEDS OF LENIN WILL LIVE FOREVER." "LENIN LIVED. LENIN LIVES. LENIN WILL LIVE." So contends the Soviet poster and slogan-making industry. Inside Russia, Lenin never died, as a portrait of him in a store front window in 1978 testified. The dates below the portrait were 1870-1978. Lenin is immortal, theatrically so, for he has been fashioned as the god of this new revolutionary world.

Historically speaking, Lenin died in 1924. By 1930 a permanent mausoleum of red granite and black labradorite was ready as a depository for his body. Each year millions of people, both Soviets and foreigners, make what may be considered a sort of pilgrimage to Lenin's resting place in Red Square. They wait in line for hours, just to catch a glimpse of the man that their government refuses to let them forget.

The militia and plainclothes security men that patrol Red Square heighten the sensational effect that the entire ritual so perfectly lends itself to. With each advancing step toward the tomb, the megaphone blasts out louder and more frequently the command to keep in line with your partner. Those who disobediently fall out of step, or don't move along fast enough, are immediately reprimanded. *"Bystro! Bystro!"* becomes a familiar sound, and a new addition to the foreigner's Russian vocabulary. Everyone obeys and the procession moves forward quickly toward its ultimate goal.

Silence becomes profound those last few minutes before one enters the mausoleum. Those who dare break the natural silence that enshrouds the few remaining steps before this monument of monuments are told in no uncertain terms to

234

Revolutionary Man on the Drawing Board

be still, and it doesn't take an advanced degree in Russian to understand the meaning of the sharply spoken command.

After hours of waiting, the viewer is permitted but a few seconds to gaze at what the Soviets claim is the embalmed body of Vladimir Ilich Lenin. The corpse is physical testimony to the revolutionary events that changed the course of both Russian and world history. Whether the body is authentic, or as is sometimes claimed, a wax reproduction, is irrelevant. The realistic-looking image of Lenin lying in a crystal sarcophagus, creates an awesome sense of power and suspense, which apparently is the desired effect. Here lies the body of the creator of a new world, the world of Soviet communism.

The Leninist drama is superbly executed. It has everything. The staging is magnificent. What could possibly compare to the fairy-tale imagery of the cobblestoned Red Square? The props are all real, seemingly unimprovable. The plot is unusual, indeed spectacular. The entire production moves carefully and dramatically towards a suspenseful climax at the tomb. But that is the only flaw; it's a tomb, an occupied one. Precision, authenticity, mystique, power—it's all there, but the fact is hauntingly inescapable: *Lenin is dead.* The fullness of Soviet Power is limited and constrained by the divine laws of nature. The glory of the revolutionary rays beaming from the Kremlin's red stars seems to fade. Lenin cannot be resurrected by revolutionary power, nor by any human power. He remains just as he became on January 21, 1924—dead.

Precisely 2 minutes and 45 seconds before the Kremlin chimes ceremoniously ring out the next hour, a corporal and two sentries begin their methodical march from beneath the Spasskaya Tower to the tomb. Each one of their 340 measured paces is punctuated by the resonant sounds of heavy leather boots smashing against the stoned pavement of the Square.

A CHRISTIAN VIEW OF RUSSIA

Only a few fleeting moments before the Spasskaya Tower will proclaim the birth and death of another hour, the honor guard will arrive at the top of the steps of the mausoleum. The entire Square will be magically bathed in silence. And then the melody of the hour will break forth unchained. A new guard will take up its position, and time will still go on.

In the days of Holy Russia, the Spasskaya Tower served another purpose, a spiritual one. This particular fifteenth century tower received its present name by order of the czar in 1658. Commemorating the annexation of the city of Smolensk by the Russian army, a fresco of the Saviour was painted over the gate of the tower. (Hence, the adjective Spasskaya, a derivative of the word *spas,* meaning Saviour.) In pre-revolutionary days, candles burned before the Russian Saviour both day and night.

An empty rectangular square, painted all in white now covers the fresco. It contrasts with the crimson brickwork of this tower which for many has come to represent the Kremlin. But beneath its special protective coating, the once-revered image of the Saviour of Smolensk remains untouched. Like the cloud that now obscures the real Russia, this covering too shall be lifted on that great and glorious day.

But for now the public attention is on Lenin, the perfect man, "the most human man," to use the words of the Soviet slogan industry. Posters show Lenin most at ease when he is in the midst of children, calling them to his side or fondly holding a little boy or girl in his arms. "Don't go away, Lenin! Stay here with us for good" are the words from a typical children's primer on this man Lenin. The parallel to Jesus placing his hands on the little ones and blessing them is both instructive and sickening. In school, children are taught verses of songs about Lenin such as, "I've never seen him, but I still love him." They learn to revere "Uncle Lenin," the man who they are told will always remain their best friend.

Revolutionary Man on the Drawing Board

Aside from all the political hoopla about building communism, there are some clear signs that the unfolding of the revolutionary vision has at least partially begun. Russians exhibit a real sense of collectivity and a social responsibility toward each other and their government that is more than socialist window dressing. And there seems to be no question that the Soviet government has played a part in fashioning such a mentality.

The signs of social responsibility inside Russia abound. On all surface public transportation systems, the honor system is in effect. Passengers are obliged to drop their kopecks inside the fare box and turn a little manual knob to take their receipt. Sinless communism, however, like Soviet Man is still in the drawing board stages. And so, like the *druzhinniki* that are responsible for keeping Russians sober, the Soviet institution that goes by the name *Kontrol*, does its best to keep Russians straight. Periodically, an unimposing woman in casual dress clothes will make her way through the bus or trolley flashing her official-looking metal badge and asking to see passengers' receipts. Those who are caught violating the revolutionary order are made to shell out a ruble on the spot. Judging by my experiences, however, the Russians are a rather honest bunch when it comes to paying their own way.

This sense of social consciousness is, as we have already seen, also manifested in the cultural pride that Russians have for keeping their metros clean. In a society where the collective takes precedence over the individual, dropping a wrapper on the ground is not doing your own thing, but offending someone else's sensibilities. Growing up, children are taught one of the most basic political lessons: "Remember, you aren't the only person in this world."

The public Russian, usually ready to genuflect before authority, is often vigilant to protect those rights that accrue from membership in the great collective. Russians have a responsibility to correct those who have gone astray from the straight and narrow revolutionary way. An example:

A totalled drunk on a crowded metro train slumps his head onto the shoulders of the passenger next to him. An irate young man responds to this intrusion by straightening the drooped head and coarsely rubbing the ears of the wretched soul who is obviously paralyzed by a half-liter or so of Russian vodka. Coming out of his stupor, the drunk begins to yawn and is quickly reprimanded for being uncultured.

A few minutes pass and a young boy who flanks the drunk on the other side now becomes a prop for the resting head. This little Russian is already aware of the duties of a Soviet citizen and knows that what is happening is not so much a violation of his individual rights, but an infringement on the rights of the collective. And so, absolutely within his authority, the nine-year-old boy, without compunction, flops the twisted neck to the other direction, regaining his right to sit unannoyed on the metro train that belongs to *everyone*.

"Getting involved" seems to be a very Russian way of expressing the feeling of community responsibility.

Coming out of my metro station stop, Aleksandr Nevsky Square, adjacent to the Moskva Hotel, I watched what looked like the beginning of a healthy brawl between two young Leningradians. Each of the contestants was busy sizing up the other and had begun the initial pushing, shoving and name-calling, a warm-up to what was to come. A couple of bystanders were already in the process of trying to mediate. The few Russians coming up from the escalator on this late Sunday evening immediately got involved, at first just reprimanding the bigger man who was quickly putting the moves on his smaller adversary. When the real swinging began, there must have been seven or eight Russians, mostly young and middle-aged, intervening and demanding that the fighting stop.

Revolutionary Man on the Drawing Board

As I looked on from a careful distance watching the mysterious Russian collective do its thing, this woman standing beside me shouted, "You're a man, help them put a stop to it!" I must confess the command went unheeded. I was afraid to get involved. This was the rule that I had been taught in the very non-collective American society, where the individual reigns supreme.

There were numerous other signs, too many to elaborate here, that spoke to me of a culture radically different from my own. For example, the public telephones where officially only three-minute conversations are permitted. And if you do your own thing for too much longer, you're likely to hear the sound of a coin tapping against the glass pane of the booth. An impatient comrade is waiting. The sign hanging in a Moscow cafeteria, "To Save Bread Is The Duty and Responsibility Of Every Citizen." The many times that I asked for change for the subway fare and ended up the recipient of a five kopeck dole from a hurrying passenger.

However one chooses to evaluate these signs of the Soviet times, one thing is certain. There is still much that must be done before communism can makes its grand entrance onto the Soviet stage. Breaking up brawls and keeping litter off Soviet streets are admirable qualities in and of themselves. But as we all know only too well, leopard spots go deep, deep below the skin. Reforming man is tough, and often discouraging, work. It demands that the Soviet government work non-stop toward this futuristic goal. Unfortunately, it does.

Russians live on a stage where a theatrical drama entitled "Approaching Communism" is re-enacted daily. Even in the privacy of the home one cannot escape the penetrating reach of the revolutionary word. Each evening television towers beam their air waves into millions of flats, and much of the programming format is taken up with depictions of work.

A CHRISTIAN VIEW OF RUSSIA

The screen will not merely show one's fellow comrades working, for that would be too ordinary. It wouldn't be uplifting. It wouldn't do anything for the creation of the Soviet Man. No, my friends, these Russian stars are building communism.

A chairman of a *kolkhoz*, a collective farm, or a director of a factory, will explain in an interview how the collective is striving to fulfill the government set plan. And then for a good few minutes, at least, the audience will be treated to the footage of combines reaping wheat.

The curious family member who wishes to glance through any of the nearly eight thousand mainly two- to four-page Soviet newspapers, already has a good idea what's in store. Page one, for instance, will feature a photograph of members of the Russian proletariat taking off a few minutes from their duties to smile at the photographer. And what do they have to say for themselves? You guessed it, that they just love to work. Well maybe it's not as obvious as that, but when you read between the Cyrillic lines, that's the message, pure and simple.

Man is called upon to glorify work, and work in turn, in the form of communism, will glorify man. But the problem is all too apparent. Work, or *rabota*, as the Russians call it, is not always, indeed is not usually, such great fun. There is a relevant parallel here between Soviet propaganda and our own Western television commercials. Take for instance, the one that shows the cheerful housewife happily washing the kitchen floor with the new, improved formula "Presto Clean." She is happy as a lark or, in the Soviet context, a Russian worker. Who says work is drudgery and so much sweat and toil? Well, for beginners, the Bible. "With sweat on your brow shall you eat your bread . . . ."[1] To know this

---

[1] Genesis 3:19 TJB

Revolutionary Man on the Drawing Board

scriptural truth, Russians don't need God's Word. Sore muscles, aching backs and tired feet—they all suggest that on this matter of *rabota*, somebody is telling a bold-faced lie.

The coming of the ideal political world, which the laws of history foretold, is what motivated a group of idealistic revolutionaries, who called themselves *Bolsheviki*, to attempt a coup d'etat against Russia's provisional government almost three-quarters of a century ago. Since that fateful day, Russians have been told that communism will be victorious. But the waiting for the triumph of communism goes on and on and on. The mantle of hope is passed along to each new generation. According to the new Soviet Constitution of 1977, the U.S.S.R. has entered a new historical stage. Socialism will begin to fade, allowing communism to make its long-prophesied entry into a waiting world.

"What's the difference between right now and when you'll have communism?" I asked a Communist Party member, who at least pretended to believe that a grand new world is coming.

"Now," she explained, "a person spends as much money as he can afford, that is, as much as he makes. But under communism there won't be any money at all. People will just take what they need."

The neat little explanation challenged me to ask how the new order will deal with the variable called human nature, that has been around as long as man.

"But," I countered, "won't a person take, say five loaves of bread, even though he may only need two or three?"

The senior university professor seemed amused by the question. She pointed out that under communism, human greed will no longer plague society.

"You don't understand," she asserted, "a person who needs only two loaves will take only two, for he will understand that others too need bread."

A CHRISTIAN VIEW OF RUSSIA

I knew enough about Russia and Russians to realize that the prophecy I had just heard was nothing more than a bit of fine acting. It was a flare for showmanship that comes naturally to the Russian people. For today, lip service to communism is part of what it takes to live in Revolutionary Russia.

A joyous new world may be on the horizon, but the Russians are not waiting with bated breath. Human nature may be about to be transformed, so that a man who needs two loaves of bread will not be tempted to take five or fifty-five. But there are few today in Russia who expect to see that day.

Russians live in the present and leave the futuristic world of communism to the imaginations and machinations of the Soviet propaganda industry. I found that most Russians treated the prophecy of a communist society in much the same way.

"No one even thinks about it," a middle-aged cabbie told me as we sped through the streets of Leningrad. "It's just a big joke," he grinned. "You know the old proverb, 'Your own shirt is closer to your body.' Money, money, money, that's all that matters to me."

Igor, a twenty-three-year-old train announcer explained, "Look, we just laugh about communism. No one really believes it will ever come. The main thing that we need is something better right now, today, like higher salaries." He shrugged his shoulders somewhat dejectedly, but with a Russian grin said, "Only if they'd up our salaries, that's all."

Communism is not only a farce that tickles the Russian funny bone, it is also a grand deception that can provoke anger. My friend Boris just about hit the roof when I teased that maybe he'd have communism in 200 years or so. I struck a very sensitive nerve.

"I don't want to wait any 200 years," he loudly complained, as his wife Maria seemed to get a big kick out of the idea.

Revolutionary Man on the Drawing Board

"Look," he said, abruptly pointing to his father seated at the dinner table across from him. "His father worked and waited for communism so that he could enjoy it. And my father worked and waited so that our family could have a better life. Well, I don't want to wait any longer." He continued to speak quickly, at times nearly shouting. "I want a better life now for myself and my family. I want money and all the conveniences in my life time, and I want it right now."

Throughout this book, I have tried to point out some of the external parallels between Christianity and communism. When we get down to brass tacks, when we separate the wheat from the chaff, everything boils down to one great issue. Is man self-sufficient? Is he the master of his own destiny? Is he his own god, his own saviour? For those who know the Lord, these questions are merely rhetorical. Jesus is Lord and Saviour; He is everything. For the Marxist, these questions have a rich ideological basis. They must answer "yes." Man is supreme. God and religion are "the opium of the people." The lines of distinction are tightly drawn. There is no mistaking the other's position.

And so the true Marxist must continue to wait for the last act of the great political drama to take place. He looks forward to that day when groaning men and women can at last shed those awful leopard spots.

The Christian, on the other hand, recognizes that he's a sinner, but also knows that he's forgiven. While eagerly awaiting "the catching away" of the Church, he praises the Lord and enjoys the fruits of Redemption right now. For as Our Lord and Saviour Jesus said, "Neither shall they say, Lo here! or, lo there! for, behold, the kingdom of God is within you."[1]

---

[1] Luke 17:21 KJV

243

14
Novgorod, 1981

When Jesus therefore saw his mother, and the disciple standing by, whom he loved, he saith unto his mother, Woman, behold thy son! Then saith he to the disciple, Behold thy mother!
(John 19:26-27 KJV)

It was the summer of 1981. I had just returned to the U.S.S.R. after a two-year absence. It was good to be back, to meet again with old friends and to rekindle my desire to raise up Jesus as Saviour of Russia. But this time, there was something very different about Russia, or maybe I had changed and not the country. My growth in the Lord at home in the States had made the grand Soviet experiment seem so much emptier, so much more meaningless than it ever had before. I seemed to be able to see with greater vision the demonic, spiritual bondage that communism really is. The darker side of the revolutionary life was a hundred times darker than before. But the light of the Lord shining on the Russia of old was so brilliant and dazzling that Holy Russia seemed transfigured before my very eyes.

The dialectical confrontation between light and darkness appeared to take on real visual form. As far as my spirit was concerned, the battle between good and evil was being fought out in a kind of three-dimensional color. I had never before experienced Russia in such a mystical way.

It was also a powerful therapy that resurrected an old, old anxiety. It was time to again climb back up on my watchtower, and, like Habakkuk, wrestle with the Lord. According to the argument of my human insight, Revolutionary Russia was climbing higher and higher into the sky, its state and spiritual power growing by leaps and bounds. "Lord, isn't it yet time to turn the tables around? This heavy atheistic society, it's too much! These poor people don't have a chance to learn about you. Soviet Power seems to have everything all wrapped up. Why have you allowed it?" Well, I'm sure He has heard such words spoken before, many times before. There was no answer to my plea, no explanation for Russia's predicament, just a spiritual heaviness that was so uncomfortable to bear.

August 22, 1981 was a tremendous day in my life. I was then in the ancient city of Novgorod, noted for its spectacular treasury of Russian art relics dating back to the eleventh century. Just after supper at my hotel, I asked Ann, a young girl on my tour, if she'd like to accompany me to the Russian Orthodox church on the other side of town. She knew some Russian and this was her second trip to Russia, evidence of her love for the country and its people. Together we set out for the Church of St. Philip the Apostle, having no idea of the wonder of what lay ahead.

The first stroke of divine providence was that we were not too late for the evening service. A few of the *babushki*, noting our foreign dress and demeanor, welcomed us warmly, bestowing Ann with a bunch of gorgeous flowers. Passing along our Christian greetings, we left St. Philip's and headed back to our hotel.

The clock was now turning toward the ninth hour, yet a gentle northern light continued to illuminate the museum city. It was time for the Lord to act, and did He ever!

Once we were out on the street, a sudden stillness

surrounded us like a cloud. The quiet of Soviet streets was solemn. The sky had turned a menacing gray. The crisp country air had become unnaturally heavy. Nature was about to explode.

The countdown began with each hurried step towards the too-distant tram stop. Grandmothers too quickened their pace. Together, we sought for shelter from the coming of the storm. And then it happened in a second's time.

Chunks of crystal-like hail rushed from the heavens in a sweeping downpour. Lightning flickered across the revolutionary sky. In this sea of ice, you couldn't even see your hand in front of you, but it made little difference. We all had our hands clamped securely around our heads, trying to ward off the pelting, punishing hail. The winds unleashed a terrible fury, holding those of us who tried to run in almost paralyzing positions. Broken branches from rugged trees were flung about like so many twigs, dancing to the rhythm of a seemingly uncontrollable power. Nature was showing who was boss.

And then, as if nothing had ever happened, the calm of Novgorod reappeared out of nowhere. The air was now wet and refreshing. The trees, looking a little limp, dripped the excess water onto the wet earth below. Symmetrical designs of melting ice now lay on the paved streets. But otherwise, all seemed back to normal in the revolutionary state.

Ann and I emerged from beneath the shelter of an apartment building. We were soaked, maybe just a bit shook up, but very much alive to what God had done. We shared our impressions of what it all meant; we wondered and were in awe. The mystery we had just witnessed led us to a brief interlude of prayer. As we took our final steps back toward our waiting hotel, we thanked the Lord for showing us that Russia, Revolutionary Russia, could be overcome by such a mighty display of pure power. We both knew we had heard

A CHRISTIAN VIEW OF RUSSIA

His voice in the ancient city of Novgorod.

August 22, 1981 was an extraordinary day for yet another reason, one that I became aware of only months later. It was the original feast date of the Immaculate Heart of Mary, instituted by the Roman Catholic Church in 1944 to commemorate the twenty-seventh anniversary of the Fatima apparitions.

During the summer of 1917, Mary appeared in Fatima, Portugal to three simple shepherd children. Calling herself the Lady of the Holy Rosary, she appeared as a radiant young girl in her mid-teens. Perhaps this image was to represent the chosen virgin at the time of the Divine Incarnation. Prayer, penance and sacrifice for the salvation of the entire world was the heart of the Marian message. For the children of Fatima, the reality of eternal damnation and "the great sea of fire" was as terrifying as it was real. Mary sadly told of how "many souls go to hell because no one is willing to help them with sacrifice."

In July 1917, only a few months *before* the historic Russian Revolution would take place, Mary gave to the little shepherds of Fatima, and to the modern world, a remarkable prophecy. If her message went unheeded, the Holy Virgin foretold that "Russia will spread her errors throughout the world, bringing new wars and persecution of the Church." Is not this revelation a prophetic commentary on nearly three-quarters of a century of world history?

The Lord had alerted His people of the threat of evil to come, but the prophecy also gave cause for great hope. Mary promised at Fatima that in the end her Immaculate Heart would be victorious. "The Holy Father will consecrate Russia to me and she will be converted." In 1952 Pope Pius XII consecrated the Russian people to the Immaculate Heart of Mary. Considering the special place that the Mother of God holds in the Russian Orthodox faith, the consecration seems so fitting.

Novgorod, 1981

Today in Revolutionary Russia, the Russian Orthodox Church sets aside twelve special feast days. These holidays recall particular events in the lives of Jesus and Mary. The four feast days that honor Mary are the Annunciation, the Assumption, the Birthday of Our Lady and the Presentation of the Virgin Mary. Despite the official reign of atheism, the Russian people have not forgotten their heavenly Mother.

In the Russian Orthodox liturgy on the Feast of Our Lady of Kazan, Mary's powerful intercession in Russian history is recalled. She is invoked as the "Protectress of the Russian Land," "Weapon Fearful for the Demons" and "Hope of Those Who Had Lost Hope." With Mary by her side, Russia need not despair. Her Golgotha shall pass; a glorious resurrection shall be hers.

For Roman Catholics and Eastern Orthodox alike, Jesus' last words to His mother and the Apostle John hold great significance.

> *When Jesus therefore saw his mother, and the disciple standing by, whom he loved, he saith unto his mother, Woman, behold thy son! Then saith he to the disciple, Behold thy mother!*[1]

The summons to console the Immaculate Heart of Mary is a specific and honored way to show devotion and love to the Merciful Mother who grieved on Calvary's hill.

Should any of us be surprised that the loving Jesus would ask that we come with compassion to his sorrowful, sorrowing mother? And is it really so unusual that this same Mary, who became a sanctified vessel of the Holy Spirit in Nazareth two thousand years ago, should again play a central role in the Church's final victory over the forces of evil?

I must confess here that my personal relationship with the Saviour first grew out of my devotion to Mary in my teen

---

[1] John 19:26-27 KJV

years. How well do I remember the mystical experience of being led to Jesus through Mary. And how vividly do I recall how quietly she decreased and how gloriously Jesus increased in my spiritual life. Mary was always present, assuredly pointing the way to her Divine Son.

For me, the feast day of the Immaculate Heart of Mary will always take on the proportion of divine power and majesty as I remember Novgorod, 1981. And too, it will remind me of Mary's enduring promise for the conversion of the great Russian people. At Fatima, Mary asked that a special prayer be recited after each mystery of the rosary. "O my Jesus, forgive us our sins; preserve us from the fire of hell, and bring into heaven all souls, especially those most in need of Your mercy."

It is in this prayer that I see the unfolding of the victorious vision of Fatima. For it is in Jesus—Saviour, Redeemer and Lord—that Russia will indeed resurrect to be filled with a mighty outpouring of His Holy Spirit.

15

Victory Day

In the end of the sabbath, as it began to dawn toward the first day of the week, came Mary Magdalene and the other Mary to see the sepulchre.

(Matthew 28:1 KJV)

There is one day each year when the "Great Patriotic War" is joyfully remembered. It is May 9, officially proclaimed in the Soviet Union as "Victory Day." On this day, the somber tone of the war years gives way to a splendid celebration commemorating the war's end. The ritual is inescapably religious. Twenty million Soviets, mostly Russians, were sacrificed for peace and, in the Russians' eyes, world peace. Victory Day celebrates the deliverance of the motherland from the Nazi invasion.

War veterans can be seen before this great Soviet holiday flocking to Moscow and Leningrad. Delegations and congresses fill up all available hotel space. Reunions, parties, Russian and Soviet spirits, recollections, laughter, joy and tears is what Victory Day is all about. New slogans and banners are put up to enhance the spirit of excitement and enthusiasm. The wearing of war medals, a tradition which is observed year-long by veterans, now takes on special significance.

A CHRISTIAN VIEW OF RUSSIA

Driving into Leningrad from the airport on May 9, I could feel the spirit of the Leningradians. Red flags rippled in the crisp spring air all along the airport road leading to the Leningrad War Memorial. Loudspeakers were in place, and propaganda and music added to the emotion of the gathering. The crowds filling the war memorial overflowed onto the streets, forcing us to detour along another route. All of Leningrad was revolutionary red; scores of flags and banners were everywhere. This time the color of crimson did not seem at all contrived or artificial. It stood as a symbol of the eternal heart, not the passing Revolution.

At Hotel Leningrad the restaurant was filled to absolute capacity with those who had miraculously survived the great siege. Spontaneous songs of celebration seemed to cover up the tragic memories that I too often had seen Russians relive. The wounds of the war were closed, at least temporarily; the pain was deadened by the free-flowing liquor. The haunting spirit of war, of foxholes and labor camps, of savagery and death, no longer possessed these war veterans.

As I passed through the restaurant, a group of Russians called me over to their table, and poured me a full glass of bitter vodka. Their toast to world peace was a refrain I had come to expect; it was as perfectly Russian as the straight alcohol I drank to the hope of peace.

The foreign currency bar that night was an unusual place. The Russian bartender and barmaid had dropped their professional image and began to compete with their foreign customers, downing screwdrivers and cognac. "To peace forever," the young barman hailed, raising his glass high before his evening drinking buddies. While the barman was hand-wrestling with his foreign comrades, the barmaid was flirting. Such conduct under ordinary circumstances would have been considered uncultured and forbidden. It just wasn't done, ever! But this wasn't a typical day. Russian patriotism

Victory Day

and pride reigned above Soviet order. Russians were recalling a great, great victory. Their motherland was now free, saved from an enemy that tried so brutally to destroy it. Celebrating this event was enough to transform the restrained public Russian. It was a time to rejoice. The night of darkness and terror had given way to light, freedom and rebirth.

Boris Pasternak, one of the greatest poets of the twentieth century, writes of another Victory Day, a day of ignominious death, a day of triumphant Resurrection. In his epic novel, *Doctor Zhivago*, which has never been published in the Soviet Union, Pasternak gave the world, "*Magdalina*, Magdalene."

In the final stanzas of the second poem, Mary Magdalene, prostrated beneath the cross, is overwhelmed by the gory and glorious scene she beholds. In the terrible transformation of the moment, she looks forward to the dawn of Resurrection.

It is my prayer that the Russian nation, in their remembrance of the great war, will find their Saviour and their day of Victory.

Organizations With Ministries
Behind the Iron Curtain

Open Doors
With Brother Andrew
P.O. Box 2020
Orange, CA 92669

Russia for Christ, Inc.
P.O. Box 30,000
Santa Barbara, CA 93105

Eastern European Bible Mission
P.O. Box 73
Walnut Creek, CA 94597

Persecuted Church Commission, Inc.
P.O. Box 1340
Kingston, NY 12401

Slavic Gospel Association
P.O. Box 1122
Wheaton, IL 60187

Lithuanian Catholic Religious Aid, Inc.
351 Highland Boulevard
Brooklyn, NY 11207

Committee for the Defense of Persecuted
Orthodox Christians, Inc.
P.O. Box 9669
Washington, D.C. 20016

Selected Bibliography

SOVIET SOURCES
I. Guidebooks

Chernov, Vladimir. *Moscow: A Short Guide.* Translated by J.C. Butler. Moscow: Progress Publishers, 1979.

An informative handbook which takes the reader on a comprehensive tour of Moscow. The perceptive reader will sense how dramatically Russian life has changed since the Revolution.

Doroshinskaya, Y., and Kruchina-Bogdanov, V. *Leningrad and its Environs: Guidebook.* Moscow: Progress Publishers, 1979.

A highly recommended book for anyone planning to visit Leningrad.

Levitsky, H. *Kiev: A Short Guide.* Translated by Angelia Graf and Christopher English. Moscow: Progress Publishers, 1980.

The chapter entitled "War Memorials in the Hero-City" illustrates the importance the Soviet government has given to preserving the memory of World War II.

Persianova, O. *The Hermitage: Room-to-Room Guide.* 2nd ed., rev. Translated by John S. Heyes. Leningrad: Aurora Art Publishers, 1975.

A compact source of information on some of the major works of art contained in the Soviet Union's largest art museum. The variety and scope of West European paintings dealing with religious motifs might be of interest to some art enthusiasts.

II. Encyclopedias

Garadzha, V.I. "Religion." *Great Soviet Encyclopedia.* 3rd ed. 1978. Vol. XXI.

A comprehensive summary of the Soviet view of the nature, history and purpose of religion.

Glagolev, V.S., and Evdokimov, V.I. "Atheistic Education." *Great Soviet Encyclopedia*. 3rd ed. 1973. Vol. II.

An informative article showing the importance that the Soviet state attaches to atheistic education.

Golikov, G.N., and Kuznetsov, M.I. "Great October Socialist Revolution." *Great Soviet Encyclopedia*. 3rd ed. 1974. Vol. IV.

The last section of the article is entitled: "The worldwide historical significance of the Great October Socialist Revolution." It is a good example of the kind of propaganda barrage that Soviet citizens are subjected to.

Minkovskii, G.M., and Sakharov, A.B. "Crime." *Great Soviet Encyclopedia*. 3rd ed. 1979. Vol. XX.

The purpose of this article is to show that unlike capitalist societies the Soviet Union has been able to do away with the root causes of crime.

Ovchinskii, S.S. "Volunteer Public Order Squads." *Great Soviet Encyclopedia*. 3rd ed. 1975. Vol. VIII.

This short article describing the activities of the public order squads reflects the official concern that order be maintained in every sphere of Soviet life.

Petrenko, F.F. "Criticism and Self-Criticism." *Great Soviet Encyclopedia*. 3rd ed. 1976. Vol. XIII.

A very useful article which helps to understand the problem of dissent and criticism in Soviet society.

III. Documents

"The New Soviet Constitution of 1977: Official Text." In *The New Soviet Constitution of 1977: Analysis and Text*. Ed. Robert S. Sharlet. Brunswick, Ohio: King's Court Communications, Inc., 1978, pp. 73-130.

Chapter 7 of the Constitution, articles 39 to 69, describes the rights and duties of Soviet citizens.

"The RSFSR Law on Religious Associations of 1929 (as amended by Decree of the Presidium of the Supreme Soviet of the RSFSR of June 23, 1975." In *Review of Socialist Law*, I (September, 1975), 223-34.

Review of Socialist Law is published in Leyden, The Netherlands. A complete copy of the amended 1929 law may be obtained from: Dr. Janis Robins, 11 Ludlow Ave., St. Paul, MN 55108.

Selected Bibliography

IV. Pamphlets

Kononov, A. *New Year in Sokolniki: Lenin Among Children*. Translated by Fainna Glagoleva. Moscow: Progress Publishers, 1975.

> Representative of the type of teaching material used in Soviet schools, this primer is about Lenin's visit to a children's New Year's party in Moscow in 1919.

USSR: 100 Questions and Answers. Moscow: Novosti Press Agency Publishing House, 1980.

> A popular pamphlet containing the official answers to the questions most often asked by foreigners visiting the U.S.S.R.

V. Short Stories

Grin. A. [Alexander Stepanovich Grinevsky] *Crimson Sails: A Fantasy*. Translated by Fainna Glagoleva. Moscow: Progress Publishers, 1978.

> An imaginative fairy tale about how a young girl's dream of romance and happiness comes true.

NON-SOVIET SOURCES

I. General Books

Cornforth, Maurice Campbell. *Dialectical Materialism: An Introduction*. Vol. II: *Historical Materialism*. 2nd. ed., rev. New York: International Publishers, 1971.

> A scholarly treatment of Marx's theory of the development of society designed for the serious student of Marxism.

Dmytryshyn, Basil. *A History of Russia.* Englewood Cliffs, N.J.: Prentice-Hall, Inc., 1977.

> A recommended book for the beginning student of Russian history.

Fedotov, G.P. *The Russian Religious Mind*. Vol. 1: *Kievan Christianity: The Tenth to the Thirteenth Centuries*. Cambridge, Massachusetts: Harvard University Press, 1946.

Fedotov, G.P. *The Russian Religious Mind*. Vol. II: *The Middle Ages: The Thirteenth to the Fifteenth Centuries*. Edited by John Meyendorff. Cambridge, Massachusetts: Harvard University Press, 1966.

> Fedotov's two volume scholarly classic painstakingly traces the development of the religious consciousness of the Russian people.

A CHRISTIAN VIEW OF RUSSIA

Gerhart, Genevra. *The Russian's World: Life and Language.* New York: Harcourt Brace Jovanovich, Inc. 1974.

A unique and admirable handbook containing a great deal of specific information about Soviet life not found elsewhere. Students of the Russian language will find this book enormously helpful.

Grant, Michael. *The Fall of the Roman Empire: A Reappraisal.* Radnor, PA.: The Annenberg School Press, 1976.

Some of the reasons Grant offers to explain why Rome fell appear useful in identifying the basic problems and weaknesses of the Soviet Union.

II. Narratives and Novels

Deyneka, Jr., Anita and Peter. *A Song in Siberia.* Elgin, Illinois: David C. Cook Publishing Co., 1977.

A comprehensive and well-written account of the daily trials and spiritual victories experienced by a congregation of believers in Soviet Siberia.

Dostoevsky, Fyodor. *The Brothers Karamazov.* Translated by Andrew R. MacAndrew. New York: Bantam Books, Inc., 1970.

A long and highly complex novel which examines among other things the nature of suffering and evil.

Pasternak, Boris. *Doctor Zhivago.* Translated by Max Hayward and Manya Harari. "The Poems of Yurii Zhivago" translated by Bernard Guilbert Guerney. New York: Pantheon Books Inc., 1958.

Pasternak's epic novel set in the context of the Russian Revolution concludes with some brilliant religious poetry which is both symbolic and inspirational.

The Way of a Pilgrim and The Pilgrim Continues His Way. Translated by Helen Bacovcin. Garden City, New York: Image Books, 1978.

The great spiritual classic about an anonymous Russian peasant's pilgrimage through 19th century Russia. A highly recommended book especially for anyone interested in the spirituality of the centuries-old Jesus Prayer.

Selected Bibliography

III. Pamphlets and Journals

Marx, Karl, and Engels, Frederick. *Manifesto of the Communist Party*. New York: International Publishers Co., Inc., 1948.

Claiming that the history of mankind has been one of class struggle, the *Manifesto* calls on the workers of the world to rise up and forcibly overthrow the capitalist system.

"Young Russia to Young America." *Sparks*, V, No. 4 (October-December, 1981), 4-5.

This stirring appeal for help from Russian Orthodox believers in the Soviet Union provides some interesting insight into the Russian people's search for and experience of Christ. *Sparks* is a quarterly journal of the Institute of Slavic Studies, a division of the Slavic Gospel Association, P.O. Box 1122, Wheaton, IL 60187.

IV. Bibles

Authorized King James Version. The Open Bible Edition. Nashville, Tennessee: Thomas Nelson Inc., 1975.

The Jerusalem Bible. Garden City, New York: Doubleday & Company, Inc., 1966.